GROW YOUR FOOD FOR FREE

(well, almost)

Great money-saving ideas for your garden

DAVE HAMILTON

First published in 2011 by

Green Books,
Dartington Space, Dartington Hall,
Totnes, Devon TQ9 6EN

Reprinted 2012

Photographs by Dave Hamilton unless otherwise credited.

Design by Jayne Jones
Cover illustration by Ellie Mains

Illustrations by Ellie Mains

ISBN 978 1 900322 89 8

Printed on ON Offset paper
by Cambrian Printers, Aberystwyth, UK

GROW YOUR FOOD
FOR FREE
(well, almost)

CONTENTS

DEDICATION

This book is dedicated to Nick Gooderham, an inspiring teacher and good friend.

ACKNOWLEDGEMENTS

I would like to give extra special thanks to my partner Ellie Mains. Not only did she put many hours into the sometimes difficult job of illustrating the book, but she also put up with me throughout the writing process and provided much-needed tea, hugs and love.

Special thanks go to Amanda Cuthbert for providing the idea of this book and endless help and advice throughout. Thanks to all at Green Books for being the world's friendliest publisher.

A BIG thanks to Lou and James Brown for Lou's photos and James's endless practical advice.

Thanks go to all my contributors – James Adamson, Mark Boyle, Chris Eaves, Tony Kendle, George Kestell, James Brown, Nicky Scott, Pippa Rosen and Ben Moss.

I would also like to thank staff and students on the Duchy/Schumacher horticulture course, especially George, Bill, Bethan, Dyane and John, and of course Nick, to whom this book is dedicated. They all happily fielded my questions, which helped to hone the information presented in this book.

Further thanks go to: Cath and Ben, for lifts to the Mecca that is Newton Abbott tip; Adam, for keeping me sane; Jenny and Alison, for being good sounding boards for ideas (and for listening to me rabbit on about the book); Laurel, for her laugh and lifts; Francis, Ian and Joni, for morning tea and chat; Graham from Bridgetown Stores, for snacks and laughs; and Simon, for his mum's cake.

And finally, to Reuben and Robert, who always wanted to get a mention in a book.

(The biggest thanks of all go to anyone who has bought this book, and an even bigger thanks to anyone who may have bought more than two copies.)

INTRODUCTION

When you are about to shuffle off this mortal coil, would you like your memories to be of those drives to an out-of-town retail estate? Will you think fondly of that time you argued with your partner all day and filled up the back of the car with all the things you thought you needed for your new vegetable plot? Or perhaps you'd like to reminisce about the day your new shed was so late being delivered that you spent an hour on hold to a call centre?

As your grandchildren gather around your deathbed, you could regale them with stories of the time your new fence plunged you so far into your overdraft that you had to take on a part-time job just to pay off the interest. It would be such a loss for shared wisdom such as this to miss a generation.

A well-tended garden holds as many memories as a photo album, and you, as the gardener, choose what goes into that album.

The difference between building a productive garden with what you have around you, rather than buying everything in, is rather like the difference between a home-cooked meal and a microwave dinner. A garden that relies on the garden centre or garden mega-store will look like countless others, cost money

Free garlic — from cloves saved from last year's crop.

and use up dwindling resources. This is in marked contrast to a plot with a self-built shed, bench and raised beds, and crops grown from saved seed. The latter will be a totally unique reflection of your personality, quite unlike any other garden. What's more, you will be able to save yourself a small fortune as you 'grow your food for free' . . . (well, almost).

PART 1

GETTING STARTED

Whatever the age of the gardener and whatever his or her level of knowledge or experience, every one will tell you "I'll get it right next year." I always bear this in mind whenever I take on a new vegetable plot or continue with an old one for another year. Each year we try our best and each year there are successes and failures, but with any luck there will be more of the former than the latter!

In terms of getting it right, throwing money at a garden is never going to be as effective as taking a step back, assessing what's already there, and seeing what needs to be brought in and what needs to be done.

Chapter 1
· · · · · · · · · · · · · · · ·

YOUR GROWING SPACE

If I assumed that everyone reading this book had identical horticultural starting blocks, it would be akin to assuming that every reader is my height, weight and age, has a similar income, eats the same kind of food and wears the same kind of clothes as I do. Even my identical twin brother differs from me in his gardening style and where he gardens (he also differs in weight, food preference, clothes and income!).

So I have to assume that no two gardeners, or the gardens they tend, are alike, and any row of gardens is testament to this. As the years go by, gardens change dramatically from their original construction, depending on the gardener or gardeners who tend them. This is even more true of allotment sites, with their patchwork display of crops, trees, paths, sheds, flowers, fruit bushes and fences.

I've moved home a lot in the last few years, and everywhere I went I put down a vegetable patch – be it in a home garden, on an allotment or (by invitation) on someone else's land. It was sometimes only for six months, sometimes a year or two, but each time it was different and I learned something new. The gardens I inherited came in all shapes and sizes, from a tiny balcony or front yard to vast jungles that provided few clues to what lay beneath the thick undergrowth before I hacked it back like some intrepid explorer.

No two gardens are ever the same.

So, from experience, the most important thing to consider when designing a garden for very little (or no) money is that it has to be adaptable. As soon as you open your eyes to the world of DIY gardening and/or salvaging materials, things can get a little . . . well, let's just say a little . . . creative.

This kind of gardening is akin to cooking with what you have in the cupboard rather than buying in ingredients. Instead of buying in raised beds, you may begin with a deep bed system and then, over time, if the wood turns up, the raised bed can be put into place. Or you may even decide you no longer want raised beds as the deep beds seem to be doing a pretty good job! You might have wanted to lay a brick path but then discovered that a friend is digging up his or her patio. The patio slabs might be just the right size for the job, so why splash out on buying materials when suitable free ones are there for the asking?

It helps if garden plans are as organic as the plants within them – growing over time and adapting to changing conditions and budgets.

This kind of gardening is more resilient to changes in your lifestyle and income, as it is also to changes in climate and in society as a whole. No one knows what the future holds for us in these uncertain times, so having a garden that can not only feed you but also not require any further economic input will stand you in better stead than one that requires you to throw money at it year in, year out.

One of the aims of this book – apart from saving you money – is to start you thinking a little differently about how and where you garden. It is not so much about teaching you to garden per se. Many of you will find that you can just garden at home, which is fine, but not possible for everyone, and it is by no means the only option. All you really need is a desire to garden – then, in my experience, if you are determined enough, and if you keep your eyes and ears open and remain optimistic, something will come your way.

Some options when considering where to garden are as follows. Each is discussed in detail in the following pages.

- Home garden
- Indoors
- Allotment
- Garden share
- Landshare
- Community Supported Agriculture (CSA) scheme
- Volunteering
- Guerrilla gardening

HOME GARDEN

The ideal situation is a growing space where you live. A home plot means regular attention, fresh produce when you want it and no travelling time. For those with a busy lifestyle this has to be the best situation, as a garden benefits from the 'little and often' approach

Edible ornamentals

In the past I've chosen to grow ornamentals with an edible use, to mix the aesthetic with the practical. I've grown things like *Sedum spectabile* (the young leaves can be eaten in salads and it is fantastic for pollinators), nigella (edible seeds), mallow (salad leaf and egg substitute), evening primrose (edible flower) and nasturtium (edible everything) mixed in with seasonal vegetables and herbs in a bed surrounded by a chive border.

as much as it does from attention for hours on end. Once established, even a large productive garden may need only 20 minutes a day – and I've found that if those 20 minutes are not too far from a kettle and a well-stocked biscuit tin, somehow extra time is usually found and helpers are more likely to come by.

The style of planting in a home garden can sometimes be slightly different from that of a garden away from the home. The garden may be seen as an extension of the house, and its overall aesthetic can be as important as the

amount it produces. Many people choose to have a more cottage-garden-style garden at home, with a mix of flowers and shrubs alongside their fruit and vegetables.

Having a garden at home, no matter how small, is of course a lot easier than travelling to one. Lack of soil need not be a problem, as pots can be placed on patios, on concrete, on gravel or on small balconies. I've even made large planters out of pallets and sat them on a gravel garden that otherwise had no soil.

Try to think positively: what has the space got going for it? Is it south-facing? Private? Low maintenance? How can you make the most of what's there? If there is no room to spread out, can you go up? Can raised beds be built where the soil is poor or non-existent? If

there is an ugly old patio, is there sufficient soil underneath for alternate slabs to be taken up and the soil underneath planted?

Even the most artificial, concrete-covered of gardens can have something going for it.

Tips for tenants

As a tenant gardener you really have to read the seed packets and gardening books to work out how many days you have between sowing and harvest. There is little point in sowing crops that might take a year to mature, such as parsnips or purple sprouting broccoli, if you will be gone by the time they are ready to harvest. Quick crops, such as fast-growing salad leaves, are best, since even in a six-month tenancy you will be able to make a number of harvests.

Making the most of a small garden. *Photo: Lou Brown*

There is also the option of growing in pots and taking these with you when you move. This only really works for small pots, as larger ones, once they are full of soil, water and growing crops, can be nigh-on impossible to move. I was devastated when I realised there was no way I could lift my old Belfast sink planted up with herbs. The sink weighed enough before it was planted up, let alone afterwards!

You also have to consider how you are going to move and how far (if you know in advance). If moving somewhere in the same town you should have no problem making a number of trips to pick up your plants. But moving out of an area may mean one trip and one trip only!

INDOORS

You may well grow indoor houseplants, but perhaps seldom think about growing indoor vegetables. Yet a surprising amount of produce can be grown indoors, on windowsills, in well-lit porches, in conservatories and under skylights. Modern homes are quite often full of natural light in the daytime and are heated in the winter, making them the perfect growing place for an indoor vegetable garden.

Of course, large vegetables such as trailing squashes won't be suitable for indoors, but plant breeders are cottoning on to the fact that people are growing in pots and are constantly bringing out new compact varieties of our favourite vegetables. I saw first-hand the variety of things people grew inside when I worked as a postman in Oxford. As I delivered the mail I couldn't help but nose around and see what people were growing – jungles of vegetables reached up towards the light in top-lit stairwells; south-facing porches were proudly housing tomatoes, chillies and aubergines. On the rare occasion that I saw the back of people's houses I saw conservatories brimming with more veggies than the average greenhouse!

It helps to find areas with the most natural light possible, preferably with that light coming from above. On windowsills some plants can become etiolated, that is, stretched, elongated and contorted as they reach towards the light. Regular turning can help, as can raising the plant up if it's on a low windowsill.

Crops to grow indoors

- **Tomatoes, chillies and aubergines** Small bush varieties are suited to windowsill

Tenants' karma

Excuse the hippy term but there really is no other word for it. I believe that you should always leave a garden in better condition than when you found it. Even if the next tenants don't garden, what have you lost? You will have improved your local environment, harvested a season's worth of fresh produce and got some worthwhile exercise.

If you've been renting for a while, especially in a city, you may notice that there are certain houses that are *always* up for rent. I know – I've gone to parties in the same house hosted by completely different people. The high volume of tenants can be for a number of reasons but quite often it is simply because the houses are pretty horrible places to live! But it is just these kinds of horrible houses that really benefit from having a garden that is taken care of. It just takes one person to break the cycle of neglect and one more to continue working it. An understanding landlord may even drop the rent for a well-tended garden. You won't be upsetting a nasty landlord by not doing the garden; you'll just be making life difficult for the next tenants if they want to grow there.

A windowsill can act like a miniature greenhouse.

Where to garden if you don't have one

Modern living arrangements push us into smaller and smaller houses or flats, where gardens become a luxury rather than a given, so it's not surprising that growing spaces can be hard to find. Landlords in major cities will happily charge more for a home with an 'outdoor space', even if that outdoors space is a north-facing patch of concrete. There is of course a lot you can do indoors or in very limited outdoor spaces. However, it is easy to forget that gardening doesn't have to be done on your own land – there are many options open to those looking for a plot of land to exercise their green fingers, some of which are discussed in the following pages.

growing; larger and trailing plants to porches and conservatories. They will need to be grown where the temperature doesn't go below 10°C (50°F). They can become etiolated (see above) so are not suitable for windowsill growing unless on a very well-lit sill.

- **Herbs** These can be grown on a kitchen windowsill so they are to hand when cooking. Basil, mint, chives, thyme and parsley are all suitable for home growing.
- **Salad leaves** Try either whole lettuces in flowerpots or a tray of mixed leaves. Winter leaves such as rocket, mizuna and mibuna can all be grown on a windowsill.
- **Mini root crops** Compact varieties of beetroot and carrots have been developed, and Japanese varieties of turnips are no bigger than a ping-pong ball. They will need to be in a large trough rather than a small pot.
- **Citrus fruits** Dwarf varieties of citrus fruits can be grown indoors in pots. Bear in mind

that growing from seed can be unpredict-able – the resulting plants may grow up to 3m (10ft) tall.

ALLOTMENT

For the benefit of those who have never heard of one, an allotment is a small parcel of land, usually public but sometimes private, rented out to an individual or a family to grow their food. In parts of the world outside Britain they are often called 'community gardens'.

I've found allotment growing to be one of the nicest ways in which to grow my own produce. A lot of resources, such as communal muck and leaf piles, can be shared, and there is nearly always someone on hand to give advice (whether it's needed or not!).

Waiting lists are long, and it's worth putting your name down for an allotment as soon as you arrive in a town. Two-, five- or ten-year

Pros of working in a group

- **Plays to strengths** Some like to dig, some can weed very efficiently, some act as the brains working out problems, and some can act as brawn whenever heavy work is to be done. Working as a group means you will always play to the strengths of the group rather than the weaknesses, so even if you aren't the best gardeners in the world you may make up for it in other ways (even if it is just making a good cup of tea and a nice cake!).
- **Spreads costs** There is often no need to buy lots of tools and lots of seeds individually – a hedge-trimmer may only come out once a year, so do you really all need one each? Likewise, do you personally need all 50 tomato seeds or all 20 courgette seeds in a pack?
- **Provides holiday cover** Sharing the work on a piece of land also means that holidays are covered naturally. As long as everyone doesn't want to go away for the same two weeks in August there will always be someone around to do the watering.
- **Gives time benefits** With all the will in the world, you sometimes don't get a chance to get out and garden as much as you want to. The benefit of working with a group means that a plot may not go to rack and ruin if you don't manage to be there day in, day out.

Some will naturally do a lot more than others, and I've found that a 'harvest if you put the work in' scheme seems to work.

Cons of working in a group

- **Disputes** It can be hard enough for couples to get on at times, let alone groups of ten or more! Many growing groups try to pre-empt disputes by writing an agreement up first. It may sound needlessly official (although no doubt some in a group will jump at the chance to create a bit of bureaucracy and admin), but in the long run it could stop a whole scheme from falling apart.
- **Hard feelings** In my experience, groups with an ethos of 'I did this, why aren't they doing that?' will never work. Resentment and bad feelings don't make for happy, willing workers. Instead, try to cultivate a feeling of 'They did that, perhaps I should do this' by playing up to the most productive in the group rather than down to the least. If you choose carefully who you work with, it shouldn't come to this kind of petty situation. Nevertheless, humans are humans and disagreements do arise, even with every precaution you may put in place. The best approach is to try to quash any dispute before it explodes, as it is far easier to put out a spark than a fire.

A well-earned meal can be a great way to get together.

waits may seem interminable, but in two, five or ten years' time you will be grateful you decided to put your name down. Besides, people's circumstances do change and a predicted five-year wait can sometimes be just two or three years.

Available plots often seem to be the most neglected and, tragically, I've seen many people come and go very quickly as they get overwhelmed by the amount of work they feel they need to do. The best advice I was ever given was to not do it all at once. Instead, I cut all the vegetation down to ground level and covered what I could with weed-suppressant material or cardboard (the latter needs topping up as it rots). I worked half the plot in the first year, only reaching full cultivation after about two years. My brother always likes to tell people to work backwards – looking at what you've done rather than what you need to do.

Alternatively, if the work does seem all too much, there really is no need to take an entire allotment. Full-size allotments can be split into half, thirds or quarters and shared out amongst friends or offered to others on the extensive waiting list.

Let's get together

With few exceptions, mammals are social creatures. Meerkats live in 'clans' or 'mobs' of around twenty, and baboons live in groups of between ten and two hundred. Humans also evolved in groups or tribes rather than singly – there is strength in numbers, and having contact with others has been shown time and time again to typically reduce stress and increase well-being. There are also many other advantages to working in a group – see opposite.

GARDEN SHARE

In the very early stages of this book I hit quite a major snag – I didn't have a garden! Although my partner and I did have some outside space, it was not enough to grow the sort of things I wanted to, or to build some of the projects necessary for a book of this kind. However, help was at hand from a neighbour of ours who lived a stone's throw away from our maisonette.

Our neighbour was a very keen gardener, but like many people these days didn't have time to keep his garden the way he wanted to. He jumped at the chance to share his space and the produce it would hopefully give. So, with our growing experience and his land, we suddenly found ourselves with not only a space for growing but also a good friend just around the corner. I was lucky to know our neighbour quite well before he offered the garden, and he knew us enough to trust us both with his back garden key. This is of course the most convenient way to start an informal garden share, but if you wish to find a space, or offer yours out, becoming a member of a garden-share scheme could be the most logical approach.

Many towns and cities run garden-share schemes, the details of which can be found in the usual sources of local information, such as on local noticeboards and/or on virtual or online noticeboards such as www.gumtree.com. If you find that your town doesn't have one, then you could consider setting one up – See the Transition Town Totnes website for more details (http://transitiontowntotnes.org/gardenshare/startupscheme).

Garden shares can help bridge the gap for those who have no garden of their own or are on a long waiting list for an allotment. There are also many benefits for the garden owners. Some elderly people find that keeping a

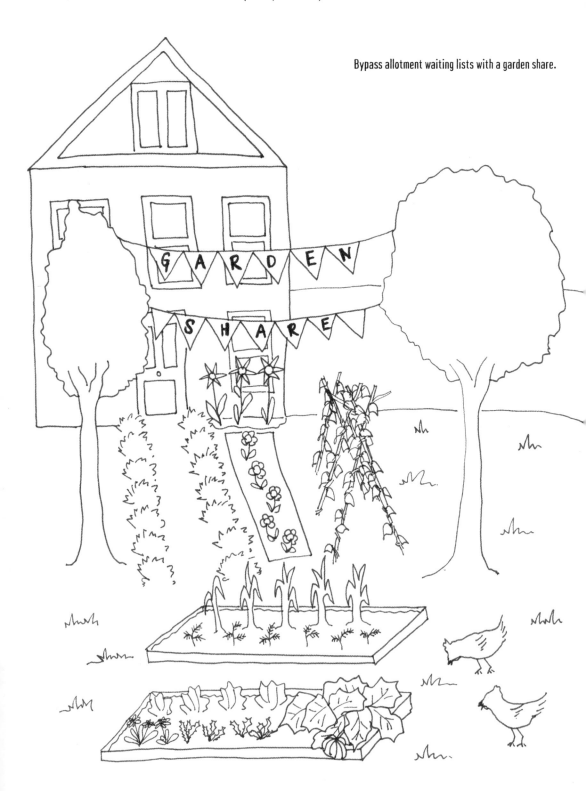

Bypass allotment waiting lists with a garden share.

Totnes garden-sharer Jenny, in her well-tended garden.

garden maintained is too much of a challenge and they are forced to put in low-maintenance measures, such as gravel or decking. In extreme cases gardeners may even move away from a family home as the upkeep of the garden is simply too expensive.

So having someone tend to an overgrown garden can make a real difference, both financially and to the well-being of a garden owner. A friend of mine tends the garden of a woman in her 90s and finds himself also checking on her health – both out of compassion and in view of the risk of losing his growing space!

As with all human relationships there can be setbacks and misunderstandings in garden shares, but Lou Brown, the garden-share scheme coordinator in Totnes, believes that these happen far less than you may imagine.

Reasons for offering your garden

- Neglected areas of the garden can be utilised
- A share of the fresh produce
- No need to install expensive low-maintenance features (such as gravel)
- New friends may be made or existing friendships built on
- Increased sense of community

Reasons to share someone else's garden

- Often no need for initial investment in tools
- No long waiting lists
- New friends may be made or existing friendships built on
- Increased sense of community
- Sometimes the work is shared

"All I can say is that the experience has been profoundly positive and there have honestly been no drawbacks. All the gardeners and the many garden owners have worked and shared their spaces with respect and commitment. Sure, there have been a couple of gardeners who haven't put in the work and have been disappointed, but inexperience and lack of time has been the worst of it – and these cases are astonishingly rare!" Lou Brown, Totnes garden-share scheme coordinator

LANDSHARE

Aside from garden shares, landshare schemes are on the rise. In the UK a landshare directory has been set up at www.landshare.net, where members can post if they need or want land. This can include everything from large pieces of agricultural land right down to small private gardens. The directory covers all of the UK and it seems to be growing daily.

Some areas of the country are much better represented in the directory than others, and, unsurprisingly, it seems that cities have an abundance of growers looking for land rather than people offering it.

Landshares can range from plots as small as a back garden to fields of considerable sizes. The pros and cons are similar to those of a garden-share scheme and are as unique as are the people who offer the land. There seems to be a lot of positive feedback on the scheme, so with luck its success will continue – and I'm sure that even if this particular scheme doesn't, something similar will take its place in the coming years.

COMMUNITY SUPPORTED AGRICULTURE SCHEME

According to the Soil Association there are well over a hundred Community Supported Agriculture (CSA) schemes in the UK, at various stages of development. Some are very small, comprised of a few allotments where members do all the growing themselves. Others are large farms with over 200 members, producing large quantities of meat and veg. Some have been led by farmers who seek a dependable market; others by communities where social and environmental concerns about food have been motivating factors.

Community Supported Agriculture is one of the most recent and perhaps best examples of groups working together. James Adamson, Founder and Coordinator of Sims Hill Shared Harvest, Bristol, tells us more about them, drawing from his own experience in North East Bristol – see opposite.

VOLUNTEERING

It often seems that those with time on their hands generally have no money and those

Willing workers taking a rest at a work day at Chagford CSA.
Photo: Boz Kay

About Community Supported Agriculture

James Adamson, Board member and co-grower of Sims Hill Shared Harvest, Bristol

Community Supported Agriculture (CSA) has been steadily gaining popularity since its conception in Japan several decades ago. There it is known as *teikei* – 'food with a face'.

Principles of CSAs

CSA is a broad term which manifests in many ways depending on the land, growers/farmers and community involved. There are, however, a few key principles that make CSA stand out from conventional consumer culture.

- CSAs have members rather than customers, and these members commit to financially supporting the running of the farm by weekly, monthly or annual subscriptions. Subscriptions cover all the running costs of the farm, such as wages for growers, seeds and land rental. In exchange for this investment, members receive an equal share of all the produce (usually veg but sometimes eggs, dairy products, fruit and meat).
- This unique form of food production fosters beneficial relationships between people, farmers and the land. For its members this means the opportunity to truly know the origin of their food, see how it is produced and have a say in how the farm is managed.
- Farms become not just places to grow food but social hubs, where friends gather and take part in work days and seasonal celebrations.
- For farmers, growers and landowners CSA presents a viable economic model. Investment and commitment from the community can make a massive difference, especially for small farms where margins are narrow.
- All CSAs are built on trust, sharing the risks and the benefits of locally sourced food. They present a refreshing change to supermarket shopping, with active participants rather than passive consumers.

Case study: Sims Hill Shared Harvest, Bristol

Sims Hill Shared Harvest (SHSH) was born following a very successful public meeting held in Bristol to gauge if there was enough interest to run a CSA in the city.

Bristol City Council gave its full support to the venture, offering a large site of some 6 acres (known as Sims Hill) in Frenchay, North East Bristol. The site is part of a fertile strip, stretching out into the hinterland and historically used to grow food for the city. In recent years the site has been neglected and underused, and it seemed fitting to restore the land to its former productivity.

In the summer of 2010 a second public meeting was held to present the work and achievements of Sims Hill Shared Harvest. It was well attended and

we launched the project as "a members-owned-and-led CSA that will:

- provide quality fruit and vegetables grown using natural farming methods
- offer opportunities for education, work and recreation to the wider community
- work to include and support people who are socially or economically marginalised
- build community life through creating a relationship between food and its production."

The farm will be managed using a standard CSA model, where members contribute to the costs in exchange for a share of the harvest, but SHSH represents a lot more. Some of the core principles are taken from permaculture and community

(Cont'd)

(Cont'd)

development models, so there is a strong emphasis on education, inclusion and equality as well as environmental stewardship. All members will be encouraged to have their say on how things are run, and the legal structure of the farm promotes this.

So far 120 households have expressed an interest in the project, and over 40 are already directly involved. Our first members' meeting was held in January 2011, and we have started a workshare scheme through which people can do a few hours' work for their share. By year 3 we will have reached capacity, supplying 100 households with veg. By then Sims Hill will look quite different. Not only will it be immensely productive but there will be ponds, more trees, and spaces for people to come and enjoy being close to the land and each other.

For more information on Sims Hill Shared Harvest please visit http://simshillsharedharvest. wordpress.com or email simshillsharedharvest@ googlemail.com.

Two (or more) growing spaces

If you're lucky enough to have more than one growing space but in different areas then you have some quite unique choices to make. It makes sense to use each plot differently rather than having two identical plots. Many people with two allotments choose to grow fruit on one and vegetables on the other. This makes sense, as each have different requirements at different times of the year. The fruit plot, for example, will need less regular attention than the vegetable plot, but you may need to spend some time pruning it in the winter when there is little to do on the vegetable plot.

A friend of mine owns a field a few miles from his home and has a small garden plot at home. On his field he has a small orchard and grows potatoes and other vegetables that don't need daily care. At home he grows things such as salad greens, herbs and tender vegetables that he wants to have in regular supply and that need a little more attention.

with money generally have no time. In many ways a lack of time can lead to a much more impoverished existence than a lack of money, and giving time to someone can be much more appreciated than giving them cash (although I wouldn't object if anyone reading this wants to send me a big cheque).

One of the most enriching things you can do with your time is to volunteer, and there are countless gardens and organisations with gardens in need of someone to give up their time. I found that as soon as I made the choice to volunteer there was so much around that I could pick and choose where I wanted to go and what I wanted to do.

The sort of work I did was as varied as the people I met – I ended up doing everything from constructing a green roof with a group of filthy-mouthed but very entertaining long-term unemployed to building a cob Wendy house with a professional photographer and an out-of-work actor to potting seedlings with a wannabe rap artist.

On the whole the sort of people I met were intelligent, funny, well-rounded individuals who wanted to make a bit of a difference to their community. Volunteers, especially those keen to work on the land, can make a huge difference to an area. In Detroit, USA, derelict housing blocks are being turned into productive gardens to feed locals who otherwise have no access to fresh vegetables.

I'm still in touch with many of the people I volunteered with and would strongly advise anyone moving to a new town or city who is finding it hard to make friends to go and find a community project, city farm or local public garden that would benefit from his or her help. Many places will have evening sessions in the summer and weekend sessions all year round, so even those in full-time employment can squeeze in a few hours.

I've found that quite often these organisa-tions are so glad to have you on board that you'll receive a generous share of the produce in return for your volunteer hours. These are often organically grown, well-cared-for vegetables that would cost a fortune to buy.

On some volunteer placements you can try out new equipment and tools, and/or work on unusual plants and in unusual locations (such as in botanic gardens, arboretums or city farms) that would normally be well outside of your normal set of circumstances.

It's a sad fact of life that many organisations disappear not through lack of funding but through lack of volunteers. Recruiting volunteers has been likened to herding cats, and it may seem that some places advertise for volunteers in the same way that the Vogons advertised the destruction of the Earth in Douglas Adams' *Hitchhiker's Guide to the Galaxy*. However, local newspapers, library noticeboards or direct contact with an organisation can be good ways to find out about ad hoc or regular volunteer opportuni-ties, or just ask around in your local area.

It is a very rewarding way to garden: turning up somewhere where they will always be glad to see you is a real boost to the self-esteem.

GUERRILLA GARDENING

Guerrilla gardening can brighten up the dullest, most neglected patches of our city streets. The grey urban landscape can suddenly be transformed by the wash of colour from flowers, shrubs and even food plants. What's more, as there is zero rent or yearly subscription to pay, it can be a totally free way to garden.

If I can't give them away, I use up any extra seedlings or unwanted seed by guerrilla planting. I heard a lovely story once of someone who would see sunflowers appear all over her neighbourhood right through her childhood. It wasn't until she became an adult that she found that her father had been sowing seeds in neighbours' gardens every year as he loved the flowers so much. This just goes to show how such imaginative gardening can have really worthwhile effects.

Pros of volunteering
- Learn new skills
- Share produce
- Free plants, seeds, pots and compost on occasion
- Make new friends
- Improve employment prospects and enhance CV
- Work in interesting environments
- Increase happiness

If it looks like it's meant to be there it will generally get left alone.

Seed bombs

I first became aware of seed bombs from reading David Tracey's brilliant book *Guerrilla gardening: A manualfesto*. Seed bombs are a great way to introduce plants to otherwise inaccessible places. In my adaptation of the seed bomb 'recipe' in David's book, I use a vegetable such as a potato or small squash about the size of a tennis ball (or grenade), then hollow it out to hold the horticultural contents. You could also use an already-hollow vegetable such as a pepper.

Seed bombs are most useful for flowers, but self-seeding salads such as land cress and rocket can also be sown this way. If allowed to run to seed, both these plants will quickly become naturalised and add to the variety of edible 'wild' plants.

Guerrilla planting and vandalism

Guerrilla-planted plots can get vandalised, but this is rarer than you may imagine. Contrary to popular belief, vandalism is rarely planned and it is rarely malicious. Often it is nothing more than a case of something in the path of someone with more testosterone or alcohol (or both) in their system than they can handle. Planting away from busy pubs and clubs, planting out of reach or just making something look like it is meant to be there can go a long way to ensuring that it is left alone.

Contamination

Guerrilla-planted food can carry all the same risks as foraged food in urban areas. There is a risk of contamination from rats, dogs, cats and even humans. Any food plants should be washed thoroughly or, preferably, washed *and* cooked before eaten. Leafy greens take in a lot of air pollution. Unless there is some kind of barrier, such as a hedge or fence, between the road and the plants then they will contain these pollutants.

Guerrilla gardening and the law

Technically, guerrilla gardening is illegal and can be classed as criminal damage. Its advocates often play up the dangerous side, but if caught you are much more likely to get a telling off than a conviction. You may have the moral high ground and the support of local residents, but in the eyes of the law you are in the wrong. To be on the safe side, avoid areas with CCTV or even ask for permission first.

If you look like you are meant to be there, nine times out of ten the police will ignore you. A team with fluorescent jackets in broad daylight looks a lot more legitimate than a team dressed in black at 2am.

HOW TO MAKE A SEED BOMB

1 Using a sharp knife, cut the top off your vegetable and hollow it out in the same way you would a Halloween lantern. It should be cut in such a way that the cap can be replaced. Or pull off the stalk of your pepper.

2 Coat the base of the bomb with a moist, rich potting compost – use a funnel if the top hole is small. If you wish to sow wildflowers, use spent potting compost as they prefer an impoverished soil.

SEEDS

COMPOST

4 If sowing 'hungry' plants such as sunflowers, add some slow-release fertiliser pellets. (This may not be necessary if the compost is rich enough.)

3 Add the seeds on a small piece of wetted tissue paper.

5 Top with more moist compost.

6 Find somewhere to throw your bomb!

Chapter 2

....

PLANNING

Once you've established where you are going to grow, it helps to take a detailed look at the site. This will give you a complete picture of your plot before you start and will help you work out what will thrive where, what plants might be suitable or what might be simply too big. It will also help you to tot up the number of seeds you might need, making life easier when you come to acquire them.

Whatever you decide to do with a garden, making plans and assessing the site before you begin will save you time and money in the long run. However, be aware that there is such a thing as over-planning, which can take time away from important tasks and hold you back in the growing season. The key, as with most things, is to strike a balance.

DRAWING A PLAN

A plan will help you decide the best position for any structures, paths or other permanent fixtures. It can be a work in progress across a year or two – you may put in only annuals in the first year and structures and perennials from the second year on, when you have a more complete picture of the garden.

Things to include on a plan
To get the most out of a garden, consider drawing a plan to include all its different

environmental as well as physical characteristics. These include factors such as:
- the direction of the wind
- the position of buildings, trees and shrubs
- the amount of sun/shade each area or each bed receives
- the location of the water supply
- any permanent fixtures – manholes, drains, washing lines, etc.

The process can be somewhat illuminating, even for gardens that are long established, and it can also throw up new possibilities you may not have thought about before.

For example:
- You may want to put in a new shed in an area to act as a windbreak.
- It may be worth growing various crops in a vegetable bed that only gets a couple of hours of sunlight a day, and creating another one in a sunnier spot elsewhere in the garden.

In a lot of cases you might need nothing more than a rough sketch, especially for smaller plots. However, the more detail you put in, the more accurate and full picture you will get of your growing space and the more you will be able to plant each section up to suit its conditions. The time put in on making a good plan is usually well spent!

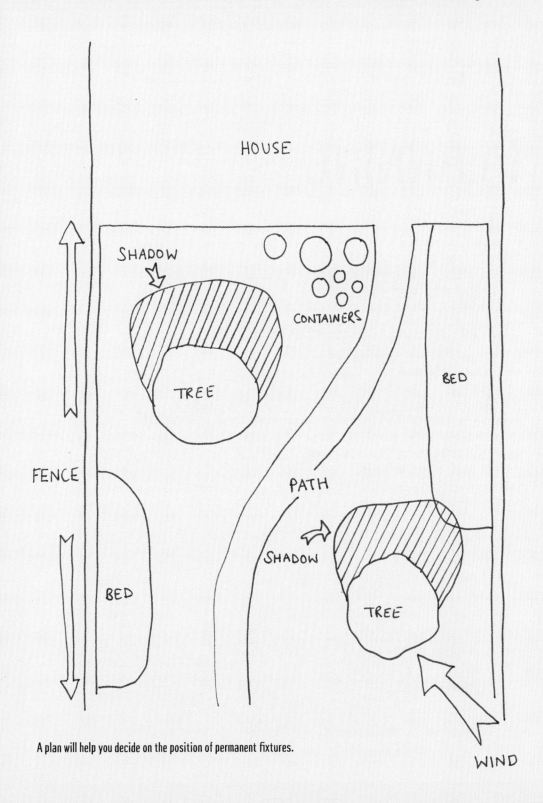

A plan will help you decide on the position of permanent fixtures.

Measuring the plot

For a small garden (under 10m [33ft] in width), measure a long wall, a side of a house, a fence or path running the length of the garden. These (in theory) should be a perfect straight line for you to position the plan of the garden around. Next, measure offsets, i.e. measure from that line at right angles running the full width of the garden. Mark the distance of anything in between, such as a tree or a vegetable bed, before marking the far side (see picture below). It is easier to do this in note form first, noting down all the distances before putting the plan together later – indoors in the warm.

You will need to triangulate larger gardens. This is not as scary as it sounds: it simply means dividing rectangular or square areas of a plot into triangles (see picture opposite). Unlike four straight sides, the sides of a triangle don't change (think of the eaves of a roof rather than four lolly sticks pinned together), which should enable you to

A good plan will always start with a tape measure.

measure up large areas without mistakes. For uneven areas of a garden, take offsets as above. Again, measure the distances between objects, plants, trees, etc.

Scale

Work out a suitable scale for your plan – 1:50 scale means every 1cm on the page equals 50cm in the garden and a 1:100 means every 1 centimetre on a page equals 1 metre. (Or, in imperial units, people tend to use a quarter scale, where ¼ inch on the page equals 1 foot in the garden.) It is easier to work out than you think, i.e. for 1:50 just divide by 50. So, on a 1:50 scale, a 1m x 2m bed would equal 2cm x 4cm on your plan. (Or, for imperial, divide by 4 and change feet to inches, so 4 feet in the garden will equal 1 inch on the page.)

Some examples are given in the table overleaf, using one garden that miraculously has everything measured to the nearest metre and another that just as miraculously works perfectly in feet and inches.

8m (24')
9m (27')
4m (12')

Triangles provide a rigid, constant shape.

How actual measurements are represented on a plan				
	Metric 1:50 scale		Imperial 1/4 scale	
	Garden	Plan	Garden	Plan
Bed	1m x 2m	2cm x 4cm	3ft x 6ft	$^3/_4$" x 1 $^1/_2$"
Tree canopy	Radius 3m	Radius 6cm	10ft	2 $^1/_2$"
Wall	15cm x 5m	0.3cm x 10cm	1ft x 16ft	$^1/_4$" x 4"
Shed	2.5m x 2m	5cm x 4cm	8ft x 6ft	2" x 1 $^1/_2$"

Putting in detail

You should include as much information as you have time for or wish to work with. The more you put in, the more informed choices you can make when planting or building in your garden.

A single plan on a single sheet will do for a basic plan, or you could make a series of plans throughout the year for more accurate data.

Weeds What weeds are growing where (can give clues to the pH and condition of the soil and will affect what food plants you may want to grow).

Soil pH If you have access to a soil pH testing kit, take samples around the garden and put this information on the plan. The soil pH can change throughout the year, so more than one measurement may be necessary.

Wind Draw arrows for the direction of the wind (In the UK, northerly winds can be cold and south-westerlies a lot warmer). As with the pH, this can change throughout the year so, again, measurements at different times will provide more accurate information.

Light and shade For a full picture this should be recorded morning, noon and afternoon and right across the year (use photocopied plans or planning software). As the seasons change so does the position of the sun in the sky, so without a 12-month plan you won't have an accurate picture.

Using digital photos

In conjunction with a software package such as Photoshop or an open source equivalent (or even paint!) a digital photo can be a great tool for judging the overall look of a garden. Take a few pictures from different angles and use the software or sketch on a printed copy any changes you wish to make.

You could use it to gauge, for example:
- what a tree is going to look like when it reaches maturity
- what visual impact a shed might make
- how a vegetable patch might look in the middle of the lawn.

Points to remember when making your plan

Changes can be monitored in your first year, so in your second year you can make a more suitable planting plan if necessary.

If you are only there on a short-term let (less than a year), a quick overall assessment might be all you need.

If you don't plan to grow any vegetables in winter you don't need to map the light/shade at that time of year.

You can cut and paste pictures from the internet over the top of the photo – rather like making a collage – to get a good idea of how things may look.

WORKING WITH YOUR SITE

Try to look at your plot with a critical but sparing eye, as the more you can leave a garden as it is and adapt what you want around it, rather than the other way round, the less time, money and effort you will need to put in.

If a garden is gravelled and exploratory removal of a small section reveals concrete, hardcore or serious compaction underneath, think about building up rather than down. Building raised beds will mean importing soil but it could work out a lot cheaper than hiring a skip to dispose of a few tonnes of hardcore.

Work with the soil type

Work with your soil type rather than against it: this could save a lot of time and money in the long run compared with the costs of importing tonnes of organic matter to improve the soil (although there is never any harm in this if you can get it).

Brassicas, corn and squashes will thrive with very little improvement on a clay soil, while root vegetables, such as carrots and parsnips, will love the loose particles of a sandy soil to push their roots into.

Similarly, brassicas prefer alkaline soils and blueberries will grow well in an acid soil.

Work with the local climate

See what's around you, what is growing well and what is struggling. Work with your climate – is there any point in sowing late-season potatoes in a rainy area when they just get blight year after year? Try planting just earlies or even an alternative root crop such as Jerusalem artichokes, or experiment with yams suited to your climate.

If you are in a drought-affected area, does it make sense to grow crops that need a lot of water? Why not grow amaranth, asparagus, artichokes (Jerusalem and Chinese) or even edible succulents rather than thirsty cucurbits?

FACTORS TO TAKE INTO ACCOUNT

We've all come up against the views of relatives around the dinner table, and after a while I'm sure we've all realised there are certain things in life you may never be able to change. The same is true for gardening. No matter how hard you try there are just some things you have to work with, rather than against. The trick is identifying those things early on and adapting to them.

Lack of light

In towns and cities it is quite common for a garden to be overshadowed by neighbouring buildings. In some gardens, including one of my old ones, this overshadowing can be so bad that the garden may be in full sun for just a few hours of the day, if at all.

My old dark dingy garden taught me a few things. First, it taught me to look at the house you wish to rent in the middle of the day rather than in the fading winter light. Second, it taught me about phototropism, which is the term for the simple fact that plants will grow towards the light.

For the squashes I grew in this grotto this was quite beneficial, as they headed out of the shaded bed and towards the light in the middle of the lawn. However, my chive and onion border leaned into the lawn in search of light and didn't look quite like the architec-tural companion planting I desired.

Beetroot can flourish in dappled shade.

Crops for shade

Lettuce
Parsley
Mint
Radish
Sorrel
Beetroot
Perpetual spinach
Perennial / Babington's leeks
Wild garlic
Good King Henry
Jack by the hedge
Siberian purslane

Crops that need full sun will seldom thrive in a shaded garden, so you have two choices: grow to the light with trailing or climbing plants, or grow crops suited to shade.

If it is trees that are causing the shade, you can try to grow vegetables that will become established before the trees come into leaf, such as broad beans and spring cabbages, along with fast-growing salad leaves. Otherwise, you can reduce the height or even remove the tree if it is your own, or politely ask a neighbour to do the same if it is not on your land. Not all tree species are well chosen, beneficial or valued.

Climate

Knowing what can grow in your particular area can save you time, money and effort. I've often seen people in the UK trying to grow aubergines unprotected outside, inevitably with very little success. There is a cost involved in getting that plant from seed to plot, and that money is wasted if you are destined to watch the flowers drop and the plant never form fruit.

Aspect

Just as you can't choose the geographic location of your garden, nor can you choose the aspect.

A lot of mobile phones have a compass application, which takes the guesswork out of navigation – or you could even just use an actual compass! However, in the absence of technology, new or old, the sun will always be due south around midday.

In the northern hemisphere, south can be determined by holding an accurate analogue watch horizontally and pointing the hour hand at the sun. The point halfway between the hour hand and 12 o'clock will point south. So, for example, at 2pm south would be at 1pm on the watch face and at 6pm south would be at 3pm on the watch. (This is because the Earth goes around the sun once a day whereas the 12-hour clock repeats twice a day, so it is necessary to halve the angle between the hour hand and 12 o'clock.)

In the southern hemisphere you point the 12 o'clock position at the sun and take the point

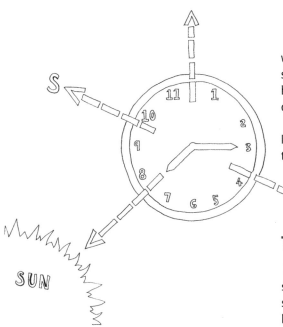

which can lead to pests such as slugs. All should not be lost in a north-facing garden, however, as lettuces, cabbages and some culinary herbs can all do well.

East-facing gardens get the morning light but things can get decidedly gloomy by the afternoon. Peas, carrots, lettuces and cabbages will all cope reasonably well in these conditions.

TIME MANAGEMENT

If you want to develop a really low sense of self-worth and suffer a big dent to the ego, start by being completely unrealistic about how much work you can do.

halfway between this and the hour hand to find south.

Neither of these methods will work in the tropics, but if you live there it's probably less of a concern which direction the sun is coming from.

The ideal aspect for a piece of land in the northern hemisphere is one that gently slopes to the south or, failing that, to the west/south-west. Most plants will thrive in these gardens, especially short-lived summer annuals such as sweetcorn (maize) and squashes, along with fruit-bearing plants such as tomatoes and cucumbers (I know, a squash is a fruit-bearing plant too!). Roots will also do well, but you might struggle with some salad greens as these can prefer slightly cooler conditions.

Problem aspects
North-facing gardens can be gloomy, and you may struggle to bring in extra light by simply reducing any large trees or shrubs that may be causing shade. These gardens may also have problems with damp conditions,

I do believe that at times it is important to push yourself, especially in busy periods such as the spring. However, knowing how much you can achieve and successfully achieving it is far better for your well-being than constantly not meeting impossible targets.

It helps to time how long a task takes so you know how long it will take in the future. If you normally spend time chatting, drinking tea, watching grasshoppers or staring into space,

Guide to mismanaging your time

- Set yourself impossible amounts of work, e.g. four hour-long jobs each day but only two hours to do them in.
- Line up more jobs behind this so you can really feel crushed at the end of the day.
- Rather than complete any one job do a little bit of each one.
- Give up the garden because it has got on top of you.

then include this time in your calculations as it will give you a realistic rather than a skewed idea of how long things will take.

MAKING GOOD USE OF THE THINGS THAT YOU FIND

Gardens and especially allotments can, to say the least, get neglected between owners. At first glance it might seem that your intended vegetable plot is nothing more than a mass of weeds. In my experience, appearances are not always that deceptive – what looks like a mass of weeds may well be a mass of weeds.

But it is important to be a little vigilant before diving in with the brushcutter, scythe, spade or rotovator – you could be doing something you may later regret. Instead, take the time to look around for any perennials that may be lurking within the jungle undergrowth. It might only take five minutes but it will be worth it in the long run, as you could discover something that has taken years to establish.

A rhubarb patch is sometimes the only evidence of the last plot holder.

Once found, try to weed around the plant or cut down the weeds and surround it (e.g. a blackcurrant bush) with a cardboard mulch and top-dress with well-rotted manure or use a feed (such as comfrey feed) during the growing season. A more drastic, but effective approach if the weeds have really taken over, would be to dig the plant during its dormant season (winter), carefully untangling roots from the weeds as you do so, and replant it somewhere weed-free. Water it in well and mulch around the top.

Be careful below the ground too. I made a big mistake in my first year of growing when I dug up what I thought to be a mass of weed roots. I was amazed at how easily they seemed to pull out and was fascinated by the shape of the roots. They were not a jumbled mass like couch grass or long like a nettle, nor were they a deep taproot like dock or dandelion. Out of curiosity I left some of the plants just to see what they were. Come the spring the patch I left began to send up spear-shaped green shoots. I instantly recognised them as asparagus and found that my hand had involuntarily slapped my forehead.

Discovering edible perennials

Experienced gardeners can look away now, as they shouldn't need any help identifying common perennials on their plot. First-timers or those still finding their feet, on the other hand, might need a little help to ensure they don't throw out the baby with the bathwater, or at least the bay laurel with the bramble. The following are some plants you may well come across whilst trying to tame your own private Amazon jungle.

- **Jerusalem artichoke** A plant grown for its tubers, which are knobbly, about the length of a finger but a little fatter, and sometimes pinkish in colour. In the winter the tubers may raise themselves to the surface and reveal themselves. If disturbed by a spade they can easily be replanted. In the spring and summer they will resemble their close relative the sunflower – the long straight stem or even the flower should be a dead giveaway. When dormant they can be dug up and replanted in a weed-free spot with a little compost or well-rotted manure added.

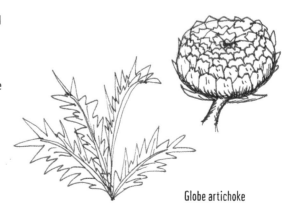

Globe artichoke

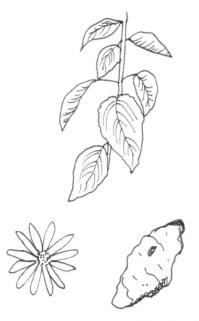

Jerusalem artichoke

- **Globe artichoke** A very easy plant to spot as it resembles an overgrown thistle (it *is* one really!). The leaves are a light dusty green with a large flower that is about the size of a tennis ball. When left unattended these plants can form large clumps and should be thinned out to just the parent plant, with any seedlings/offshoots planted elsewhere if needed. If you don't have room in a vegetable bed, globe artichoke makes an excellent architectural plant in a mixed border. If replanting, do so carefully and in the winter, and bear in mind that they don't always take.

- **Asparagus** In the winter this can be identified by its crowns under the soil surface, which look like fat floppy strings. In the spring it will pop up with the telltale spear-shaped shoots, which later give way to large very wispy fern-like growths, possibly with very small red fruits. If you can, weed around the plant and try not to disturb the roots. You can cut down the ferns as they start to discolour and cover the plant with thick black plastic over the winter. Covering it in this way should make the job of weeding a little easier – just remember to take up the plastic again in the spring when it is growing again!

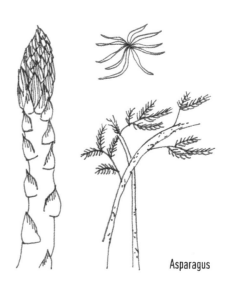

Asparagus

- **Rhubarb** You shouldn't have any trouble spotting this plant – a big leafy thing on stalks! Separate any large crowns by digging up, chopping in two and replanting both halves. Keep weed-free and top-dress with manure.

Rhubarb

- **Strawberry** Creeping cinquefoil can be mistaken for strawberries, so check that your 'strawberries' don't have five little leaves and a yellow flower before you start to really nurture them. Strawberry plants get past their best after only a few years so don't be surprised if your free plants don't produce much. Pick off the best runners, replant those and, to rejuvenate

Strawberry

the plants, remove flowers in the first year so they put more energy into the roots.

- **Raspberry** This can sometimes be mistaken for brambles. However, brambles tend to trail and run whereas raspberries grow straight upwards in canes and have fine spines rather than thorns. It can be very difficult to tell an autumn raspberry from a summer one, so if in doubt leave it and see what it does. It can be dug up and replanted in ground prepared with well-rotted manure, or you can apply a thick mulch.

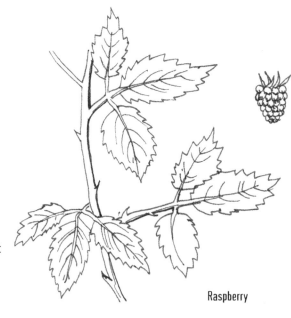

Raspberry

- **Fruit bushes** Usually quite distinctive no matter what time of year it is, fruit bushes often even have labels left on them telling you precisely what they are. There are very few weeds that will resemble a carefully placed fruit bush, so if in doubt leave it be and see what happens. Consult a guide to pruning if it has got out of hand – remember to cut dead, dying and diseased growth and never more than a third of living material in any one year. Cut the weeds down to ground level and mulch with – in this order – cardboard, newspaper and manure/compost and then leaf litter or woodchip on top.

- **Herbs** The smell should be a telltale sign: tear off a leaf, break in up in your hand and take a sniff. If you can't identify the scent, but there is one, take a look online or in a herb book to get a clear identification. Dig up what you can and replant. Mulch around the base of woodier herb shrubs such as rosemary or sage, and treat bay trees as you would fruit bushes.

ESTABLISHED TREES

The right kind of tree in the right place is always a real bonus. My first allotment had a sweet chestnut and a blackthorn (sloe) tree growing in the hedgerow. Roasted chestnuts were an unexpected treat in my house that autumn, as was the sloe gin at Christmas.

Both trees were far enough away from the land to not cause any real problem with their roots taking food away from my veggies. Also, they were on the north side of the plot and so didn't present much of a problem in terms of light – had they been blocking out the sun I would have had a real dilemma.

Problems with established trees

But you might not be so lucky: an established tree in the wrong place can rob a plot of light, restricting the growth of your veggies. Worse still, it could be growing right where you want to put your veg plot or may be blocking the light to a window. To work out whether it needs the pruning saw, the spade or the axe, or if it is best left alone, consider the following.

- **Is it blocking light to a plot?** If it is worth saving, perhaps the crown can be reduced and/or the tree trained in a way that no longer blocks the light? First, cut out dead, dying and diseased branches. For most trees (you can actually cut elder and willow right down to the base and they'll still grow back), do not remove any more than a fifth to a third of living branches – this is especially true for fruit trees. For a really neglected tree this means that the whole pruning process could take a couple of years or more. Leylandii and other cypresses can be reduced in height, but don't cut as deep as 'the brown stuff' – once the green leaves have been cut away they won't regenerate from the inner wood.

- **Is it blocking light to a window?** For small city gardens this can be really relevant. If the tree is a fruit tree you may want to consider whether the energy gained from the fruit is worth the extra cost in heat and light. There is no point in saving money by growing apples if you have to pay a large heating and lighting bill for the privilege.

- **Is the tree small?** Can it just be dug up and moved? If it is worth saving then move it somewhere else, but do think about what it will look like when it reaches full size. If you don't have room for it, maybe someone else does, so try advertising it on Freecycle (see Resources) or offering it to friends.

- **How important is the tree to the local ecosystem?** Is the tree casting heavy shade, thus preventing wildflowers and herbs from growing and reducing the garden's diversity? Or is the tree home to countless birds and insects?

- **Is the tree protected?** If you are renting, your landlord should know this. If it's your own home, check with the local authorities. Some will have interactive maps on their websites showing trees with preservation orders, but in other areas it might take a quick phone call.

- **Is it diseased?** Is it too close to another tree? If the answer to both of these questions is yes, then you might just have

TREE
BLOCKS
LIGHT

SALADS AND
HERBS ON
SUNNY WINDOW
SILL

DWARF FRUIT
TREES ALLOW
LIGHT TO
ENTER

A tree in the wrong place
can cost more than it saves
in home-grown produce.

to get rid of it. Fungal diseases such as canker can be cut out of a tree by removing infected branches. Burn any diseased wood to prevent further infection.

Removing trees

I've only ever taken down trees in a woodland situation, never in a garden. Removing large trees can be dangerous work, and more so when they are near to buildings. If you have the money then this could be the rare case where I wouldn't suggest doing it yourself. If you must do it yourself, try to seek advice from someone who has done this before, and make sure you wear the relevant safety equipment.

Feeding trees and weeding

If a tree has been abandoned for a number of years and it lies under a jungle of rampant weeds, then it might need a little tender loving care. Once the weeds have been cut back, try to prevent any more establishing by laying cardboard mulch around the base of the tree and covering this with garden compost or manure.

Nut trees

Finding a mature nut tree can be a real bonus. This tasty extra crop can be used in risottos, in a pesto or saved and eaten over Christmas.

Walnut

A large walnut tree can be as much of a blessing as a curse. If you can outwit the squirrels, then it can provide you with valuable sources of fat and carbohydrates: two nutrients that are difficult to source from the garden. Even if you don't harvest the mature nut, you can soak the immature nut in brine for a couple of weeks before pickling it in vinegar.

However, most walnut trees are grafted on to black walnut rootstock. The roots of black walnut contain a phytotoxin or plant toxin called juglone, which can affect many common fruit and vegetable plants, including those in the potato family (potato, tomato, aubergine) as well as blueberries, blackberries and apples. According to an article published by Ohio State University,[*] plants growing anywhere near the roots can be affected, which on a young tree is a distance from the trunk equal to twice the trunk's height, while on a mature tree this could be anything between about 15m and 25m (50-80ft) of the trunk.

So if you have a walnut tree you may have to forgo growing members of the potato family and instead grow squashes, beans, carrots and corn.

Prune walnuts in the late summer or autumn after harvesting the nuts, rather than in the late winter or early spring, when the sap is rising.

Hazel

You have a number of choices if you have hazel trees growing on your land:
- Manage them for the nuts.
- Trim as hedging (if in the hedgerow).
- Coppice them.

If you want to grow them for nuts, bear in mind that the nuts grow on year-old wood. Squirrels may be a problem – I've found they only really leave nut trees alone if they are next to a busy road or if the nuts grow in such abundance that they don't get a chance to harvest them all. You are legally obliged to kill a squirrel if you catch one, so if (like me) you feel you would be unable to do this then try harvesting the nuts just before the squirrels (difficult!), or just put up with a certain amount of predation. You can have a go at preventing the furry pests from climbing the trees – Martin Crawford, Director of the

* 'Black walnut toxicity to plants, humans and horses', Richard C. Funt & Jane Martin, Ohio State University Extension Fact Sheet, http://ohioline.osu.edu/hyg-fact/1000/1148.html

Moor view, less view

You may need to remove large overgrown trees that are shadowing your garden, but if the trees are on a neighbour's land this may be far easier said than done. A friend of mine lived on Dartmoor for a number of years and benefitted from a stunning view of the moors from his living-room window. His neighbour lived in a house between him and the moor and shared a similar view, reflected in the name of the neighbour's house, 'Moor view'. The neighbour was an odd fellow and, wanting to gain some privacy (in this very remote location!), decided to grow a huge leylandii hedge. There was little my friend could do once the hedge reached full height, and he ended up erecting a plaque outside his house with the name 'Less view'.

A large hedging plant won't give the neighbours any 'moor' view.

You'll often be competing with squirrels for hazelnuts.

Agroforestry Research Trust, suggests enclosing the trunk in a smooth sheet of hard material such as tree guard, starting at about 90cm (3ft) high and going up to about 2m (7ft). The squirrels won't be able to jump over it, but of course it doesn't stop them jumping into the tree from another tree.

Managing hazel as hedging means you may not get any nuts, as you could be cutting away fruiting (or nutting) wood. However, you will get a wildlife-friendly area, as there will be habitat for nesting birds.

To coppice hazel, cut right down to a stump in the autumn after the leaves have fallen. The tree will send up long straight shoots, which after six to seven years can be used in place of imported bamboo for bean supports.

Fruit trees

A well-managed fruit tree is an asset to any piece of land. Check for disease and cut out any affected branches. Prune out excess and crossing branches – this will help with airflow. The old saying advises that you should prune enough space to throw your hat between the branches. Trees in the plum genus (*Prunus*), including plums, sloes and damsons, should be summer pruned after fruiting, while most other fruit trees, including apples, hawthorns and pears, should be pruned in the winter.

Apple and pear

All types of apple, whether wild or domesticated, have a use – raw, cooked, brewed into cider or, in the case of small crab apples, made into chutney.

If you have problems with woolly aphids then rub them off with soap spray and put up a nesting box for blue tits, as aphids seem to be one of their favourite foods.

Prunus *species (peach, cherry, plum)*

There's an old joke amongst gardeners: 'Prunus, no prune us', indicating the lack of pruning required in the *Prunus* genus. You should still prune the three Ds – dead, dying and diseased – and prune out crossing branches, but do so sparingly. Prune after fruiting in the summer. In cooler climes peaches and nectarines will benefit from being trained across a south-facing wall – tie in the tree if it has become loose and prune away any stray branches.

Planting underneath trees

- Birds look for food from above, so a fruit bush planted under a fruit tree should be out of sight of their sharp eyes.
- Comfrey makes a surprising companion plant, its roots reaching nutrients the tree would otherwise miss. Use the leaves as a mulch to feed the tree.
- Under-sowing with mint will help with weed management and not interfere with the growing tree, as their roots grow at a different depth.
- Nasturtiums can be trained to run up the tree, or marigolds sown around the base. These will attract beneficial insects to prey on pests.

Chapter 3

WILDLIFE GARDENING

Striking a balance between the natural world and the plot you desire can sometimes seem like fighting a losing battle. It need not be this way, however, as the nearer you come to a natural system the less work you have to do. Attracting predators such as lacewings, ladybirds and birds can vastly reduce greenfly numbers, and attracting larger predators, such as slow-worms, hedgehogs and frogs, can help keep numbers of slugs and snails down.

A plot in balance with nature is not only a healthy one, it is also one that will be cheaper to manage as there will be no need for expensive measures to combat or protect against pests and diseases.

As with most of us, until recently much of my knowledge about wildlife gardening was based on what I'd read in populist books and magazines, my observations of the many

It's amazing what you can find in the garden. *Photo: Lou Brown*

allotments and gardens I've found myself in over the years, and finally good old fence-leaning advice from other gardeners. The knowledge passed on from other gardeners was always similar to that in books and magazines: plant native plants, grow a patch of nettles, keep it scruffy, leave the grass to grow long and dig a pond.

I've since read the brilliant book *No Nettles Required* by Ken Thompson, which confirms or dispels many of the urban myths surrounding wildlife gardening, including the following.

- 'Plant native plants.' This is not necessarily true, as non-natives can have longer flowering times and offer more diversity for wildlife.
- 'Keep a patch of nettles.' Untrue – nettles aren't exactly an endangered species!
- 'Build a pond.' True – any variety of habitat will help attract wildlife.
- 'Keep it scruffy.' Only true if it makes for a mixed habitat.
- 'Leave the grass to grow long.' True – long grass can be important for overwintering species.

I was still going by older pre-Ken-Thompson knowledge when I first took on my plot in Bristol. One of the most striking things about the plot back then was the complete lack of wildlife, large or small. In fact, with the exception of brambles and creeping cinquefoil, there was a decided lack of anything on the plot.

Over time I tried to redress this balance: I put in a pond in, around which I grew a mix of grasses and flowering plants. In places I let the grass paths and fringes grow long. I also sowed and planted clover, camomile and various other low-lying plants such as mints, valerian and golden rod around these neglected areas. In addition I companion-planted the main vegetable beds and planted and extended the two herb patches to include perennials or self-seeders such as marjoram and sorrel.

A lot of the work was intuitive but some was merely dictated by what I had to hand, what was cheap or what was given to me. Eventually a huge mix of pollinators arrived, along with a family of slow-worms, frogs and many tiny visitors I couldn't even begin to name.

Why my wildlife garden worked

It seems that through my intuition, improvisation and by generally making the most of what was there I stumbled upon many of the methods I later read to be successful for wildlife gardening.

Inadvertently I took care of the very base of any food chain, and everything above it flourished – a 'look after the pennies and the pounds will look after themselves' approach. The long grass meant that there was a place for overwintering insects, leaving some plants to seed meant small birds had food to eat, and of course the pond added an extra habitat.

Natural pest control.

THE IMPORTANCE OF A MIXED HABITAT

A crucial key to creating a wildlife garden is a mix of varied habitat. Even though many species of caterpillar rely on the nettle as food, there are a *lot* of nettles growing outside of gardens. In terms of habitat destruction we are in no danger of losing the nettle from our towns or countryside. Besides, despite what many wildlife books may tell you, there is little proof that nettles are really all that effective as breeding sites for butterflies.

There is a huge range of things that crawl, burrow, fly, run, skip, jump and walk looking for somewhere to crawl, burrow, fly, run, skip, jump and walk. Simply growing nettles for them would be a bit like playing a CD of the latest sugar-coated pop sensation to a room full of teenagers and expecting them all to like it, even the ones with dyed black hair and gloomy dispositions.

However, having a big mix of habitat – such as rocks, tall flowers, log piles, tussock grass, bare patches and flowers with a long flower-ing time – will help attract wildlife. Garden habitats should be as diverse as the crea-tures you wish to move in. Some insects will need different habitats for different stages of their lives, and providing this mix will go a long way to enabling them to thrive in an otherwise hostile landscape.

CREATING HABITAT PATCHES IN GRASSLAND

Creating habitat and attracting wildlife to a garden need not be expensive, nor does it have to be time consuming. Ladybirds, like other predatory invertebrates, seek out the shelter of long clumps of grass to bed down in for the winter. So one of the best things you can do is simply leave tussocks of grass to grow. The ladybirds will crawl out of their hidey holes in spring just in time to keep blackfly numbers in check amongst your broad beans. If scruffy tussocks isn't your thing, clump-forming ornamental grasses, such as pampas, work in the same way.

Leaving all grass to grow a little longer will help attract wildlife. The cool, humid condi-tions created by patches of long grass provide shelter for reptiles and amphibians looking for somewhere to cool down, as well as a home to a multitude of invertebrates. It is a fine balance, as it takes only a few short weeks for grass to shed seed into your well-tended, weed-free beds, but there are ways around this.

- A system of rotating areas of longer grass worked for me, allowing perimeter grass rather than grass near the beds to grow long.
- Raise the cut of lawnmower blades to around 5cm/2", as this will provide a lot more habitat than cutting grass down to ground level.
- Sow yellow rattle, a wildflower that parasitises the roots of grass, preventing it from growing too long.

A beetle retreats back under cover after basking on an old stalk.

- Encourage a wildflower meadow – mow as normal until June then leave to seed over the summer before cutting again in the autumn.
- Leave grass to grow long only near unproductive beds covered in weed-suppressant material, such as Mypex or cardboard.

It is useful to have amongst long grass common weeds such as greater plantain and spear-leaf plantain as the seeds provide a valuable winter source of carbohydrates for birds.

MAKING BASKING SPACES

For invertebrates and reptiles it is just as important to have a place to bask as it is to have a place to hide. Insects, like reptiles, are cold blooded – they need to soak up the sun's rays to raise their blood temperature and allow them to function. You may notice that some species of bee will sit on the tops of tall flowers for some time; they are not there to pollinate the flower but to warm themselves up.

So leaving tall plants, bare patches of ground, rocks or any other exposed surface for insects to bask on is a really worthwhile thing to do for wildlife in your garden.

CREATING A CHEAP WILDFLOWER GARDEN

To create a wildflower meadow on a patch of lawn, remove or rake all the mown grass each time you do a cut. The soil will be impoverished after a year of removing the nutrients that the grass would otherwise have provided, and you can now scatter-sow your wildflower seed. As the seeds can be rather small it is advantageous to mix sand with the seed to aid scatter-sowing.

Bees aren't always pollinating when they hang around on flowers.

My Oxford wildflower garden

During my early gardening days I would take long walks peering into people's gardens or going out into the countryside to seek inspiration. On one exceptionally long walk in the Coltswolds I was struck by the amount of wildflowers on verges, wasteland and hedgerows. Clearly these flowers had not been planted, but nonetheless they put on a display to rival any domestic flower garden.

Returning inspired by my country ramble I decided I would have a go at recreating a similar wildflower patch in my own back garden. At the time I had very little money (something which never seems to change!) but did have the remains of a packet of wildflower seed a friend had given to me. I scatter-sowed all the available seed on a bed that had recently grown carrots. The seed was barely enough to cover the ground, so I left the ground bare to see what would blow in – weeding out any undesirables and leaving in worthwhile plants. The results were mixed in the first year, but by the second year I had a glorious wildflower patch without spending any money.

Most wildflowers will survive in poor soil, and what nutrients were left after the carrots were harvested would have leached away by exposure to the elements. So by sowing seeds in this bed, in my naivety and poverty I chanced upon the perfect method of creating a wildflower garden on a very limited budget. The key to this method is patience, as it will take time to build up a stock of worthwhile plants rather than just dock and dandelions.

Generic wildflower seed mixes are quite common, but may not necessarily be suitable for your part of the world. There's little point growing Cornish wildflowers in the Highlands of Scotland! Instead, see what's growing in the local area and try to replicate it. Ask friends and relatives local to your area if you can look around their garden for wildflowers that have gone over and are now producing seeds. It is legal to collect small amounts of seed from the wild for private use, but you should limit this to seed from common species.

ENCOURAGING BIRD LIFE

It is important to encourage birds into the garden as they will feed on countless crop pests including cabbage white butterflies and woolly aphids. It is said that a brood of blue tits will need 10,000 insects to feed on throughout the growing season – that's a lot of pests you won't have to deal with!

For a range of bird life you will need to provide a range of food. For example, you can:
- scatter stale bread or old apples
- leave out dried seedheads of large plants
- put up bird feeders and hang fat balls
- put up bird boxes.

Be careful you are not attracting any more than you bargained for, as food left lying around can attract unwelcome visitors such as rats and other vermin just as easily as welcome ones.

Also, it is important to be consistent during the winter – birds are creatures of habit and if a feeder is there one day and not the next they may struggle to find food elsewhere during the colder months when food may be scarce.

Seedheads

The seedheads of large plants can provide much-needed winter food for visiting garden birds: leaving teasel or sunflower seedheads will provide seed high off the ground away from predators such as cats. Other blow-ins, such as evening primrose, goldenrod and mullein, can also be left to feed the birds in the colder months.

Feeders

A well-placed bird feeder can give an extra bit of interest to the garden. My Grandad liked nothing better than to eat his morning toast to the sight of countless birds feeding at his home-made bird table.

Fat balls

During the winter birds need to maintain their weight in order to survive the cold temperatures. Providing a source of fat can mean the difference between life and death for our feathered friends.

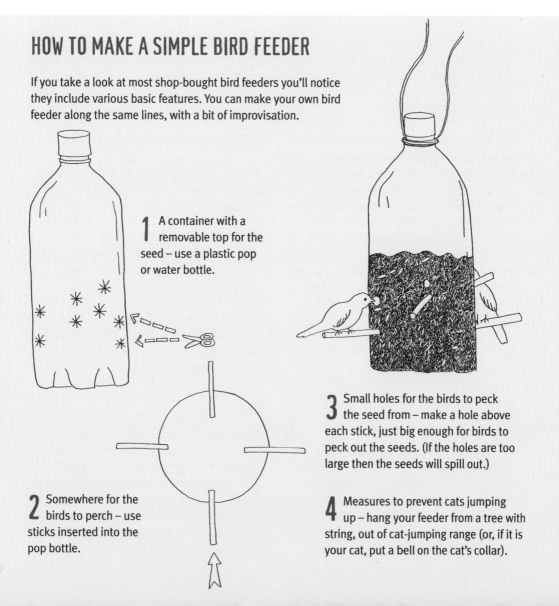

HOW TO MAKE A SIMPLE BIRD FEEDER

If you take a look at most shop-bought bird feeders you'll notice they include various basic features. You can make your own bird feeder along the same lines, with a bit of improvisation.

1 A container with a removable top for the seed – use a plastic pop or water bottle.

2 Somewhere for the birds to perch – use sticks inserted into the pop bottle.

3 Small holes for the birds to peck the seed from – make a hole above each stick, just big enough for birds to peck out the seeds. (If the holes are too large then the seeds will spill out.)

4 Measures to prevent cats jumping up – hang your feeder from a tree with string, out of cat-jumping range (or, if it is your cat, put a bell on the cat's collar).

HOW TO MAKE FAT BALLS

1 Drill a hole near the lip of a few half coconut shells and tie in a piece of string (you can use small plastic tubs in place of the coconut shells).

2 Melt a block of fat such as Crisco/Trex.

3 Mix in bird-friendly food or wild bird seed.

4 Before it cools and sets again, pour it into the half coconut shells (or small plastic tubs) and leave in the fridge to set.

5 Hang in a tree or anywhere out of the reach of local cats.

You can add almost anything you like to the fat rather than bought bird seed – just try to think what a bird might need or naturally eat at that time of year and try to recreate it. High-protein, high-carbohydrate and fatty foods are best as these are the hardest to find, especially during the winter months. Before you rush out and buy anything, take a look in the back of your cupboard, as there may well be something you've forgotten you had that would be suitable. For example:

- rolled oats
- polenta
- hemp seeds
- sunflower seeds
- sesame seeds
- linseed / flax seed.

Bird boxes

When making a bird box (see opposite), the size of the hole is critical as this will dictate what kind of bird will move in. You could contact a local birdwatching/birding group or bird charities in your area for details of your local birdlife, so you can be sure of building the right kind of box.

ENCOURAGING INSECT LIFE

Whether it is to pollinate plants or to munch up pests, insect life should be encouraged into the garden.

Bug hotels

One creature that is often overlooked in the wildlife garden is the solitary bee. These bees are just as important as honey bees or bumblebees for pollination, and are amongst the cutest insects you may ever see. They crawl into cracks and crevasses to make their homes, which can be easily replicated by making a bug hotel (see overleaf).

PONDS

Ponds are a perfect place to sit by on a warm summer's day, feeling the sun on your face and watching life dart and dash around as you contemplate the way of the world. Many insects spend their entire lives in or under water and some creatures, such as dragonflies and damsel flies, rely on water of all kinds to raise their young. Ponds are crucial in

HOW TO MAKE A BIRD BOX

Pallet planks or any spare planks of wood roughly 15cm (6") width make good bird boxes.

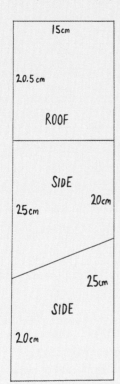

1 Cut to the dimensions suggested in the diagram.

2 To prevent the wood splitting, drill guide-holes with a thinner bit than your screws or nails. If you have them, use galvanised or weatherproof screws.

3 The top should not be glued or screwed down but hinged into place with an old piece of rubber tyre.

In the UK, the sizes of holes for different species are:
- 25mm for blue, coal and marsh tits
- 28mm for great tits, tree sparrows and pied flycatchers
- 32mm for house sparrows and nut-hatches
- 45mm for starlings.

The Royal Society for the Protection of Birds (RSPB) also suggests:
- 10cm high open front for pied wagtails and robins
- 14cm high open front panel for wrens
- 6cm low open front panel for spotted flycatchers.

(NB 2.5cm/25mm = 1")

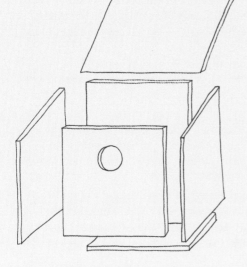

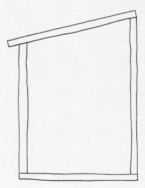

HOW TO MAKE A BUG HOTEL

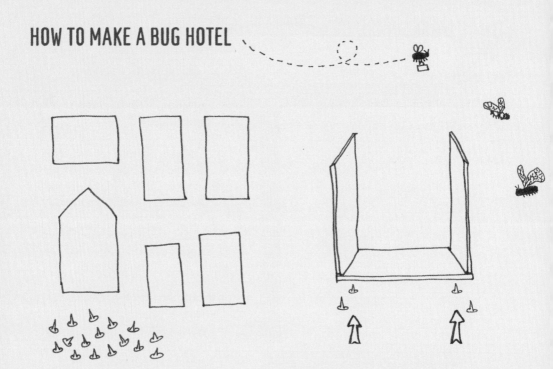

Bugs such as solitary bees don't need a fancy five-star place to live over winter. They like a bit of rustic charm in the form of bamboo or dried hogweed stems which they can crawl into and see out the cold winter months. The lengths should be around 20cm (8") and hollow throughout, not blocked by nodes.

They can be put into a wooden frame such as shown here, or into a cut plastic bottle or piece of drainpipe, again around 20cm (8") deep. Hang the hotel in a tree or the corner of a greenhouse, or sit it where it is unlikely to be disturbed, and wait for your furry guests to move in.

providing a rich habitat and thus a rich mix of life within the garden. A quarter of a frog's diet will typically consist of slugs, so this rich mix can help keep a plot in balance by controlling pest levels.

A wildlife pond and a fish pond are not the same thing. The minute fish are introduced to

a pond they quickly become top of the food chain, eating all the wildlife in sight.

Choosing a site

My old plot had a very shady corner, a little out of the way, which would turn into a big puddle whenever it rained. I considered what I could grow there for some time before the

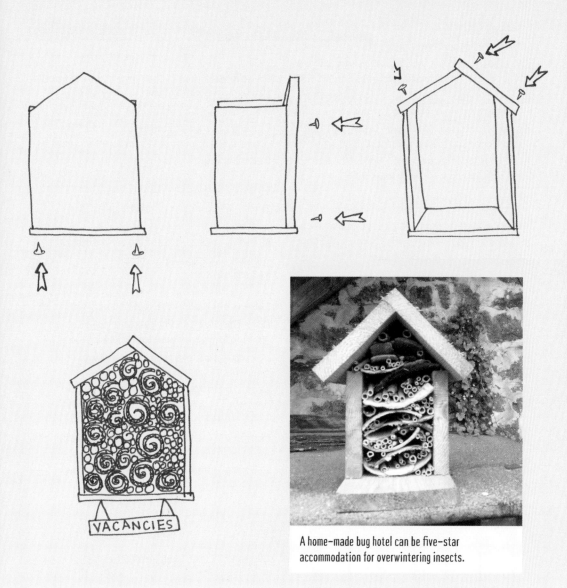

A home-made bug hotel can be five-star accommodation for overwintering insects.

obvious solution dawned on me and I abandoned the idea of growing altogether and installed a wildlife pond.

Wildlife ponds thrive in this kind of area: they need around four hours of sun a day but not much more than this, as it can lead to an over-abundance of algae. They should also be as undisturbed as possible, so an out-of-the-way corner is ideal. Leaves falling into ponds can cause problems, so ideally they should be sited away from trees (remember that even evergreens will shed their leaves throughout the year – just not all of them at once). Remember that wildlife needs to access the pond, so avoid steeply sloping sites.

Pond shape

Frogs and other amphibious life forms need to be able to get in and out of a pond, so it is crucial that the pond has at least one sloping side or stones for our amphibious friends to jump out from. Old bath tubs have high sides, meaning that you are making nothing more than a deathly prison for frogs if you use these. Bath tubs are much more suited to making planters or wormeries from.

A pond also needs to be at least 45cm (1 1/2 ft) deep, as at this depth the water is less likely to freeze solid so it provides a space for life to retreat to in frozen conditions.

You may want to form shelves on the side, as this will give you a space to rest pot plants. Imagine an upside-down Mayan pyramid as your design: this will give you an idea of the tiered levelling suitable for a range of pond plant life.

Pre-formed ponds

New or second-hand pre-formed, fibreglass or thick plastic ponds can be relatively cheap, if not free, from a recycling centre or thrown out by another gardener. Ponds made from a children's paddling pool can work in the same way as a pre-formed liner.

Pre-formed ponds should also last for a good few years, perhaps even longer than a pond made from a butyl lining. The disadvantage is that they are a set shape and you do have to prepare your hole to fit them exactly rather than shaping the liner to fit the hole.

Ponds with flexible liners

There are two types of flexible liner for a pond, a plastic or a butyl liner. Plastic sheeting, including damp-proof membranes, will degrade in sunlight and not last as long as butyl rubber.

Thicker butyl liners are expensive but they do last – they are usually guaranteed for 20-25 years or longer. As with tools (see Chapter 32), it is worth paying a larger amount for something once than having to replace it again and again. In Germany they have a saying to describe this which translates as 'I can't afford to buy cheap'. There is a second-hand market in flexible pond liners but, it seems, not such a 'fluid' one (pun intended) as with pre-formed liners. Readers in the UK might

HOW TO PUT IN A PRE-FORMED POND

1 Dig the hole a little deeper and wider than the liner.

2 Remove all stones, roots and other debris.

3 Line the banks of the hole with sand or old carpet. (Lighter soils can be sieved and used in the place of sand.)

4 Use a spirit level to make sure the pond is level.

5 Back-fill between the liner and soil with more sand to get a rough fit.

6 Begin to fill with water: the sand will compact and you can back-fill with more sand as the weight of the water compresses it.

HOW TO PUT IN A POND WITH A LINER

1 Dig your hole – make sure it has sloping angles of around 15-30° rather than straight sides along the bank (to allow frogs and other wildlife to crawl out). It should also be at least 60cm (2ft) deep with the liner in place, so dig around 7.5cm (3") deeper than this.

2 Put in a series of shelves or a shelf layer for potted pond plants.

3 Work out the size of liner you need – there are online calculators to work this out (google 'pond liner calculator'). Or, if you prefer good old pen and paper, then first measure the depth, width and length of the hole. Next work out what length and what width liner you will need using the following formula.

Liner length = (2 x maximum depth) + max. pond length + (2 x 60cm [2ft] overhang)
Liner width = (2 x maximum depth) + max. pond width + (2 x 60cm [2ft] overhang)

4 Make sure the top of the hole is level using a piece of wood and a spirit level.

5 Line it with old carpet or sand or whatever soft material/substrate you have to hand (I've used old dumpy bags / builders' bags in the past). This will 'soften' the hole, preventing sharp objects such as roots or stones puncturing the liner.

6 Put in your liner, leaving some to overhang on the surrounding area.

7 Cover the overhang with soil or stones.

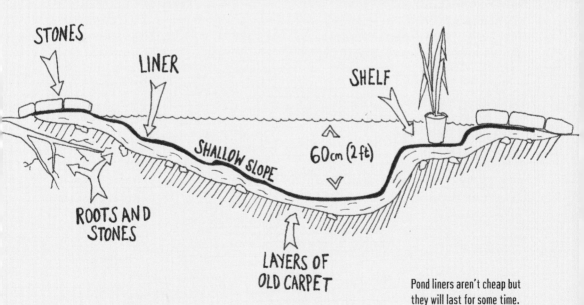

STONES

LINER

SHELF

SHALLOW SLOPE 60cm (2ft)

ROOTS AND STONES

LAYERS OF OLD CARPET

Pond liners aren't cheap but they will last for some time.

find them on www.preloved.co.uk or in the more usual places such as eBay and Freecycle.

If you have a choice between saving for a more expensive liner or putting in a cheap one then it's worth waiting and getting a good one every time.

Mending a pond liner

When you first put in a pond, save all the offcuts as these can be used to patch up any holes or tears you may get in the future. You can buy liner fixing kits, but a good non-toxic underwater glue and a length of liner will do the exact same job. Just as with a bike puncture, cover the hole completely with one continuous piece of liner and glue it into place.

Plastic sheeting glued with bathroom sealant will make a quick-fix solution if you don't have any liner, but it won't be very long lasting.

Pummelled clay ponds

Pummelled clay ponds use only natural materials and are seen as the most environmentally friendly way of making a pond. They should only be attempted on a clay site, as on light or sandy soils the water will simply drain away and the process will be an uphill struggle. The clay needs to be free of impurities such as rocks and roots, and it will help if the bedrock and water table are both relatively near the surface.

Pummelled clay *is* hard work: you need to methodically work the clay with your heels and pick out all the imperfections, systemati-cally flattening every square inch over and over. Once you've done this you need to do it again and again until every last bit of the pond is waterproof. Even then, roots could grow into the clay layer and cause it to drain.

Once in place, don't plant anything that will eventually damage the clay layer. Use pots or introduce a soil layer and shallow-rooted plants.

Filling a pond

Add a thin layer of soil before adding the water. This will provide habitat and help the water resemble a 'natural' pond for its new inhabitants.

Fill the pond and leave it for a couple of days, to check for leaks, allow it to settle and to ensure that any chlorine evaporates.

Add a cup of pond water from someone else's pond to kick-start the growth of micro-organisms. Be careful not to import any unwanted pond weeds such as duckweed or invasive weeds such as floating pennywort. This will inevitably find its way to your pond anyway and can be fished out and used as a compost activator. However, I still prefer to ward it off for as long as possible as it needs to be constantly removed to leave the pond clear and oxygen-rich, which is a bit of a pain.

Pond owners are forever weeding out ponds, so ask any you know whether they have any excess plants they might be willing to share. Always check that you know the final sizes of the plants you are growing or wish to grow, as they may take over the pond or damage a liner.

Chapter 4

PATHS, HEDGES AND FENCES

Every plot has its boundaries and on every plot you will need a way to get from A to B. The boundary materials may range from simple chicken fencing to the ornamental hedges of a kitchen garden, and the paths from mis-matched cobbles to top-quality stone.

These boundaries are part of the plot, and if built well will outlast anything else – some-times for decades if not hundreds of years.

All paths, hedges and fences will not only have to suit your needs but, ideally, also suit

Paths should be made to suit their surroundings.

their location. For an out-of-the-way allotment or a back garden this could mean a simple path made from old planks. However, a Gertrude-Jekyll-inspired kitchen garden in the grounds of an expensive country house would need a little more than a few timber planks to walk on between the snapdragons and lupins.

It is easy to spend money on this essential infrastructure of the garden. However, with a bit of careful planning, putting this part of a garden together need not be costly or too challenging.

PATHS

A good path needs to follow a 'line of desire' (see box below) or at least follow a line that makes practical sense when moving from A to B. If the task of taking a wheelbarrow from one end of the plot to the other resembles a strange Japanese game show – part balancing act, part slalom course – then perhaps the paths aren't exactly in the right place? Paths can bend and curve if you wish them too but their main purpose must be to provide an efficient way of getting from one spot to another.

Plank paths

It might be that you don't wish to have any permanent path at all, for example, if you want to maximise growing space or don't need regular access to certain beds. In such cases a simple walking plank should do the trick. Planks can be piled up out of the way and laid down as and when you need them. They spread the weight of a wheelbarrow or a person and prevent compaction, especially in wet weather.

Planks paths are particularly useful to 'no-dig' gardeners who don't wish to tread on the soil. They are usually used the most during sowing and harvesting. If you do need access to the bed all year round (and I'm sorry if this is stating the obvious), then you need to leave enough room between the plants to lay the planks.

Lines of desire

Sometimes, no matter what we tell our conscious mind, our subconscious mind convinces us into quite a different plan of action. For example, our conscious mind will see a path and it knows that this is the proposed way of getting from one point to another. It also knows that any deviation from this could compact the soil or damage growing plants. Yet quite often we may choose to completely ignore our conscious mind and, rather than take the main path, we'll jump or walk across a vegetable bed or squeeze in between a couple of fruit bushes. If done enough times this begins to compact the soil and will mark out a path other than the 'official' path.

You see similar effects whilst out walking or at large events such as music festivals – enough people traipsing in any one direction will take off the surface level of grass and compress the soil. These 'natural' paths always follow the route most taken, or the 'line of desire'.

It therefore makes sense to use these lines of desire whenever they appear on your plot rather than work against them. Once they begin to appear, they can be marked out with bamboo canes or logs on each side and either left as they are or turned into more permanent paths over time.

Pros of plank paths
- ✓ Cheap or free
- ✓ Can be easily moved
- ✓ Easy to install – just lay them down!

Cons of plank paths
- ✗ Attract slugs
- ✗ Need room for storage when they are not being used

Simple sawdust paths

The ultimate in low-tech (or no-tech) paths was demonstrated to be by James, a carpenter friend of mine (he's featured in Part 5, building his own shed – see page 221) on his allotment. He marks out where he wants to have his beds and where he wants to place his path and then removes the topsoil layer and adds this to the bed. This not only raises the level of the beds, it also adds valuable nutrients from the topsoil that would otherwise be wasted on a path (a good idea no matter what style of path you choose). Finally he covers the marked-out path with a thick layer of sawdust that he brings home from work.

Pros of sawdust paths
- ✓ Cheap or free
- ✓ Quick to install
- ✓ Low maintenance – just top up with sawdust
- ✓ Recycle unwanted material (if you have access to a regular supply of sawdust)

Cons of sawdust paths
- ✗ Rely on regular supply of sawdust
- ✗ Breeding ground for slugs
- ✗ Sawdust can migrate into beds
- ✗ Require constant topping up when sawdust rots down

A cheap and low-tech woodchip path.

Woodchip paths

Moving up the low- to hi-tech scale, the next option after a sawdust path consists of wetted cardboard or newspaper in a thick layer, or a sheet of woven black plastic or Mypex topped with around 2.5-5cm (1-2") of straw, bark chippings or woodchip. The chippings can be made yourself using a chipper or garden shredder or – as I have – obtained for free in exchange for volunteer hours at a local charity. Landscape gardeners and tree surgeons may also have surplus woodchip or bark chip available, either for free or for a small donation, as will many local councils or large parks and gardens.

I've found the cardboard-and-woodchip method works well with raised beds, as the edges of the paths are well defined by wooden structures. However, for beds without any kind of retaining structure the woodchip will gradually find its way into the

Pros of woodchip paths
- ✅ Cheap if not free to install
- ✅ Require very little skill
- ✅ Quick
- ✅ Low maintenance

Cons of woodchip paths
- ❌ Breeding ground for slugs
- ❌ Will need topping up in a year or two
- ❌ Can get slippery when wet
- ❌ Woodchip can migrate into beds
- ❌ Can bring in pests and diseases such as honey fungus

beds – lying logs along the side of the path may combat this problem.

Cardboard will rot down in a short amount of time (typically a year or two), which means it will have to be topped up. Or, as long as the soil hasn't become too compacted, you could choose to grow in the area where the path lay in the following year.

One word of warning: woodchip can contain potentially damaging fungus mycelia such as those of honey fungus. These are near-impossible to get rid of once brought in, so if you can't guarantee your woodchip isn't infected then don't use it near to trees or herbaceous perennials or, better still, consider another material for your paths.

Grass paths
Another low-tech solution is to put in grass paths. Hard-wearing grass mixes can be bought, usually advertised as being suitable for sports pitches or children's play areas. The grass can be mixed with clover, which is nitrogen fixing, to give lush fertile grass. If left

HOW TO CREATE A GRASS PATH

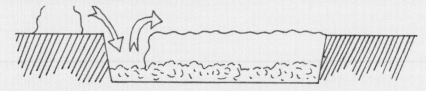

1 Double-dig or dig thoroughly to free the area of weeds or lay down weed-suppressant material and pull out any weeds left after a season.

2 Remove large stones, twigs and other debris.

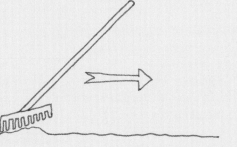

3 Rake the ground level.

to flower, the clover will also provide a nectar source for bees. Do think about how you are going to maintain the paths, i.e. if you can get a mower down them or have room for a scythe. Be aware that they may get slippery when wet.

Pros of grass paths

- ✓ Cheap to install
- ✓ Can be useful for wildlife (especially if allowed to grow over winter)
- ✓ Can be sown with low-lying herbs to increase diversity

Cons of grass paths

- ✗ High maintenance
- ✗ Can over-grow into the beds if not kept in check
- ✗ Not very hard-wearing
- ✗ Can get slippery when wet

Stepping stones

Stepping stones are ideal for forest-garden-style planting or for any large beds you may want to walk across without compacting the soil. They increase the overall planting area, making them great for small town gardens, for example, where space can be at a real premium.

I think they can add an element of fun to a garden: there is something very childlike and playful about leaping from one spot to the next. Two sunken bricks next to each other or a single patio slab can be all it takes to make a stepping stone, or any stone with a flat surface will do. These should be easy to find in skips or discarded from renovated gardens. Ask any landscape gardeners you may know to keep an eye out, or check online on sites such as Freecycle. Reclamation yards can be a good source, especially if you want more

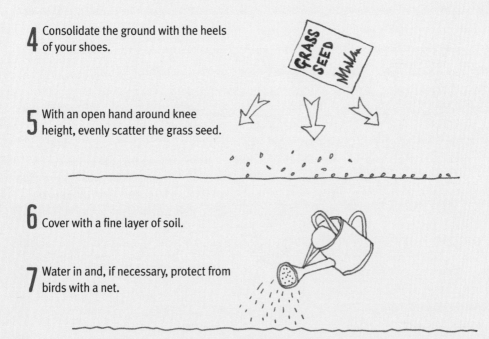

4 Consolidate the ground with the heels of your shoes.

5 With an open hand around knee height, evenly scatter the grass seed.

6 Cover with a fine layer of soil.

7 Water in and, if necessary, protect from birds with a net.

attractive stepping stones. These will vary in price depending on the source, so be prepared to haggle.

Pros of stepping stones
- ✅ Cheap
- ✅ Easy to put in
- ✅ Increase planting area
- ✅ Fun
- ✅ Materials easy to source

Cons of stepping stones
- ❌ Impossible to move machinery/ wheelbarrows across
- ❌ Can be slippery when wet

Stepping stones should be spaced to fit your stride.

HOW TO PUT IN A STEPPING-STONE PATH

1 Mark out a comfortable stride for the smallest person who will be tending the plot.

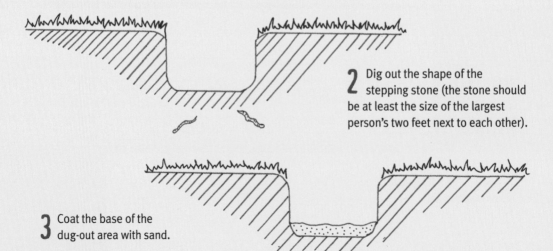

2 Dig out the shape of the stepping stone (the stone should be at least the size of the largest person's two feet next to each other).

3 Coat the base of the dug-out area with sand.

Brick and stone paths

From reclaimed bricks to patio slabs and large flagstones to tiny cobblestones, the materials used in making hard, flat, permanent paths are varied and diverse.

All create different results and vary in how easy they are to come by. Those at the upper end of the spectrum, like granite slabs or flagstones, are quite sought-after and can be costly. They are, however, very durable and are unlikely to need replacing. If someone offers you these for free, take them! – even if you don't intend to use them for a year or so.

Reclaimed house bricks, on the other hand, will usually be free but they won't last forever (although you will get a good few years out of them). Paving bricks are ideal, as they are easy to work with and durable.

You can use concrete you've pulled up from elsewhere, but you might have to be a little creative to get it to look good.

I'd recommend using a mix of materials, collecting them up over time and putting in the path when you have everything you need. Or, install it gradually as you come by more materials. This will save the expense of buying in stone and it will spread the work out.

A patio-slab path with a brick edging will be quite durable and can look quite professional,

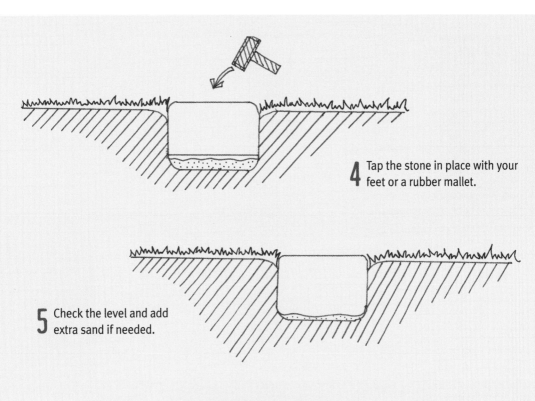

4 Tap the stone in place with your feet or a rubber mallet.

5 Check the level and add extra sand if needed.

6 Repeat for each stone (sorry for any insult to your intelligence).

HOW TO MAKE A BRICK OR STONE PATH

1 Use string and pegs to measure the length and height of the path.

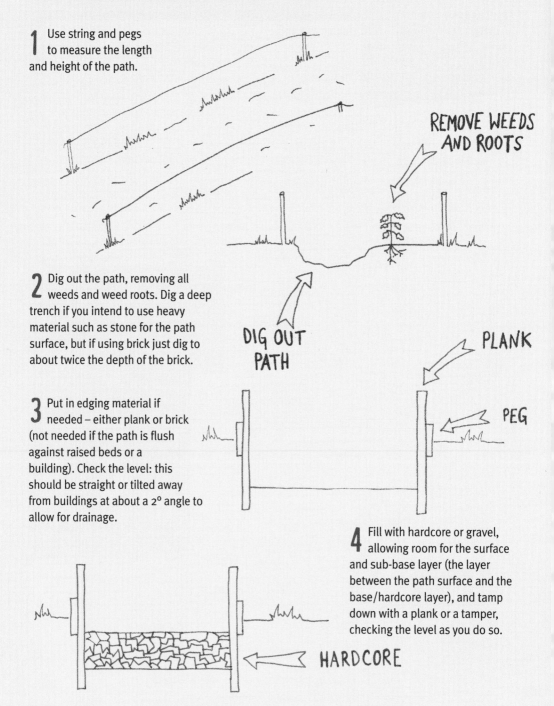

REMOVE WEEDS AND ROOTS

2 Dig out the path, removing all weeds and weed roots. Dig a deep trench if you intend to use heavy material such as stone for the path surface, but if using brick just dig to about twice the depth of the brick.

DIG OUT PATH

3 Put in edging material if needed – either plank or brick (not needed if the path is flush against raised beds or a building). Check the level: this should be straight or tilted away from buildings at about a 2° angle to allow for drainage.

PLANK

PEG

4 Fill with hardcore or gravel, allowing room for the surface and sub-base layer (the layer between the path surface and the base/hardcore layer), and tamp down with a plank or a tamper, checking the level as you do so.

HARDCORE

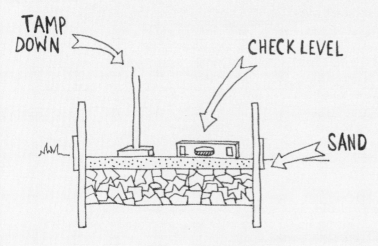

TAMP DOWN

CHECK LEVEL

SAND

5 Top with a layer of sand (or use scalpings and then sand), tamping down and checking levels as you do so. For larger stones you may choose to use a dry mortar mix here.

6 Press the stones into the sand in the pattern you require, carefully tapping them in place with a soft-headed mallet or a wood board. Check the levels of each one and only move on to the next when they are perfectly level.

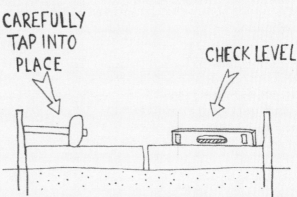

CAREFULLY TAP INTO PLACE

CHECK LEVEL

FILL IN GAPS WITH SAND

7 Fill in the gaps with more sand (or mortar if using), ensuring the bricks/stones are tightly in place.

8 If you suffer from a short temper, make up with everyone you lost your temper with during the path-laying process – if necessary cook an evening meal, preferably of humble pie.

HUMBLE PIE

as will a more 'crazy paving' approach with mix-and-match materials, if it is done well. I've sourced paving bricks from a landscape gardener who was removing one path for a client only to put in a new one almost exactly the same. He hadn't the room to store them and I was able to take them away.

If you need to cut stone, the ideal tool to have is a diamond cutter, but in the absence of this use a stone chisel and mallet. Work from the underside up to ensure the surface of the stone remains the right size. When cutting free recycled material you can afford to have a few 'practice' strikes until you get it right, and by the end of the path you should have it down to a tee.

Installing a hard path

There are many ways to put in a stone or brick path, and methods will vary depending on the materials you choose or have to hand. Reclaimed bricks are perhaps the easiest to come across, the easiest to put in place and arguably have the least environmental impact.

For larger stones or patio slabs you may choose to use concrete or lime mortar between the slabs to prevent movement and to reinforce the path. Concrete accounts for 7 per cent of the world's carbon dioxide emissions, making this a questionable approach in terms of sustainability, and it can also crack – making it, unlike unbound sand, hard to repair.

If you decide to use lime you should bear in mind that it is extremely corrosive and so you should wear gloves and be aware that your clothing may get damaged.

The method for installation is described in the box below. Bear in mind that the larger and more hard-wearing you need your path to be, the deeper the level of hardcore required.

Pros of hard paths
- Very hard-wearing
- 'Frame' a garden very well – nice aesthetic
- Good for moving machinery or wheelbarrows
- Permanent
- A lot of material is diverted from landfill

Cons of hard paths
- Can be costly to install or hard to source all the materials for free
- Take some skill or at least patience to fit

For small garden paths, especially those that aren't on light soils, a layer of hardcore might not be necessary.

HEDGES

For a professional look for little cost you can't beat an all-natural hedge to mark out a boundary or frame a vegetable bed. They may take some time to fully establish but in the long run they not only benefit the wildlife but can also shield a garden from the noise and pollution of a busy road.

The choice of hedging material ranges from hardy evergreen shrubs and native trees to low-growing herbs or conifers. What you choose really depends on what you need the hedge for – if it's to act as a windbreak or to block out the sound of traffic, for example, then you need something that will grow quite tall, such as a mixed planting of native trees or a conifer hedgerow. If you want a low continental or Victorian-kitchen-garden-style hedge then consider using box hedging or a row of low-growing herbs such as lavender or sage.

Take into account what will perform well in your area – have a look around your neighbourhood, see what others have planted and see what's thriving. In the Isles of Scilly off the coast of Cornwall, for example, there is one plant that dominates the hedgerows as it is perfectly adapted to the maritime climate. Surrounding many of the gardens are large hedges of *Pittosporum*, a non-native genus but one that grows well in the sandy soil and is tall enough to act as a shelter from the strong coastal winds.

Hedges from cuttings

Cuttings are the best way to procure free hedging and can be very simple to put in.

A Cornish friend of mine simply takes lengths of box wood 30cm (1ft) or less and about the thickness of a pencil. He cuts the bottom and the top to the nearest bud, making a sloping cut on the top, and simply pushes the lengths into the ground where he wishes to have a hedgerow, allowing around 30cm between each plant. He claims a very high success rate with this method, despite it going against all conventional advice.

Getting cutting material

Walking into a formal garden or park with a pair of secateurs will get you a lot of source material but it may also get you a criminal record. Doing the same but with the permission of the gardener or park keeper will provide the same material without the risk – they might even do it for you. You could also ask over the fence if you see a neighbour pruning, or talk to any gardening friends you may have – most will no doubt be more than willing to help you out with some cutting material. Hardwood cuttings are best taken from late summer / early autumn onwards – see page 191 for more details.

Hedges from whips

If you decide to buy in your hedging material, an economical option is to buy it as 'whips' or bare-rooted seedlings. The price comes down the more you buy, so either plant a large area at once or ask if anyone else wants to go in on it with you.

Hazel, buckthorn, holly, box, alder and beech, to name but a few, can be bought this way – check online, or try a local tree nursery.

Edible hedges

Hedgerows can make an extra-productive area with the minimum of effort. Elder, hawthorn, sloe, hazel, blackcurrant, roses (especially those with large hips such as rugosa/Japanese roses) and redcurrant all have edible fruit and all can grow quite happily around the periphery of a plot. Take as cuttings or simply drive cut material into the ground as you prune the plant after fruiting.

Roses give way to tasty hips.

HOW TO PLANT A 'WHIP' HEDGE

1 Mark out with pegs and string where you want to put the hedge. Remember to allow for growth over an existing path. Planting is best done in the winter or early spring (unless the species are evergreen, in which case any time will do).

2 Clear the area of weeds, including any nasty perennial roots.

3 Dig in the spade, push it forward, pop in the whip behind the spade and lift the spade up to allow the soil to cover the whip. Firm in the whip, and repeat for each plant.

4 Allow around 45cm (1 1/2 ft) between plants.

5 Water in and then mulch around with whatever mulching material you have available.

6 Keep weed-free and water in dry weather until established.

Beech makes excellent hedging material: it grows at around 30-60cm (1-2ft) a year and is relatively cheap. The leaves should stay on the hedge after they have turned brown, making it perfect if you want a little privacy.

FENCES

Fences are seen as permanent structures and can therefore be subject to planning permission. For fences under 2m (6ft) away from a highway, however, no planning permission is needed, but those bordering a highway may need permission for anything over just 1m (3ft).

Concrete or no concrete?

Conventional wisdom dictates that posts should be set in concrete, as without it they can't possibly stand up to the elements. It is true that fences and other structures put in using concrete can last a long time, and that they are durable and easy to erect.

However, concrete is not without its problems. Quite apart from its environmental impact (see page 64), newer cuts of timber contain a lot of moisture and as they dry they decrease in size. If not properly dried, wood will shrink as it dries out and wobble about in a concrete hole like a loose tooth in an infected gum. Conversely, in wet weather, concrete will hold on to moisture, which will be taken up by the wood. This can turn it spongy, leading it to rot and aiding the leeching of any preserving agents that may be contained in the wood.

Even large wood thinnings can be made into a fence.

HOW TO SET A POST WITHOUT USING CONCRETE

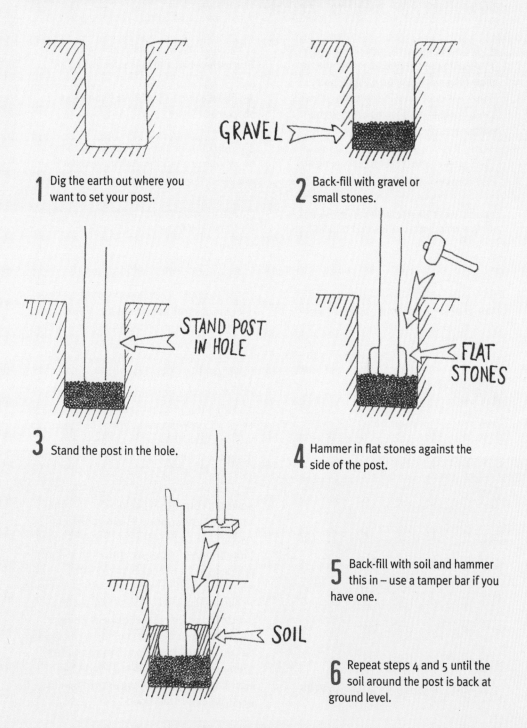

1 Dig the earth out where you want to set your post.

GRAVEL ⟹

2 Back-fill with gravel or small stones.

STAND POST IN HOLE ⟸

3 Stand the post in the hole.

FLAT STONES

4 Hammer in flat stones against the side of the post.

5 Back-fill with soil and hammer this in – use a tamper bar if you have one.

SOIL

6 Repeat steps 4 and 5 until the soil around the post is back at ground level.

It takes a lot of work to dig up concrete when it is no longer needed and there is very little you can do with it other than send it to a landfill site or use it as hardcore. I've always tried to avoid using it and instead use compressed earth or a mix of compressed earth and stones to hold post and poles in place.

I've found that posts set like this will occasionally need a little adjusting from time to time but this can be done with a hammer and a handful of stones – try doing this with concrete! I have never tried this method for really large structures, although both the arbour I built and all my sheds are still standing. If you're not convinced by this then fine – stick to concrete!

Pallet fences

A pallet is almost a complete fence just waiting to be put up. You *can* fix pallets

HOW TO CREATE A PALLET FENCE

1 Remove the planks from the underside of the pallet. This is fairly easy to do with a crowbar (see page 112).

2 Remove the blocks.

3 This should leave you with one complete 'fence panel'.

4 If you wish you can saw the tops into decorative triangle shapes or round them off like a picket fence.

5 Paint (if need be).

6 Attach to posts driven into the ground.

directly to posts dug into the ground, but this can look unsightly; alternatively, you can do some minor tweaking to turn them into an attractive length of fencing.

Natural fences

A vegetable plot can be framed beautifully by a naturally woven fence. Hazel hurdles or woven willow fencing can help garden boundaries to really blend in with their surroundings, making it hard to know where the plants end and the fence begins. They are not difficult to make, although it can take a while to master the art. Consider finding a course in your area, as although the skill is fairly easy to pick up, it is hard to learn it from a book.

Spent corn-stalk fences

I used to have a couple of dwarf apple trees, situated just off the main path, at the top of my allotment plot, on the bank of a hill. These used an otherwise unproductive space and they marked where my allotment started and the shared land ended. Or so I thought. Unfortunately, not everyone on the allotment saw the trees as being within the boundaries of my plot. They were late-season apples and most disappeared into the greedy hands of passers-by well before they were ripe.

At the time the only thing I had to hand to mark the boundary and protect my fruit were corn stalks (maize) left over from that year's harvest. The corn had been subjected to an indecently early harvest by the local mouse population!

Rather than see these events as two defeats I used the spent corn stalks as fencing, weaving them round straight poles of wood as you would with a hazel hurdle, but with the upright poles spaced much closer together. It took a fraction of the time it would have taken to make most other types of

HOW TO CREATE A NATURAL FENCE

1 Dig upright poles into the ground at about 60cm (2ft) spacing, or on light soils secure them by drilling holes into something heavy such as an old railway sleeper.

2 Using green / freshly cut wood of a small diameter for horizontal poles, weave each through, slalom-style, and push down.

3 Repeat with the next horizontal pole, weaving the opposite way through the uprights.

These will last a season or two, maybe more; lashing up the ends should increase durability.

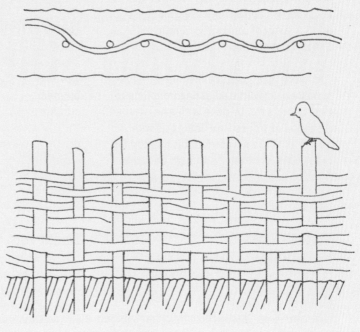

fencing and was still standing when I came to leave that allotment site two years later. It did mark the boundary very well and the following year I had a bumper crop of apples. Rather ironically, it was also a bumper year for my girlfriend's grandmother's apple tree, and that year we had more apples than we knew what to do with!

If you take corn stalks from a field, bear in mind that in the US (and other unlucky countries – perhaps even including the UK if the government has its way) you may run the risk of bringing in genetically modified corn kernels on to your plot along with the stalks. You should remove and burn any corn that germinates from imported kernels.

Salvaged fence panels / mismatched wooden fences

There are countless reasons why people throw away perfectly good fencing: fashions change, people wish to improve their gardens, or perhaps they just want to build a wall or put up a hedge instead. For whatever reason, fence panels do seem to pop up in skips surprisingly often. You may not be able to find a complete matching set of fence panels in a single skip, but it is amazing what a lick of paint and some clever planting can do to disguise a higgledy-piggledy fence (you might even prefer it that way). Though for fencing that is to separate two gardens you may want to check whether your neighbours share your taste in salvaged boundary structures!

Chapter 5

THE LIVING SOIL

Do you have one of those friends who cowers at the sight of a vegetable and somehow seemingly survives on a diet of cigarettes and junk food? How do they look?

If they are out of their twenties so no longer have youth to disguise their lifestyle, they no doubt look pretty awful. This is down to the simple truth that if we eat nothing but junk food, we look and feel pretty lousy. The same is true for the vegetable garden. A bad 'diet' will show up as small yellowing plants, prone to disease – the horticultural equivalent to a Victorian street urchin. A plant's 'diet' can be vastly improved by good soil, but in poor, nutrient-deprived soil you will get these botanical Tiny Tims.

A gardening friend once boasted he never fed his soil. He claimed that the soil (on a former market garden) was so rich and nutritious he didn't need to. However, subsequent years proved that this fertility wasn't to last: his yields soon dropped and his crops began to struggle. Finally he decided to start putting some goodness back into the land and eventually things started to perk up again.

Beneath the surface of your vegetable plot is an ecosystem consisting of millions if not billions of living, breathing, organisms. Many of these 'unlock' nutrients from the soil, which in turn are taken up by your plants.

Depletion in micro-organisms will have a knock-on effect further up the food chain, and you'll see a lack of worms and other 'macro' fauna in the soil. This is often characteristic of gardens in new builds, where much of the living topsoil has been removed. It is imperative that you breathe some life back into these soils: this is usually done by adding lots of organic matter.

Most problems arise when we see the soil as a dead medium – just something our plants need to anchor themselves in and not a living entity. As a living thing the soil needs to eat. In a closed system such as a woodland, nature provides all the nutrition a soil may need in

Manure added in the winter will add texture to a plot – but if you need the extra nutrition, add in the spring.

the form of decaying plant matter. However, in an annual food production system very little is worked back into the soil yet much is taken out. Improving the soil not only provides structure but also feeds the soil.

IMPROVING THE SOIL WITH BULKY ORGANIC MATTER

A wise gardener once said to me that, when it comes to the soil, no matter what the problem is, the answer is always "add bulky organic matter".

Any gardening book will give you detailed advice on how to identify your soil type and then how to correct it. Nine times out of ten the answer will be to add a lot of organic matter, usually in the form of compost or farmyard manure.

I've mainly worked with heavy clay, which, left unimproved, takes a long time to heat up in the spring, can crack during dry spells and during wet weather gets so sticky it turns boots into platform shoes. All this reduces the window of time in which you can actually work on such soil. The only way to really get around this is to somehow incorporate organic matter to slowly improve the soil.

So if organic matter is really the solution to all gardens' ills, then where do you get it from?

Farmyard manure

I used to get mine from a local city farm; at first they gave it away for free but after every vegetable grower in the area cottoned on to this fact they began to charge for it. Charging for manure seems to happen only if there is high demand. Quite often there is more manure than a farmer knows what to do with, and it can be free to collect if you take only small amounts at a time.

Horse stables are an excellent source: each horse can produce around 8 or 9 tonnes of manure every year. That's around 22kg or nearly 50lb a day – multiply that by the number of horses and that's a lot of poo!

In 2008 there was a problem with manure which resulted from farmers using a new herbicide called aminopyralid. This led to crop failures on land where infected manure was applied. No doubt, in due course, farmers will be lured into using the next 'safe' chemical by clever chemical company marketing. To be on the safe side, try to source your manure from an organic farm or, failing that, ask the farmer what chemicals

Soil types and the effect of adding bulky organic matter	
Type of soil	**Improvement from organic matter**
Clay soil	Improves drainage, prevents waterlogging and prevents cracking when dry.
Sandy soil	Helps retain moisture and nutrients.
Silty soils	Prevents waterlogging and improves drainage.
Alkaline/chalk soil	Helps lower the pH. With chalk it will also retain moisture and increase the amount of workable topsoil.
Peaty soil	No need to add any, but you may need to drain the soil. However, it is very unlikely you will have a peat soil. In the unlikely event that you do, choose plants that thrive in acid soils rather than seek to alter it, or grow in pots.

More than one compost bay is usually needed to prevent over-filling.

have been used that year and make up your own mind about whether you want to risk using the manure. To be on the safe side you could test it on a small area before putting on the whole plot.

Garden compost

Compost is the ultimate in recycling – using last year's crops to improve this year's soil. What's more, if you make it yourself it is completely free. Making compost is quite a simple process when you know how, and I go into more detail a little later in this chapter. In many areas of the UK (and no doubt elsewhere) local councils will take your kitchen and garden waste and sell it back to you in bags. Some local authorities, however, haven't got the infrastructure to sell on bags like this and instead will pile it up and allow people to take what they want for a donation. A quick call to the recycling department will reveal what is done in your area.

Mushroom compost

Spent mushroom compost is expensive to buy; the only cheap way to get it is direct from a mushroom grower or by making it

Weeds as compost

✻ Soak perennial weeds in a bucket of water as you pull them up and leave them for a month or so (if not more). Then bag them up in thick black plastic bags, tie up the bags and leave to one side. This should be left to compost for a year or so and can then be dug in to improve the soil.

✻ Alternatively, store perennial weeds under very thick black plastic to deprive them of light. The plastic should not let any light in whatsoever, so woven plastic won't work. Again, leave this for a year or so before adding to the compost heap or putting back on the soil.

yourself. Most mushroom growers have now realised that they can sell their compost to gardeners rather than give it away (and who can blame them? – mushroom growing can be hard work with little financial reward).

Improving your soil using a spent grow-your-own kit, however, is surprisingly easy. Old grow-your-own mushroom kits can be broken up and used as a mulch around larger plants such as cabbages. This will give you an extra few flushes of mushrooms (a companion crop!) and the mycelia will improve the soil by aiding the breakdown of organic matter. As the mycelia feed on only dead material, they won't compete with your plants.

Spent hops

My local pub has a micro-brewery situated around the back. Called the Albert Inn, the pub has a picture of Albert Einstein outside and its own beer is amusingly named 'Real-ale ativity' on site. (Now if that's not worth a few free drinks, I don't know what is.) As a result of this on-site brewing, the pub produces a large amount of spent hops, which it is more than happy for gardeners to take away. The spent hops can be spread as a thick, weed-suppressing, fertilising mulch across the garden or composted and added later. They can smell rather unpleasant but be patient, as this smell soon goes away.

Larger breweries may also offer the same service, but check with them first (you may be able to do this via their website if they have one) before turning up expectantly with a wheelbarrow.

Peat

Peat is not only expensive but also very environmentally destructive. It should therefore not even be considered as a soil improver. In any event, it is a pretty useless one as it breaks down very quickly.

Stack or bag up leaves for at least a year before using in a compost mix or to improve soil structure.

Leaf mould

Leaf mould is free to make but doesn't contain a lot of nutrients. It will, however, improve the structure of the soil. There is more about leaf mould and how to make it in Chapter 27. One-year-old leaf mould will make a good rough mulch for winter over brassicas, and by spring this will have been worked into the soil.

Wood ash – soil improver and fuel

In rural Yucatán, Mexican farmers still use the old ways of clearing land to grow their squash, beans and corn. They hack down the jungle undergrowth and set fire to it. Once the fire has burnt out they will dig the ash into the soil before planting these three crops, often referred to as the three sisters.

With my mild obsession with all things Mayan or Mexican I wanted to recreate this system, but found that in inner-city Bristol I was sadly lacking in thick, dry Mexican jungle plants. Instead I built a series of fires across a couple of the beds using all the scrap wood, newspaper and cardboard I could find. Most of the paper and cardboard came straight out of people's recycling boxes and the wood

Cooking on the plot saves money, and you don't have to go all the way home for lunch.

came from nearby skips. I made sure I didn't use green wood as it would smoke like mad, causing a lot of pollution.

To save on fuel bills at home, I would bring along a pan, noodles and some miso paste. I would make myself a lunch of noodle soup with fresh veggies picked straight from the allotment or foraged from hedgerows (hop shoots are especially good in a noodle soup!). After a series of these controlled fires I had coated the entire surface of the bed with wood ash, burning out a lot of the weeds as I did so. I then dug in the ash and later planted my corn. The corn did exceptionally well that year and I put that down to my mimicry of Mayan farming techniques. However, wood ash is not without its problems – see box, right.

IMPROVING THE SOIL – A HISTORICAL PERSPECTIVE

In days gone by, especially in rural areas, there were no sewers, no weekly waste collections and sometimes no local shops to buy fresh food and vegetables. Nowadays society would go to pot without these seemingly essential services. But back then people not only made do but thrived, combining the solutions to all these problems in the method described by George Kestell – see box opposite.

Wood ash – a mixed blessing

Around 25 per cent of wood ash is calcium carbonate, so although the ash will add some nutrients, mainly potassium, to the soil, its main effect on the soil is to alter the pH to more alkaline. Brassicas thrive in a slightly alkaline soil. However, most plants thrive in mildly acidic soil (pH 6.5-6.8), and a too-alkaline environment can harm them. Too much calcium in the soil can lock up valuable nutrients, so wood ash should be used sparingly. The writer and organic gardener Allan Shepherd recommends no more than 1kg for every 9m² (1lb per 44ft²) a year.

A modern approach

Variations on this theme can still be practised today. A bean trench can be installed during the late winter or very early spring. Quite simply, a trench is dug to about a spade's depth and the topsoil put to one side. The trench is then lined with cardboard and filled with compost before being back-filled with the topsoil. Climbing beans are then planted (or sown) into the topsoil later in the season. By the time the beans really start to root, most of the material in the

Grandfather's cabbage patch

George Kestell, Head Gardener at Pine Lodge Gardens and Tutor at Duchy College, Cornwall (www.georgethegardener.com)

In the mid-1980s my grandfather died in the same cottage, the same room and even the same bed in which he had been born nearly 90 years before, and with him died a lifestyle straight out of Victorian times. The farmhouse was no more than a two-up, two-down cob cottage purchased by his great-grandfather in 1850 and had no plumbing. Water was carried, by my granny, from a well some 100 metres across the field. The toilet was a covered enamel bucket kept and used at the bottom of the stairs.

The cabbage patch was the other side of the orchard behind the cow yard and was under constant cultivation. It was not large, some seven metres by four, but it kept them supplied in 'greens'. There was always an open trench in the soil and granny would empty 'the bucket' and take all her kitchen waste and ashes to the trench and cover over what she had put in with the shovel that lived by the trench. Entrails from the poultry prepared for the table were also

deposited in the trench, as was the contents of the ditch that drained the cow yard above it. After 130 years of this practice the soil was rich and black and grew very healthy cauliflowers, Brussels sprouts, broccoli and cabbages.

The deep roots of cabbage prefer a rich soil to tuck into.

trench has begun to rot down, providing valuable nutrients.

The idea of using human waste via a 'bucket' might not appeal to our modern sensibilities, and nor may it stand up to modern environmental health standards! It needs to be properly composted to break down all pathogens, and even then it should really be used only on fruit bushes and trees rather than leaf crops. However, many are now seeing the benefits of using human waste as a resource, and they choose to use it on their gardens. The Humanure Handbook by Joseph

Jenkins (see Resources) goes into more detail about such methods.

Human waste should not be used in a conventional composting system as very high temperatures are needed to break it down, and it should also be left for much longer (usually around two years) to kill all pathogens present. Composting toilets – essentially boxes with a toilet seat above them – are the modern equivalent of a bucket. They are allowed to fill before being removed and sealed off for two years for the contents to be transformed into rich compost.

COMPOST

Compost is one of nature's miracles. You pile up all your dead plants, food scraps, cardboard and twigs into a container, perhaps pee on it and turn it a couple of times, wait a while and – hey presto – out comes a rich, nutritious soil improver.

I find it truly magical stuff and I'm constantly amazed how a well-mixed heap can make vast piles of organic waste simply shrink into next to nothing in what seems like a very short space of time. This alchemy is caused by millions, if not billions or trillions, of micro-organisms all feeding on what we would otherwise throw away.

Garden centres sell bags of the stuff, yet all gardeners can make their own with very little effort.

Making compost

Anything that was once living (in this epoch) can be composted. So that excludes plastics, fossil fuels and man-made fibres but includes food scraps, cardboard and paper (once a tree), garden trimmings, and clothes and fabric made from natural fibres.

It is important to see your compost as a living thing which, just like you, needs something to eat, something to drink, air to breathe and warmth. It also needs a balance of nitrogen and carbon, which for simplicity's sake can be seen as recently dead material (nitrogen) and long-dead material (carbon).

So a heap of just kitchen scraps will be too wet and will not have enough air running through it. It will look slimy and might well smell pretty awful. This can be solved by adding cardboard, straw, twigs or shredded newspaper – in other words 'brown' ingredients – and material to separate layers and

add a bit of air to the heap (twigs and corrugated card will help here).

A heap that doesn't seem to do anything, just sits there refusing to rot down, might be at the other end of the spectrum and be too dry and too carbon-rich. It can help to pee on this heap quite regularly, to add both moisture and nitrogen. Fresh leaves will also help, perhaps comfrey or nettles if they are growing nearby. Both plants grow back quite quickly, so more than one cut a year can be made.

Making a compost bin

I've never bought a compost bin, yet I've managed to have one in almost every plot and garden I've ever worked on. In one tiny back yard in Northampton I made a 'dalek'-style compost bin from an upturned plastic bin, with the top (technically the base) cut off. The lid rested quite neatly on the cut-off top

Putting together a pallet compost bay.

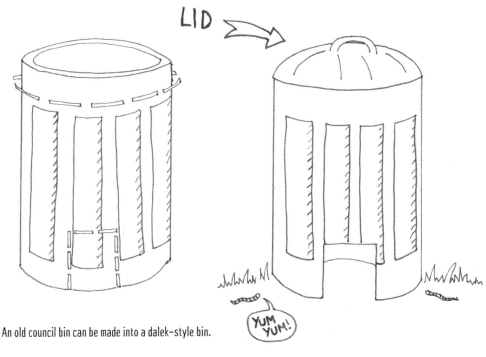

LID

YUM YUM!

An old council bin can be made into a dalek-style bin.

(base) and I pulled fresh compost out from a flap I cut in the base of the bin.

In another house I used a pallet, sawn in two and placed in the corner of the garden so the fence could make up the other two sides. For bigger gardens you may want to use whole pallets, which can be lashed or nailed together. The compost can be covered with an old carpet or with sheets of cardboard.

Some people experience problems with rats in compost bins – rats are attracted to all food waste, including vegetable scraps, but more so to cooked food, meat and fish. So if you do find rats to be a problem, use some sort of sealed bin. (There are plenty of types available to buy but you can also try adapting a dalek bin, for example, by attaching chicken wire across the base.) Another option is to use a Bokashi bin (see box overleaf) as a first-stage composter before adding the waste to your outdoor bin. Rats tend to go for compost

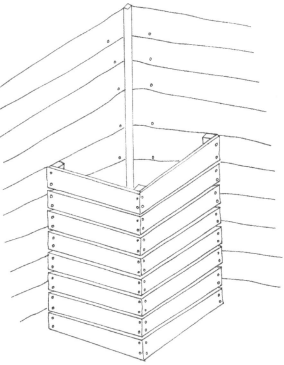

A solid fence can make two sides of a compost bay.

Composting in a small space

Nicky Scott, author of *How to Make and Use Compost: The ultimate guide*

It is possible to compost your fruit and vegetable scraps and plate scrapings (even dairy, fish and meat in small quantities), even if you live in a flat, especially if you have a balcony or any outside space. You can use a wormery for composting, or a Bokashi system for fermentation.

Wormeries

With no outside space at all it is still possible to have a wormery. I have kept compost worms inside for a time, although you do need to keep a low-wattage light on at night or you will find them wandering in the dark! The route to success with worms is to get it into your mind that your aim is to be a worm breeder rather than treating them as your waste-disposal route. In other words, the worms' needs are paramount. These are the key things to remember:

- You are not making compost — you are worm farming.
- Worms can eat only about half of their body weight per day in ideal conditions, so do not over-feed: add a small amount of food at a time; don't dump a whole week's worth in.
- Worms like it cool, moist but not water-logged, so add woodchip or some twiggy material to create some airflow and encourage drainage. You don't want a build-up of anaerobic (airless) conditions,

which will lead to smelly greenhouse gases; keep it aerobic (airy). You can also add paper and cardboard — not too much, just enough to soak up excess liquid.
- Tap off liquid continuously and make sure that the tap does not get gunked up. You can use this liquid watered down as a plant food (foliar or direct on the soil) – dilute with at least ten times the amount of water to a weak tea colour.

When your wormery is full, dig out the top layer and the majority of the worms, which should be just underneath this layer, and put to one side in a wheelbarrow or on a board or sheet. Then dig out the rest: you can bag it up to use when you are ready but make sure the bags don't get any water in them. It doesn't matter if there are a few worms left in the compost. If there are lots of worms in it, spread it out on a large plastic sheet and gather it into little conical piles. It's best to do this on a sunny day. The worms will go to the bottom of each pile, so have a tea break and then go back with a couple of buckets: put the top of each pile in one bucket and the worms from the bottom in the other, then pop them back into the compost bin along with the fresh layer of material from the top – easy!

Worms are actually best suited to the maturation stage of composting, so if you want to use

bins only in the winter, as a source of warmth, so be more vigilant at this time. If rats are too much of a problem for open bins, you may have to switch to a sealed compost bin. It's worth trying to adapt an open bin in the first instance, but rats can be persistent little blighters!

TO DIG OR NOT TO DIG?

Once you have your soil improver you need to decide whether to dig it in or not. The methods, single- or double-digging, are described in many gardening books so I don't feel the need to go into detail here. Both methods a wormery as a single-stage system, be careful to add food in small amounts and be prepared for the appearance of flies due to fresh material breaking down before the worms can get to it. Although any type of food waste – cooked, raw, meat or dairy – can be added to a wormery, this is worth bearing in mind. The best arrangement for a small space may be a Bokashi system (see below) coupled with a wormery – you can add more Bokashi compost at a time to a wormery than fresh material, but should still be careful not to add too much at once.

You can make a wormery from all kinds of containers: stacking storage containers, half barrels, old wheelie bins and dustbins. Just remember that you need good drainage and a well-fitting lid. My most trouble-free wormery is a half a plastic barrel with holes drilled in the base and an old dustbin lid that fits snugly.

Bokashi systems

Bokashi systems can be used in conjunction with wormeries or composters. Bokashi is an airless fermentation system using anaerobic micro-organisms selected by a Professor Higa in Japan. Not all anaerobic microbes cause putrefying smelly conditions – many have been used in food fermentation and preservation.

Bokashi is useful as a 'first stage' composting system for food waste, which is then added to a normal compost heap when it has fermented sufficiently – about two weeks – to not cause problems with vermin. If you want to use the end product directly on your garden, leave it to ferment for at least six weeks. The end product isn't strictly compost, but it is a valuable fertiliser.

You can add any type of food waste to a Bokashi system. Making a Bokashi system is easy, although you have to buy the microbes (usually called 'EM' or 'effective micro-organisms'; check out www.effectivemicro-organisms.co.uk). It can even be kept in the kitchen; although there is a slight smell, most people don't mind it.

- Get hold of four large (approx. 10 litre / 17 pint) containers, such as the sort that ice cream comes in. You are making two separate nesting sets of containers, so you will need just two snap snap-on lids.
- Drill plenty of holes in the bottom of two containers so that liquids can drain into the bottom containers.
- Put the container with the holes in it into the one without holes.
- Put your waste into the top container, sprinkle it with Bokashi micro-organisms, push the material down firmly to squeeze out any liquid and remove as much air as possible, and put the lid on. As the waste ferments, liquid will drain into the bottom container and can be watered down (10:1) and used as a plant feed.
- When the first container is full, swap the set for the second pair of containers and leave to ferment for the necessary period of time (see above).

help break up heavy soils by exposing them to frosts, and they allow soil improvers to be worked in thoroughly, kill off weeds and expose soil-borne pests to predators. However, advocates of no-dig gardening claim that we are just beginning to understand the interactions between all the forms of life that live beneath the soil, and that through digging these life forms are disturbed. These include mycorrhizal fungi, which make complex associations with the roots of plants, allowing them to take up nutrients from a much wider area.

Nick Gooderham's South Devon 'No Dig' market garden.

Some people complain of compaction and puddles of water on no-dig beds, so the method doesn't appear to be right for everyone. Also, the volume of compost needed is quite high, so can be difficult to obtain.

As with all gardening techniques, people will argue from both camps as to which system is the best. Without trying it out for yourself you won't know which works best for you. I've found that if the ground is free of weeds, gently working in manure to the top few inches seems to work fine and there is no need to double-dig every year. I've also found that not digging works well for larger-scale field systems.

It is doubtful that you will ever get everything right every year with gardening, and a range of techniques can be the key to success. You might want to try one or two no-dig beds for a few years and see if they work for you – it could save you a lot of time (and backache) in the future. And if it doesn't work you can always return to hard labour!

HOW TO MAKE A NO-DIG BED

1 Hoe off surface weeds and remove all perennial weeds in the autumn once the main crops have been harvested. Cover with cardboard.

2 Add around a 5cm (2") (or more) layer of compost or well-rotted manure. Rather than dig this in, leave it and let the worms and micro-organisms take it down for you. Plant up in the spring, adding more compost if need be or add a little concentrated chicken manure with each plant or seed.

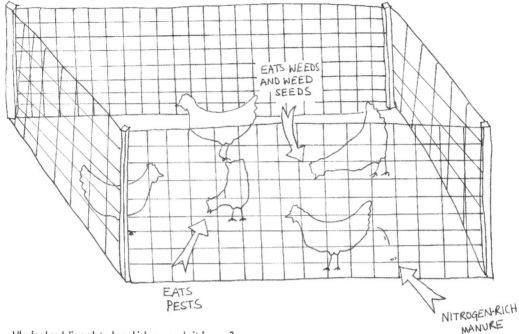

EATS WEEDS
AND WEED
SEEDS

EATS
PESTS

NITROGEN-RICH
MANURE

Why feed and dig a plot when chickens can do it for you?

Chicken tractors

My introduction to the chicken tractor came from a man called Nev who joined the www.selfsufficientish.com team quite early on in the website's creation. He has been clearing land in his suburban garden on the outskirts of Sydney this way for years and swears by it.

Working land that has had chickens on it is an absolute dream. Weeds are at a minimum and the soil is nitrogen-rich, perfect for crops.

Using a chicken tractor

- An area is enclosed by a movable fence and chickens are put in during the day.
- The chickens scratch around in the dirt munching on soil-borne pests such as grubs, cutworms, gnats, flea beetles and slug and snail eggs.
- They also feed on weed seeds and help rid an area of all but the most deep-rooted of weeds.
- They poo on the land, enriching the soil as they do so.
- The fence is moved and the process begins again.
- The top crust of poo is removed and added to the compost heap (mixed with brown waste, e.g. cardboard), and if there is still a strong smell of ammonia a little more is removed. The ground can be roughly dug over (although this may not be necessary).
- Crops are sown either directly into the ground or sown once a little compost or leaf mould has been spread over the surface.

Chapter 6

WATER

Water is essential to all life forms but animals have the advantage over plant life as, relative to plants, they can control their intake of water. If plants can't take in enough water from their surroundings, they rely on us for their survival.

Filling a watering can or turning on the hose every time your crops need a drink is convenient but comes at a cost. It takes a lot of energy to treat water and deliver it to our taps, and the pressures on our water resources are increasing all the time. Water meters are becoming the norm in the UK, and worldwide we are seeing a rise in hosepipe bans and water-saving measures. Sources of clean fresh water across the world are becoming scarcer and the situation can only get worse in years to come.

Water is essential to all life — including vegetables!

In order to conserve this precious resource and save money, edible gardeners have to think carefully about how they will water a plot. Tap water shouldn't be the only source of water – rainwater should be collected, and when water is used this should be done as efficiently as possible.

HOW MUCH WATER?

How much water your garden needs will depend on many different factors. A clay soil will retain much more water than a sandy soil and gardens in areas of high rainfall will need far less water than those in arid regions. Plants will give you quite prominent clues if they are getting thirsty: usually they will wilt and in extreme cases they may drop their fruit before it ripens. You can get an idea of how much water may be needed by poking your finger in the soil to see if it is damp. Or you could set up a rain gauge to find out if there has been adequate rainfall. Rainfall of 2.5cm (1") per week is enough for most plants, but squashes, cucumbers and beans may need a little more.

HOW TO MAKE A DIY RAIN GAUGE

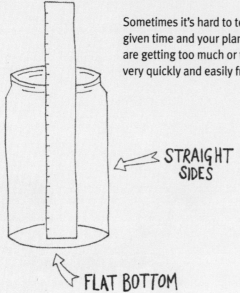

STRAIGHT SIDES

FLAT BOTTOM

Sometimes it's hard to tell just how much water has fallen in a given time and your plants may not indicate straight away if they are getting too much or too little. A simple rain gauge can be made very quickly and easily from recycled materials.

1 Take a jar or similar container with straight sides and a flat bottom.

2 Either attach a ruler to the jar, starting at the zero mark, or mark off centimetre or inch marks with a permanent marker or waterproof pen or paint.

3 Lash the jar/container to a pole and wait for the rain.

Water-saving tips

We live in times of unexpected drought or freak heavy downpours, and we can't rely on previous seasonal estimates for anticipating rainfall. To ensure growing plants get what they need, we need to conserve rainwater whenever and wherever we can.

✳ Water only in the morning or evening, as this minimises evaporation losses and the risk of scorching as a result of water on leaves.

✳ Aim the hose or watering can right at the base of the plant to localise watering.

✳ Dig a crater for thirsty crops such as squashes, to retain more water.

✳ Mulch around your plants to minimise evaporation.

✳ Avoid sprinklers altogether – far too much water is lost to evaporation. Instead consider installing a drip irrigation system, as these direct water where it is needed and save you a lot of time. Depending on the size of your garden the initial cost may be offset against future water bills.

✳ Check you are not over-watering plants – look for signs such as leaves turning yellow and dropping, roots rotting and the appearance of mould.

✳ Add compost! Compost will help clay soils drain and sandy soils hold on to moisture. Ensure that there is plenty in the soil before you start planting or sowing and, if you have enough, mulch with it a couple of times a season.

COLLECTING RAINWATER

I've used all sorts of things as water butts in my time, from storage crates and dustbins to old whisky barrels. The type and size of the container you'll need depends on your water requirements and the size of the roof the water runs off. A tiny shed providing water for a 2m² (22ft²) plot is unlikely to need a 1,000-litre (220-gallon) container, although it would be wise to store more than you need to cope with prolonged dry weather.

A container of at least 550 litres (about 120 gallons) is suitable for the average garden shed or greenhouse servicing a small garden of around 50m² (540ft²), but it will run dry if there is little or no rain in the growing season. An allotment or garden of around 100m² (1,080ft²) will need at least a 1,000-litre container, especially if there is no mains water backup. There are of course many factors affecting how much water is needed – rainfall, the types of crop, the amount of evaporation loss – so these figures are only a rough guide.

WATER BUTTS

Walk around any large allotment site and you will see how ingenious people can be when it comes to collecting rainwater. Water butts are a low-cost, low-tech way of harvesting rain-water and can be set up to collect water from the downpipe of a house, shed or green-house. Important factors to consider when choosing a container for a water butt are:

- It doesn't leak!
- A tap can be fitted or you can plunge a watering can into the top.
- It can withstand extremes of temperature.
- It will not let in any light or, if it is clear, the outside can be painted or covered (if light gets in, algae can form inside).
- It has not contained hazardous waste.
- You have somewhere to put it.

Make it big enough

With water meters becoming the norm it is worth considering getting a water butt much larger than you need simply for your garden. The excess water can be used for washing a car, flushing the toilet or filling ponds, or it can even be filtered and used in place of drinking water.

Where to get it

There is a huge choice when it comes to water butts, both bought and found, and many of these are no more than a recycled container with a tap attached. There are companies that specialise in selling second-hand containers (see Resources for one example), usually cheaper than new water butts but still at a cost.

Every roof is a potential source of water.

If you don't mind cleaning them out, you can go directly to source and get ex-food or ex-drink containers from:

- large-scale caterers
- restaurants and cafes
- factories
- nursing homes and hospitals
- vineyards or distilleries (who will no doubt charge!).

Having worked in them I know that warehouses and factories can be an Aladdin's cave of discarded goodies – go round the back and you are likely to find large storage containers, perfect to act as water butts. Be sure to ask before you take anything though, as otherwise it is technically stealing (even if the items have already been thrown away).

A quick look on the internet or in a local business directory will give you the numbers of companies that may have raw ingredients delivered in bulk. Don't expect to be treated with the same kind of customer service you'd get in a five-star hotel, but state what you want clearly and most people will be happy for you to take away their scrap containers. A lot of companies now have to pay to dispose of their waste, so as long as it doesn't inconvenience them they really won't mind you taking away their rubbish.

Where to put it

Ideally, a water butt should be positioned on a rainwater downpipe near to a vegetable patch. A small garage or shed roof is usually large enough to fill up a good-sized container, such as a 200-litre (44 gallon) oil drum, if not more. A house roof will fill a 550-litre (120 gallon) container with no trouble at all, and additional butts may have to be added if you want to really make use of all the rainwater.

If you are lacking a building to collect water from then you may need to construct one. A wood store or a shelter to sit under is ideal – this needn't be anything fancy, just four posts with a roof over the top. Alternatively, large troughs or lined ditches can be effective in collecting rainwater. However, their large surface area will be prone to evaporation loss in warm weather and can also be breeding grounds for mosquitoes and algae.

The butt should be raised off the ground so a watering can will happily fit between the ground and the tap. You can buy stands to raise your water butt off the ground, but these are quite unnecessary as a couple of concrete blocks will do the trick.

Fitting a tap

A water butt can be left open at the top for a watering can to be dipped in, but in most cases it will be more convenient in the long run to fit a tap.

The choice of taps include:

- standard metal bathroom/kitchen/ garden tap
- a tap from an old home-brewing barrel
- a water butt or worm bin tap.

A tap and its fittings.

HOW TO FIT A TAP

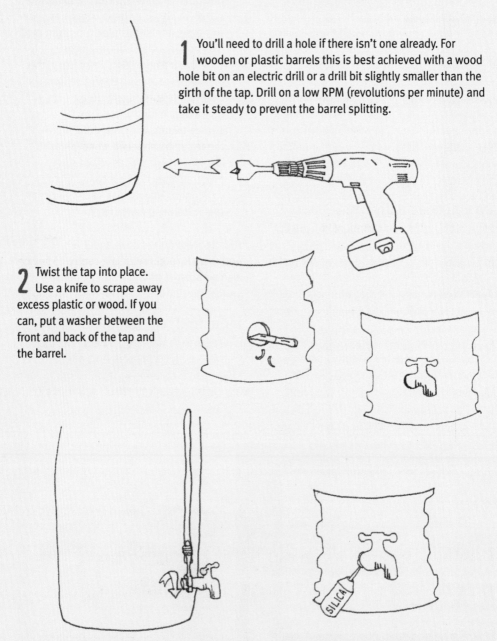

1 You'll need to drill a hole if there isn't one already. For wooden or plastic barrels this is best achieved with a wood hole bit on an electric drill or a drill bit slightly smaller than the girth of the tap. Drill on a low RPM (revolutions per minute) and take it steady to prevent the barrel splitting.

2 Twist the tap into place. Use a knife to scrape away excess plastic or wood. If you can, put a washer between the front and back of the tap and the barrel.

3 Screw on a back nut inside the barrel. If you can't reach inside, try using a long-armed spanner or a spanner tied to a stick.

4 Test the barrel out before a rain shower and seal up any leaks with bathroom sealant/silicone.

Fitting a water butt to a downpipe

Some rainwater downpipes can simply be cut and a water butt placed underneath. You will need to put an overflow in place and collect excess water in an extra butt or two. Or you could have the excess water diverted directly down the drain. You will also need to make sure you have enough room for the water butt and that the position is not annoying a neighbour (for example, someone living in a flat might unwittingly site the butt outside a neighbour's window). If it is, you may need to fit a diverter to the rainwater downpipe.

Do you need a diverter?

A diverter is a small attachment you put on the rainwater downpipe, which diverts some water to the water butt and allows the rest to continue down the drain. There are a few factors to take into account when considering whether to install a diverter.

- An iron pipe will require considerable work to cut and this is really not recommended – diverters are really suitable only for plastic pipes.

- Putting a diverter on the rainwater downpipe means you can, to some extent, put the butt somewhere convenient. For example, if the downpipe runs right next to a front door and there simply isn't the room to fit a butt there you can run the diverter pipe around the corner and the butt can be tucked around the side. A diverter also means you won't need to source overflow barrels straight away; these can be attached when you find them or when you can afford them.
- Diverters may be the most suitable for continuous downpipes, which run from the guttering straight to drains.

Diverters are quite cheap and it is possible to find them in larger recycling centres. They can also be bought fairly cheaply from hardware stores; these will come with full instructions.

Industrial bulk containers (IBCs)

These large containers hold 600-2,000 litres (132-440 gallons), although 1,000 litres (220 gallons) is the most common. They're usually attached to a pallet and set in a wire cage.

No matter what size your butt is, someone will always have a bigger one!

HOW TO ATTACH A DIVERTER

1 The diverter feeds into a hole made in the side of the water butt, measured to the diameter of the piece of hose you wish to use. This should be around 10cm (4") from the top of the butt.

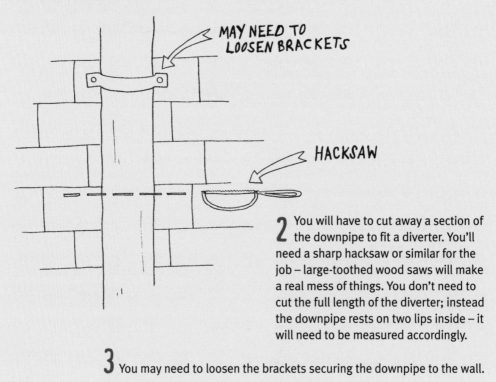

MAY NEED TO LOOSEN BRACKETS

HACKSAW

2 You will have to cut away a section of the downpipe to fit a diverter. You'll need a sharp hacksaw or similar for the job – large-toothed wood saws will make a real mess of things. You don't need to cut the full length of the diverter; instead the downpipe rests on two lips inside – it will need to be measured accordingly.

3 You may need to loosen the brackets securing the downpipe to the wall.

They weigh roughly 60-80kg (around 130-180lb). Their weight and size mean you will need to enlist the help of friends to move them.

Industrial bulk containers can sometimes have been used for hazardous waste – see box on page 90.

Anyone tending a full-size allotment plot or a large garden should consider butts of this size. They can be unsightly for domestic use, so you might want to screen them with a hedge, some fencing or a wicker/hazel screen.

IBCs are often clear, which will encourage algal growth – to avoid this cover or paint the sides. If they are in constant use this should be minimal, but it will still present a health hazard as it can attract pests and diseases.

Most IBCs have a huge tapped valve at the front, and the pressure when full will send water gushing out at quite a rate. They therefore need a small tap or a hose attachment fitted. These don't cost much and can often be bought online or from suppliers of second-hand industrial containers.

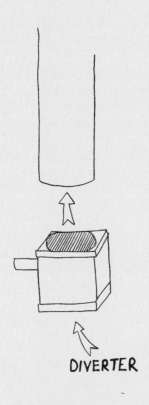

DIVERTER

4 If you have one, fit the rubber splash guard and then slot the diverter in place.

5 Use sealant or waterproof tape if you spot any leaks once the diverter is fitted.

You will have to drill an inlet hole into the top of the container. Some people choose to remove the entire top of these containers, but this does lead to evaporation loss and potential contamination with leaves, algae, mosquito larvae and other pests.

Blue barrels

These ex-food containers are quite common: they range in size from tiny ex-mango-chutney containers, at 30-50 litres (6.5-11 gallons) up to around 210-240 litres (46-53 gallons), with a couple of sizes in between. Some companies supply these as water butts with taps fitted, but it is more likely that you will have to fit one yourself. They sometimes have the bonus of coming complete with a sealable lid, which can make fitting an inlet pipe much easier. A removable lid or open top is useful for adding liquid feeds, e.g. a submerged sack full of manure or a couple of buckets of nettles and comfrey (not suitable near a house due to the smell!).

Metal drums

You are quite likely to find these abandoned

Has it contained hazardous waste?

If a container hasn't been cleaned out, you will need to know its previous contents before you clean it. Some IBCs may have contained hazardous chemicals, so wear protective gloves, mask and goggles. By law any hazardous contents must be indicated on the container, as shown below (taken from the *IBC Utilisation Guide*, published by Francis Ward).

The most important thing to look out for on these labels is the pack/package group, typically an X, Y or Z, or Group I, II or III: these indicate what was once in the container.

Group Z indicates low-grade hazardous materials, mainly food; often the safest bet. Extreme and moderate hazardous waste groups will need researching – the potential contents are too varied to list here. Don't let this put you off: sometimes all it takes is a little vinegar or bicarbonate of soda to clean the barrels out and local recycling centres often take hazardous waste – but don't take anything you don't think you can clean!

Extreme hazard	Moderate hazard	Low hazard
Group I	Group II	Group III
Pack (or Package) Group X	Pack (or Package) Group Y	Pack (or Package) Group Z

in all sorts of locations: they come either covered (known as a closed-head drum) or uncovered (an open-head drum). Closed-head drums have only a small inlet/outlet hole, which means that they are not always suitable for water butts (unless bought new or already cleaned out). The open-topped sort with a removable lid are perfect, as they can be cleaned out and liquid feeds can be

added (see 'Blue barrels', page 89). There is much debate about taking rusty water from old metal barrels used as water butts and putting it on food plants, but there seems little evidence that it will do you or your plants any harm and it has been suggested that the iron is in a form that the plants cannot take up.

Wooden barrels

In terms of aesthetics, wooden barrels are arguably the wisest choice for the discerning gardener. Needless to say, they come at a price. They have become quite sought-after in the second-hand market but can be found cheaply with a bit of determination. Check local wineries or distilleries, wood recycling projects or the usual sources of second-hand

Keep it wet

✳ A water butt (or planter) made from a wooden barrel should never be left empty as it can fall apart if it dries out and will be almost impossible to fit back together.

goods such as your local recycling centre. If you take the winery/distillery approach, check their website before you call as they may have a policy on second-hand barrels. You may be one of a long line of people who've asked already and you could get a frosty reception from the receptionist (trust me on this one!).

Barrels also make attractive planters and, combined with a wooden-barrel water butt, they can add rustic charm to any garden.

Plastic packing crates / recycling crates
These rectangular boxes seem to turn up in discount stores across the world. The older ones were made of quite strong plastic which (unlike the more recently made ones) seemed to hold up in outdoor conditions. I used one as a backup water butt for around six years – it would have been longer but I accidently put a fork through it. They are a mixed blessing as they don't hold much water and their large surface area leads to evaporation loss. However, they are quite easy to come by for free and, as they are not very tall, they can be squeezed straight under a downpipe with no need for extra fittings. Watering cans can be filled by dunking rather than a tap being fitted. I've found crates to be a useful stopgap until something else comes along.

IRRIGATION

A good irrigation system provides a plant with water right where it needs it and losses are reduced to a bare minimum. These systems come in handy on larger plots where hand watering may be impractical, or in dry climates where water conservation is imperative.

Clay pot irrigation
Records indicate that clay pot irrigation has been around for quite some time, first used by the ancient Chinese and later by the Romans.

It can be up to ten times more water efficient than surface irrigation and, as the water seeps through a porous clay pot, it can filter out large particles including salt. This method is particularly suitable for areas of low rainfall. It is important that the pots are unglazed, and if you have the facilities to make them yourself they should be fired at temperatures below 1,000°C (1,832°F). Like all good ideas the method is as simple as it is effective (see overleaf).

Because the water is supplied to a localised area, clay pot irrigation is also useful for container growing. The irrigation pots only need topping up once a week, making this method ideal for those who have busy weeks but are able to work at weekends, or for anyone wishing to go on holiday! You can apply feed using this method as long as it isn't in a concentrated form (e.g. pure comfrey feed or pure seaweed feed that hasn't been watered down).

Plant pot and plastic bottle irrigation
There are adaptations of the clay pot method more suited to cooler climates such as in the UK, northern Europe and the northern states of America.

The first method uses a flowerpot filled with gravel or small stones in place of the clay pot. The pot will need filling more often than the clay pot as the water seeps through at a quicker pace. However, it still supplies water at a controlled rate and most of the materials are very easy to come by.

Another adaptation is to use a plastic drinks bottle, normally 2 litres (3.5 pints), with holes pierced in the lid and the bottom cut off (or holes pierced in the bottom and the top removed – whichever is easier to top up with water). Only half the bottle needs to be

HOW TO INSTALL CLAY POT IRRIGATION

1 Dig a hole about three times as wide and twice as deep as the pot you are using.

2 Back-fill some of the hole with compost and bury the clay pot up to its neck before filling the rest of the hole so it fits snugly without wobbling – some of the neck can be sticking out of the hole.

3 Sow seeds of small plants such as lettuces, salad greens or radishes in a circle around the pot or a larger plant (e.g. tomato) to one side of the pot.

4 Fill the pot with water once a week and a place a small stone or specially made lid over the top to prevent evaporation.

5 As the clay is porous, water will gradually seep out through the sides into the soil and provide a slow, steady supply to the plants.

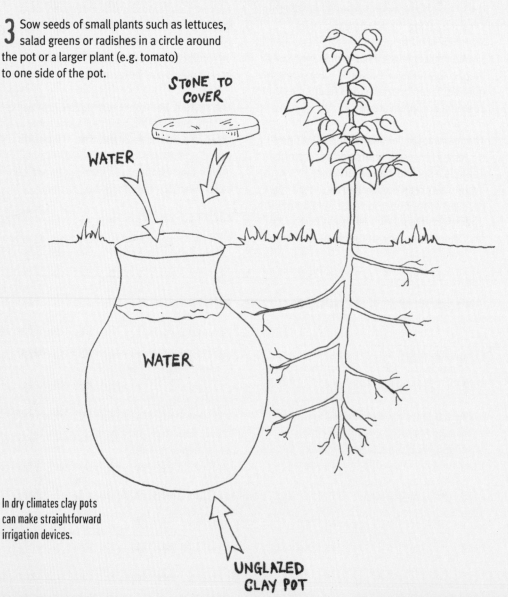

STONE TO COVER

WATER

WATER

In dry climates clay pots can make straightforward irrigation devices.

UNGLAZED CLAY POT

submerged rather than the whole thing. The bottle will need topping up every few days or so. The cut-off base can be placed upside down inside the bottle or a flat stone can be use to prevent evaporation. Again, this method is very suitable for container growing and liquid feed can be applied via the bottle.

Leaky pipe system

A leaky pipe system drips water to a bed over a period of time. In a true leaky pipe system the flow of water is regulated by an electronic sensor, making these very expensive. Technically speaking the system described in the box below is not a leaky pipe system but more of a way to direct water right where it is needed. It can be made for a fraction of the cost of a bought system.

The more advanced leaky pipe irrigation systems come with filters and regulators. There is a second-hand market for this kind of system as occasionally they are sold cheaply or given away when horticultural companies upgrade or go out of business. Check your local press, free newspapers and online.

Wicking irrigation

I first heard about wicking irrigation from an Australian friend called Cath – the compost-obsessed wife of my oldest friend Matt. Melbourne, like many parts of the continent, suffers serious drought conditions, making saving water of the utmost importance.

Wicking beds are most useful in warm, dry conditions, but at present in the UK we have high rainfall across most of the country so wicking beds would not be necessary on a large scale outdoors. However, container growers could experiment with the system, as could those growing under cover in greenhouses and polytunnels.

The system works on the principle that water will travel or 'wick' upwards if stored low down in a bed or plant pot. These types of irrigation systems can be made quite easily out of recycled materials and can be scaled up or down to almost any size or shape.

Some systems also include an area for worms, which recycle kitchen scraps and feed

HOW TO MAKE A DIRECTED PIPE SYSTEM

1 This system can be rigged up fairly easily over the top of raised beds using a PVC (polyvinyl chloride) pipe.

2 Cut holes directly where you will be planting, e.g. every 30cm (1ft) for cabbages at this spacing.

3 Bung the PVC pipe at one end and attach a hose to the other.

4 For more than one bed, connect pipes up with lengths of old hose.

5 The hose is switched on when the water is needed; the pipe supplies it directly to the plants and saves you having to constantly unravel the hose reel.

HOW TO MAKE A WICKING BED

1 Find four empty plastic bottles of equal shape and size (1-litre tonic or cola bottles are best – could be a good reason for a party!). Using a sharp pair of scissors (you may need a grown-up to help you here), cut the tops and bottoms off three of the bottles and fit these together to make a pipe.

2 Lay the pipe flat and cut a hole in the side of it to fit the third into it as an upright. Alternatively, use a length of agricultural piping instead of the three bottles and attach a length of PVC pipe to it as an upright, cutting a hole for it in the piping.

3 Using a pin, make a number of holes in the horizontal pipe. As pipes can get clogged, use old sacking or porous weed-suppressant material to allow water out but not soil in.

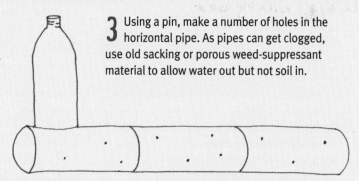

4 Place the L-shaped pipe you've made into a poly-styrene fish/vegetable container. Punch holes at the far end of the container, either side of the pipe, for drainage. For a large raised bed (see Chapter 30, pages 213-14, for how to construct this), lay waterproof material down first, lay the agricultural pipe above it and drill drainage holes into the raised bed.

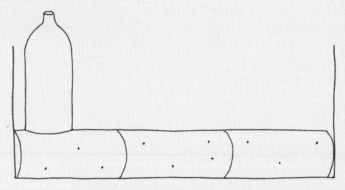

growing veggies at the same time. The worms come up to feed on the scraps and then travel into the beds, feeding your plants and aerating the soil as they do so.

GREY WATER

One of the great gardening debates that still goes on amongst environmentally friendly and/or penny-pinching gardeners concerns the use of grey water. Some say never to use it on vegetable or fruit beds and others say it is fine, especially if you use environmentally friendly washing products. The middle ground seems to be:

- not to use grey water on leaf crops
- not to water tomatoes and other fruit-bearing crops from above with it
- not to use it on any crops that are eaten raw
- alternate its use with tap water or rainwater

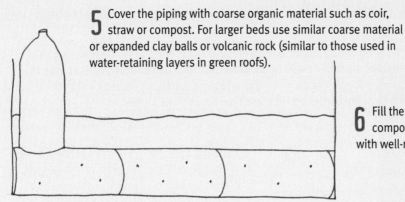

5 Cover the piping with coarse organic material such as coir, straw or compost. For larger beds use similar coarse material or expanded clay balls or volcanic rock (similar to those used in water-retaining layers in green roofs).

6 Fill the bed with potting compost or topsoil mixed with well-rotted manure.

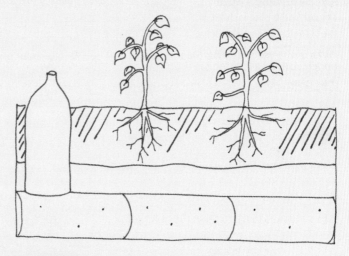

7 Plant your seeds or sow seedlings. For seeds you will need to water normally for the first couple of weeks until the plants establish roots.

8 Water into the upright about twice a week or when the pot/bed dries out.

Please bear in mind that I've made only preliminary experiments with a wicking bed – how effective it is as a means of irrigation is not tried and tested by me. It could well be worth experimenting with, but do try it on a small scale before you dive in and decide to grow everything this way. (And please do let me know the results!)

- never use it if you have washed oil from your hands or body
- never use it if you have recently washed up meat or washed cooking oil down the sink.

The main concerns with grey water are as follows.
- It may contain potentially dangerous pathogens from food waste or contaminants such as oil, meat or cooking oil.
- Washing powders and liquids may contain chemical contaminants which can damage crops and stay in the food chain.
- It can be highly alkaline, which will damage acid-loving crops (blueberries, etc.).

I'm not in favour of being prescriptive about what you should and shouldn't do in the garden. I once told an 87-year-old gardener that I had read that growing watercress in still water can lead to potentially fatal liver flukes. He'd been growing watercress in a bucket in his garden every year for almost 60 years with no ill effects!

So issues like the use of grey water have to be decided for yourself. Filtering out food particles and oil with a sand filter (fill a bucket with a layer of large stone, then gravel then sand) can help but it won't eliminate every-thing else dissolved in the water. Mulching around the plants once you've used dishwater can also help, as this should provide a barrier between rotting food particles and the things that like to eat rotting food particles.

Whether or not you think the risks are exaggerated or understated depends on what research you read. Personally, if it was unfiltered I would only use bathwater and dishwater on fruit trees and then only if there had been minimal use of bubble bath, etc.

Rainwater will always be the best possible option for use on your plants. Rather than waste grey water, if you do decide to use it then perhaps use it to flush the toilet rather than to water prize vegetables?

MULCHING

Mulches are one of those 'minimum input for maximum output' techniques that make permaculturists weak at the knees.

A good mulch will:
- block light from weeds, preventing their growth and germination
- retain moisture by limiting evaporation
- if using compost, manure or comfrey it will also provide a feed
- help regulate heat – cool in the summer and warmer in the colder months
- protect soil from erosion
- provide a barrier against predators.

Except for sheet mulches, such as cardboard and plastic, a mulch should be around 7.5cm (3") deep to prevent weed growth and to conserve water. You can use a variety of materials as mulch.

Black plastic

It is possible to get second-hand woven black plastic (such as Mypex) from farmers, growers and gardeners: it may have holes and tears in it but you can get around this by doubling it up or covering the holes with cardboard. It benefits the soil by warming it up in the late winter and early spring and will keep weeds at bay by forming a barrier. Whole areas can be cultivated by leaving black plastic down for a year before peeling it back to reveal weed-free ground ready to plant into.

For the water-wise it reduces evaporation loss – plants can be either sown or planted

Black plastic retains moisture — good for thirsty plants.

through holes made in the plastic. Some people like to plant potatoes underneath it: when growing foliage starts to raise the plastic up they cut it open to allow the leaves to poke through and soak up the sun.

Squashes and other cucurbits benefit the most from these types of mulches, and I've found it goes some way towards preventing powdery mildew at the end of the season.

The main downside to planting through plastic, other than the environmental cost of its production, is its tendency to provide a home for slugs. Early squash and courgette plants are especially prone to this and I've

Killer clippings

✱ If you are still slightly stuck in the past and use herbicide and weedkiller on your lawn, never use your grass clippings as mulch on a fruit or vegetable bed.

lost whole plants overnight to these slimy pests. See Chapter 29, page 210, for more on using black plastic.

Grass clippings
As with most things in horticulture there are many and mixed opinions about using grass

Drought-tolerant veg; thirsty veg

Specially adapted varieties of common crops such as sweetcorn (black Aztec corn) and tomatoes (those grown in the Middle East and Spain) can withstand prolonged dry conditions, as can everyday annual vegetables such as onions, turnips and kale.

In warmer climates some food plants, such as chaya, or tree spinach (which can also be grown in the UK), edible cacti and cassava are naturally adapted to grow in drier conditions.

Some perennial vegetables are adapted to dry conditions as they are slow growing and their roots can seek out moisture over a long period

of time. These include sea kale, Jerusalem and Chinese artichokes and asparagus.

At the opposite end of the scale, some vegetables are very thirsty and can require huge amounts of water. Members of the squash/cucumber family, including cucumbers, melons and courgettes, come into this category, requiring water in large amounts. Digging a sunken bed or growing thirsty plants in their own specially dug crater will help, as will mulching around them.

Sunken beds can help retain water in a dry climate.

clippings as mulch. Unless you wish to make a wildflower meadow, the best choice is to leave clippings where they were cut, allowing them to decompose back into the soil and feed the grass. Failing that, they can be used on the compost heap mixed with drier 'brown' waste.

As mulch, grass clippings will prevent weed growth and can retain heat and moisture. They can heat up quickly as they decompose, which may cause damage to the roots of some plants. They can also get matted and slimy. Rather than use them as a mulch, grass clippings can come in handy to earth up potatoes. This should be done at levels of no more than 5cm (2") at a time.

Compost

Compost really is miracle mulch – it holds moisture in and improves the soil life, structure, drainage and water-retaining capacity all in one go. I sprinkle a good layer of compost over a garden bed if ever I'm working in someone else's garden – the contrast of dark compost against green foliage is a great way to frame any work you may have done.

Cover over the bed if you have it in abundance, otherwise just coat around fruit bushes, trees and perennials and get busy making some more!

Cardboard

Cardboard is very cheap and easy to obtain. My old allotment was in an area that had kerbside recycling, which meant I could take all the cardboard I wanted on my way to my plot. Cardboard can be used as a base layer for mulches such as manure and woodchip (see below) or on its own. If topping with compost or manure it will not need weighing down but if used on its own you will need to cover it with rocks, bricks, wood or whatever you can get your hands on.

Manure

Manure can be used to mulch around mature fruit trees and bushes or around perennials such as rhubarb. It should be well rotted before applying, so may need stacking before you use it. It can be used just on its own but is best used in conjunction with cardboard to really keep the weeds out and moisture in – spread a layer of cardboard and then pile the manure on top.

Woodchip

Woodchip mulches should really be used only on top of some kind of barrier such as cardboard or black plastic. Woodchip is mainly carbon and in order to break down properly it needs nitrogen. When used as a mulch around plants it can rob them of this essential element.

Chapter 7

TREASURE IN THE TRASH

In the past, builders made houses with what was already in the landscape. Aberdeen, for example, is built from local granite; the villages surrounding my home town of Northampton are made from the local sandstone; and in parts of Cornwall cob cottages would have dominated the landscape.

Gardens would have no doubt been no different, with their plants and structures reflecting those in the local area. Nowadays we are more likely to get wood from Norway than from 20 miles down the road, or stone from a Chinese quarry rather than dug out of a local hillside. However, just because we can

One man's scrap is another man's brass.

import and export building materials from all over the world doesn't mean we should!

My lack of a car has always meant I lead something of the life of a bygone age. None more so than when I'm in the garden, and I'm forced to make do with what materials are around me, either on my plot or left in skips or abandoned nearby. This is not always as bad as it sounds: gardeners are great hoarders and in each allotment or garden I've come to work on I've nearly always found the half-finished projects of the previous tenant or the scraps of projects that never happened.

True 'rubbish' or 'trash' is something that has ceased to have a function. Yet with a creative eye and a second look, many things can be given a new lease of life with an entirely new function. Even if an object can't be used in its entirety some of it can often be salvaged and used for something else.

SEPARATING THE TREASURE FROM THE TRASH

Sometimes it pays to listen to your partner, your spouse or your friends: they might just be right when they tell you that rotten, plastic-backed carpet is not worth dragging home. I've seen couples have heated rows over what they want to take home in the back of a van and I've had plenty of those kinds of 'conversations' myself – from both sides. Not everything is worth having and you may need to ask yourself whether you are considering taking home something that will later become some kind of pollution. Imagine the item in your vegetable garden; now imagine it in ten years, twenty years. Sometimes you have to face facts and realise that things are thrown out for good reason: they are trash!

At times what may seem like a great way to use unwanted items can merely be creating

problems for the future. I leapt at the idea to use up a pile of scratched CDs and obsolete computer discs to scare birds. My enthusiasm wasn't so great, however, when I found I was picking up their shattered remains for the next couple of years. To make matters worse the birds didn't really seem too bothered by the CDs and they still ravaged anything I didn't have under a net! There are far better ways of recycling CDs than littering your garden with them for years to come. In the UK, polymer recycling (www.polymerrecycling.co.uk) will take broken CDs, including the jewel case, and recycle them for you. Similar facilities exist elsewhere in the world – check online for details.

I can't pass a skip without peering in and I've found out the hard way what is best to take home and what will just clutter up the garden. I've now learned from my mistakes (well, most of the time) and I now ask myself some of the following questions to determine whether dragging a new new-found 'treasure' home from a skip is worth it.

- **Have I got room for this item?** A summer house being dismantled and thrown out might at first seem like an opportunity too good to miss, but if you've no room in your garden to put it up is it worth taking?
- **Is it plastic?** If so do I plan to use it outdoors? A lot of plastic is not UV (ultraviolet)-stable, that is to say it will break down in sunlight. Coating a greenhouse with thin clear plastic from shopping bags might seem like a good idea at the time but it won't last. They will break down into smaller fragments, scattering far and wide, polluting the soil and contaminating local wildlife. Most plastic will begin to degrade if left outdoors.
- **Is it weatherproof?** MDF and chipboard, although stable indoors, will warp and break down if left outside.

- **Is it damaged beyond repair?** This mainly goes for garden tools and machinery but could also include shattered plant pots and twisted or rusty nails/screws.
- **Will I or someone I know be able to fix it?** Or will I (realistically) learn how to fix it? If the answer is yes to either of these questions then by all means take it home. However, be really, really honest with yourself: are you likely to learn the ins and outs of lawnmower mechanics in the near future? If not, would someone else benefit from that broken lawnmower instead?
- **Will it break down into toxic compounds or leach toxic compounds?** Without a chemistry degree this isn't an easy question to answer. If something is man-made or treated try doing your homework a little. I used car tyres to grow potatoes in for years but now find that they can leach toxic compounds into the soil. The Royal Horticultural Society (RHS) now advises that tyres should no longer be used for food growing.
- **Will it be an eyesore?** Aesthetics may not matter to everyone but if something is so ugly that it will cause friction with the neighbours is it really worth taking home?
- **Is it carrying a disease?** Plants can carry fungal diseases or viruses, such as canker in apple or big bud in blackcurrants. When bringing in salvaged plants try to be sure you are not bringing in more than you bargained for!

For the most part, however, one man's muck really is another man's brass, and I'm constantly amazed by what people throw away. But remember when 'skip diving' to

always try to ask permission first, especially if the skip is in a driveway.

THERE BE TREASURE

So what should you look out for? What's worth loading into a van, balancing on a bicycle or slinging over your shoulder to carry to the plot? Below is a list of some of the things I've found in skips. It is by no means comprehensive but does highlight the range of valuable items you might find and some of their uses.

A good friend of mine called Heather often talks about skips ripening. She'll see a skip parked up in a side street and say 'give it a couple of days, it's not ripe yet'. Her eye for skips is as primed as that of any fruit grower gearing up to sell their crop, as, lo and behold, two days later the skip will fill with all kinds of goodies ripe for the picking.

The ripened items of skip treasure I always keep my eye out for are good pieces of wood – wood is by far one of the most useful things you can come by in the trash.

Skip treasure

- **Buckets/containers** There are infinite uses in the garden for good-sized buckets and containers of all shapes and sizes. They can be used as growing containers or plant pots, for making liquid feed, as trugs for weeds, for forcing rhubarb or blanching sea kale or, if they are big enough, they can be used as water butts.
- **Wood** Never pass a good bit of wood, but be careful with treated or 'man-made' wood (see next chapter).
- **Nets / net curtains** Nets and net curtains are gardeners' gold – great for keeping birds and bugs off your brassicas.
- **Sticks** Peas sticks, canes for beans, short sticks for marking out lines or for pegs . . . the list goes on.

- **Stones and rocks** Good for weighing down weed-suppressant material, nets, fleeces, pond liners, etc. Also good for paths and stepping stones.
- **Plants** A rare find in skips but not unheard of. These are of course treasure! Gardeners will always need to thin out, separate and generally rid a garden of its plants. You seldom need to pay for raspberry canes, strawberry plants or spreading herbs such as mint or marjoram if you get friendly with a jobbing gardener.
- **Windows** Old windows are just a cold frame waiting to happen.
- **Old plant pots** Just know when to stop collecting them – you can have too much of a good thing.

Chapter 8

WOOD

Wood is one of the most durable, versatile, abundant and, if sourced correctly, sustainable building materials you are ever likely to use in a garden. Wander around any garden or allotment and you'll see it being used in sheds, compost bins, fences, bird boxes, trellises, raised beds, benches, tables, supports, planters, steps . . . I could go on.

Wood can seem a daunting material to work with, yet even novice carpenters should be able to saw a plank of wood in two to make a simple raised bed or lash together some pallets to make a compost bin.

WHERE TO FIND WOOD

Salvaged wood can be quite easy to come by, especially in bigger towns and cities. Many of my DIY projects have been made from wood sourced from skips outside houses undergoing renovation, and this seems to be a good place to start.

Pallets and good pieces of wood can be found left abandoned on industrial estates or fly-tipped by the side of the road. By taking these away you are improving the local environment and recycling a material that would otherwise go to landfill. One resident of Birmingham I met some time ago sources all his wood this way and claims to have saved himself a small fortune in the process.

Recycling centres or local tips now often have a section for wood, which they sell for a nominal amount. Wood reclamation is on the rise, and centres such as the one described in the box overleaf in Bristol are cropping up all over the place.

Maybe the best things in life *are* free.

Why buy recycled timber?

Ben Moss, Co-Founder, Co-Manager and Tea Boy at Bristol Wood Recycling Project

It should be fairly easy to find somewhere near to you where you can buy recycled timber. Most towns have a reclamation yard, while a growing number of locations around the UK have a social enterprise dedicated to recycling wood. The National Community Wood Recycling Project (www.communitywoodrecycling.org.uk) represents enterprises such as the Bristol Wood Recycling Project (BWRP) and the Brighton and Hove Community Wood Recycling Project,

The Bristol Wood Recycling Project.

TYPES OF WOOD

Superficially, salvaged wood can be split into two main categories: 'man-made' and 'natural'. Pedants among you may realise that the 'natural' wood has been cut, milled and dried and is far from its natural state, just as much of the 'man-made' wood is made from pieces of 'natural' wood.

However, the distinction is there for ease of reference, as all you really want to know when rifling through a skip is whether something is usable or not!

Man-made wood
Man-made wood isn't really good for much in the garden but it is unfortunately a very common thing to find in a skip.

Chipboard / particleboard
It simply is not worth using chipboard/particleboard in the garden as it is very low-quality timber and quickly disintegrates when wet. There is very little you can do with this kind of wood other than using it as indoor shelving. A face mask should be worn if working with this material as the dust released can be hazardous.

along with similar projects across the UK, from Somerset to Glasgow. These projects make it possible to buy timber that has been rescued from the waste stream, at low prices, whilst enabling volunteers to gain important skills and work experience.

So what are the benefits of buying recycled/reclaimed timber over buying new timber? The table below summarises the basic reasons. There are huge environmental costs in transporting, milling, possibly kiln drying and distributing wood. Then, when discarded, the wood is often mechanically recycled at either a council-run tip or a waste transfer station.

Buying reclaimed timber eradicates a whole portion of these costs.

Old timber	New timber
Reclaimed timber is often well seasoned and unlikely to warp.	Kiln dried, and prone to warping and cracks.
Absolutely full to bursting with character and history.	Somewhat generic in appearance.
Social enterprise factors – volunteers; not-for-profit; tangible community benefits.	Rarely funds social enterprises (although there are exceptions to this rule).
Cheap prices: e.g. BWRP offers wood at $2/3$ the price of the cheapest standard softwood. Low overheads mean the prices are kept low.	Often larger overheads and subsequently higher prices.
A way of sourcing endangered hardwoods without having to plunder virgin forests.	Can contribute to the deforestation of hardwood forests.

MDF

Often called the modern asbestos, MDF was once heralded as a cheap alternative to timber for the DIY enthusiast. Unlike timber (but just like chipboard), MDF warps and eventually disintegrates in wet weather and as such is completely unsuitable for garden projects. If you have some spare offcuts use them in the house or shed for shelving and wear a mask when working with it.

Plywood

There are various different grades of plywood and many are perfect for outdoor projects.

Marine grade and Exterior grade plywood are both made using waterproof glues; they are considered the Rolls Royce of salvaged wood and work especially well as shed roofing.

Other grades of plywood can be useful for outdoor projects but will vary in durability and quality.

Wood–plastic composite (WPC)

As the name might suggest, this is a mix of recycled waste wood (usually sawdust) and post-consumer plastic. Despite its seemingly good environmental credentials, its durability

If only all scrap wood was as well sorted as this.

is as yet unknown and it could yet prove to be a hazard to the environment. It comes in pre-moulded shapes and is difficult if not impossible to work with. As with the other man-made woods, a mask and goggles should be worn when working with WPC.

Natural wood

Without going into too much detail as to why (and, believe me, you can on this subject), wood falls into two botanical categories: softwood and hardwood.

Soft and hard wood

Softwood tends to be faster-growing, mainly evergreen conifers; hardwood tends to be slower-growing, deciduous trees. Both have their merits and their flaws, and within each type of wood there many subcategories.

It stands to reason that a well-seasoned chunk of solid oak should last a lot longer outside than a flimsy piece of pine. However, that won't always make it the right choice for an outside job. The solid piece of oak will be extremely heavy, expensive and hard to work whereas the pine will be cheap and can be easily worked in to a whole range of gardenware.

Unless you are buying wood it is unlikely that you will have a choice in what you come by. You can, however, favour picking up certain types of wood over others, depending on the job in hand.

Some common types of wood and their uses

The chart below shows some common wood types and their uses. It is a generalisation, as trees vary depending on the conditions they are grown in. For example, softwoods grown in cool climates will grow very slowly and have growth rings close together, producing a sturdier wood than if the same species of tree is grown quickly in a warm country.

Skip diving for wood – at a glance

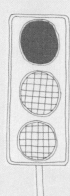

Red light – don't pick up

- **Knotted wood** Go for wood with as few knots as possible – the fewer the knots the easier it will be to work with.
- **Wood with too many nails** Nails can be removed with a claw hammer but there is a limit to the number you may be able to remove easily. If there is a choice, go for nail-free every time.
- **Wood covered in concrete** Flat pieces of wood are sometimes used to mix up concrete, rendering the wood unusable.
- **Warped wood** A little warping can be worked around but it's useless if you need straight edges.
- **MDF and chipboard** Only really good for indoor shelving.

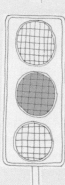

Amber light – think about it

- **Painted wood** Paint can flake off. Old paint can be lead-based. Take it only if you can remove the paint or you can use it as it is.
- **Treated wood** Use for construction projects such as sheds or fences but not for raised beds or benches.
- **Rotten wood** Good for composting or piling up in a neglected corner for wildlife, but try not to take rotten painted or treated wood.

Green light – go for it straight away

- **Untreated wood** Untreated wood can be made into a wide range of things – it is a blank slate waiting for you to transform it into something in the garden.
- **Solid doors** Very useful for all kinds of projects, especially shed building. But don't consider if made with thin panels or chipboard.
- **Posts** The wood forager's dream! Square posts are worth saving or dragging home as they can be made into fence posts, shed frames, the corners of compost heaps, pergolas . . . Round posts won't fit into a square hole but they can make good fence posts.
- **Logs** Larger logs can be burnt on a log pile or used to attract wildlife. Thinner ones can be useful for making the edges of paths or raised beds when laid flat on the ground, or can be made into legs for benches (or entire benches).
- **Planks** Check for signs of woodworm, rotting or cracks. If in good condition, pile them up and take them home. Good for panelling on sheds, raised beds, paths and benches.
- **Pallets** As long as you have space for them these will always come in handy – but avoid ones made of chipboard or ones with an angry dog tied to them.

Wood use in the garden

Type of wood	Original use	Properties	Garden uses
Ash	Rare to find salvaged (occasionally used in flooring) but commonly grown tree. Old tool handles.	Hard-wearing, good for burning, flexible, won't split.	Tool handles, benches.
Cedar and larch	Beams.	Hard-wearing, weatherproof.	Structures, fencing, raised beds, fence posts.
Douglas fir	Floorboards.	Softwood, good for building but not weatherproof – use under cover.	Garden furniture, raised beds (if untreated).
Oak	Beams, floorboards.	Rot-resistant. Splits easily.	Heavy-duty applications such as sheds, fence posts and all building work.
Pine and spruce	Beams, floorboards, pallets.	Softwood, not rot-resistant unless high grade.	Building work such as sheds if covered and weatherproofed.

USING TREATED WOOD

Left to its own devices, deadwood will fall prey to countless organisms such as insects, actinomycetes, fungi and bacteria. These all find their way to the decaying wood to seek what nutrition they can, in the same way that hyenas, vultures and maggots will clean a carcass in the Serengeti. As the organisms act on the wood it will eventually completely decompose, forming new soil as it does so.

Wood treatments aim to slow down or prevent this process. Treatments can contain:
- fungicides to deal with fungal attack
- insecticides to deal with the insects
- and – rarely – poisons dangerous to mammals to stop predation from rats.

Treated wood can be a way in which garden-ers can introduce toxins unwittingly into their garden – damaging themselves, their plants and the local wildlife as they do so. The treatments vary in both their toxicity and their effectiveness, and the older the wood the more likely toxins are to have already leached from it and thus no longer present any problems. The best option is always to try to source untreated wood and either treat it yourself or choose to leave it as it is.

When used for raised beds or any other horticultural setting, treated wood can leach toxins (including heavy metals) into the soil and eventually your food. A thick plastic sheet between the wood and the soil will prevent this. Salvaged wood, unfortunately, doesn't come with a full history of how it has been treated, but there can be telltale signs.

Heat-treated wood

Many softwoods are heat treated with

chromated copper arsenate (CCA). This penetrates into the wood, preventing attack from fungi and insect predation.

The problem with CCA-treated wood is given away in the name: arsenate can break down to arsenic, especially in acidic conditions. This typically happens at a soil pH of around 3, which is generally far too low for vegetable growing (most vegetables grow at a pH of between 5 and 7).

- You can usually spot CCA-treated wood as it has a characteristic green tinge to it.
- It is generally used to treat garden furniture, such as picnic tables, wooden decking, fencing and outdoor wooden structures.
- You are more likely to find CCA treatment on softwood rather than hardwood, but it can be found on both.

Much of the toxic component of this treatment would have already leached out of second-hand wood by the time you get it. However, the Environmental Protection Agency in the US and the European Commission both ban the use of CCA-treated wood in non-industrial environments as they deem it far too hazardous to human health! They also advise that gloves and a mask should be worn whilst handling it and that bare human skin should not come into contact with surfaces treated with it. This may be a little alarmist, but needless to say the wood should be treated with caution.

Due to its links with arsenic contamination of the soil, it is advised that you should not use CCA-treated wood for food-growing projects. If you are in doubt, use thick plastic sheeting between the edge of the bed and the soil – thick discarded manure, sand or soil improver bags work well.

CCA-treated wood is especially unsuitable for compost bins, as when organic material breaks down organic acids are released, which can not only aid the leaching of arsenic but will also help rot the wood.

Creosote

I have a very clear memory of my father treating our garden fence with creosote. More than anything it is the smell I can remember – a smell that not only evokes strong child-hood memories but one that I now know also indicates carcinogenic vapours.

Creosote has since been banned, and any recently treated offcuts of wood shouldn't contain it. However, older wood, especially fencing, could well be treated with creosote.

- Creosote-treated timber is usually characteristically dark brown, fading a little with age.
- It sometimes has a coal- or tar-like scent, even years after application.
- Creosote will leach into the soil and the water table: don't use it for any projects coming in direct contact with either.

You shouldn't burn creosote-treated wood – instead recycle it where facilities exist.

Railway sleepers

Back in the 1980s and 1990s railway sleepers (or 'railroad ties') were the salvager's dream and were even popularised on TV gardening shows. It has now been widely publicised that they contain substances hazardous to health, including creosote and the salts of heavy metals, and should therefore not be used in direct contact with the soil or perhaps on any gardening project. (Not everything that looks like a railway sleeper is a railway sleeper – you can now get 'eco sleepers', which are treated with more environmentally friendly preservatives and intended for use in gardens. However, it may not be easy to tell the difference.)

Painted wood

Paint can hide a multitude of sins, including woodworm and rotten wood – give anything painted a good look over before you take it home. Also, with older wood you can't guarantee that it hasn't been painted using lead-based paint (see below).

An electrically heated paint remover will make short work of taking paint off. However, in the absence of one of these you will need to use one of the following (listed from easiest to hardest).

- An electric sander.
- A drill with a sanding disk attachment.
- Sandpaper / abrasive paper and elbow grease (elbow grease now comes in a handy squeezable bottle . . .).

Alternatively, leave the paint on the wood, but don't use it in contact with the soil.

Lead paint

It is unfortunate that wood painted with lead-based paints doesn't come with a big sign saying 'You can't touch this'. Lead-based paints were used right up to the 1970s and subsequently banned in the UK, US, Australia and elsewhere.

Removal of the paint can be quite problematic, to say the least. The British Coatings Federation (yes, such a thing exists!) recommends the use of chemical-based, heat-based or infra-red paint removers to remove it. However, as the particles of lead can be inhaled, these should only be used with an approved, suitable dust mask.

Blow torches, sanders or plain sandpaper should not be used as these will just throw up lead particles into the air.

Once the paint is removed, all the debris has to be cleaned up using a vacuum cleaner with a special filter attached to deal with all the tiny particles of paint. All the remains should be disposed of properly by bagging up any chippings or dust, sealing the bags with tape and taking to the hazardous waste section of a recycling centre.

I'm sure I'm not alone in thinking all that sounds like a little too much effort and the best solution would be to avoid lead-based paint wherever possible.

TREATING WOOD YOURSELF

Thick pieces of hardwood will last a long time but softwoods and small cuts will not last as long. With this in mind you may want to do something to prolong their life.

Ideally you should use a natural wood preservative such as linseed/flaxseed oil (or, for the money bags, Tung oil). These are natural but expensive and can take time to dry, especially in cold conditions. This is somewhat unfortunate, as most woodworking projects take place in the colder months of the year when there is little to do on the plot.

Look for the VOC rating when choosing a wood preserver, which will range from high to low or minimal. VOC stands for volatile organic compound and refers to the solvents used in various wood preservers (and paints). Preservers and paints high in volatile organic compounds are harmful to humans, plants and animals and should be avoided. Ideally we would all use zero-VOC products on wood, but budgets don't always allow this and minimal VOC products can be used in their place.

I have found one bucket of minimal-VOC wood-preserving paint to be ample for a couple of coats of a small shed, with enough left over to paint my arbour/pergola along with odds and sods of other jobs. It comes in a wide range of colours, from green and brown to Titchmarsh blue.

PALLETS

Pallets are an indispensible source of recyclable wood for the gardener. They are ubiquitous in our modern life and represent our modern global culture like no other object. They begin life in factories and warehouses in far-flung parts of the world, only to miraculously appear in our back alleys, car parks and city canals.

Pallets are very versatile for the freebee gardener: you can use them whole to make compost bins (see Chapter 5, page 77), part-dismantled to make fence panels (see Chapter 4, page 68) or table tops, or taken to pieces to make almost anything.

Pallets are a good source of timber.

Heat-treated pallets can be identified by the letters 'HT'.

Methyl bromide

Up until March 2010 some pallets were fumigated with the chemical methyl bromide – a substance which is known to have serious effects on human health and can be damaging to the environment. These have the letters 'MB' on the pallet near the International Plant Protection Convention (IPPC) logo. Although heat-treated pallets (look for 'HT' rather than 'MB') present their own problems, I would use them in favour of 'MB' pallets.

HOW TO DISMANTLE A PALLET

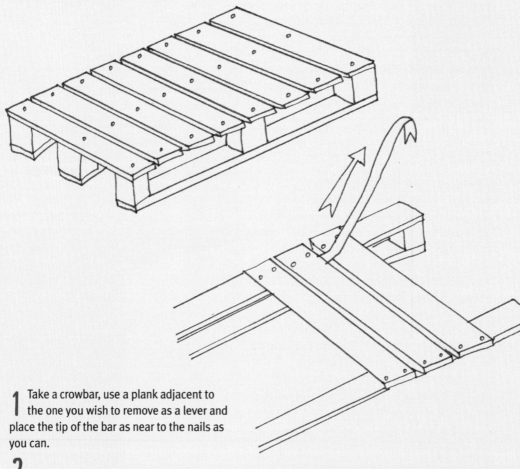

1 Take a crowbar, use a plank adjacent to the one you wish to remove as a lever and place the tip of the bar as near to the nails as you can.

2 In theory, the plank should pop off.

3 Some will come off more easily than others – no doubt the ones when nobody is watching you!

4 All but the most unwilling nails can then be removed with a claw hammer or, on traditional crowbars, the back claw.

Sourcing pallets

There is a strange phenomenon I've noticed, with both pallets and certain models of car. I first noticed this as a teenager when a friend of mine bought a red Mini Metro. Days after his purchase it seemed that every second car that passed me had somehow become a red Mini Metro. There didn't seem to be many on the road before but now there were simply hundreds of them!

Of course there hadn't been an overnight increase in the number of Mini Metros on the road, but there had been an overnight increase in my awareness of red Mini Metros. I'm sure there is a scientific name for such a phenomenon, but I prefer to call it The Red Mini Metro Syndrome.

The Red Mini Metro Syndrome seems to also work with pallets. I bet before reading this paragraph you hadn't noticed a single pallet in the streets near where you live. Yet look tomorrow and they will start turning up all over the place. They are so common in modern life that sourcing them should be quite easy.

On the slim chance that this phenomenon hasn't happened to you, then my advice is to start looking around industrial estates, retail estates, building merchants and DIY stores, or anywhere likely to have goods delivered on pallets. Most will give away pallets for nothing but some will try to charge. I sourced mine from a wholefood warehouse: they were happy to give me, for nothing, both broken pallets and ones of odd sizes they could not return.

Dismantling pallets

Unless you are blessed with magical powers and can melt nails with your mind, it is unlikely you will be able to remove all the planks from a pallet without breaking any. There is a film on YouTube of a man doing just that (look for 'How to dismantle a pallet'), but I expect he has had a lot of practice. His plank-and-mallet technique makes it look very easy, yet I've always found the machine-driven nails grip tighter than a limpet at low tide.

After a lot of experimenting I found the best method was to use a crowbar. Crowbars seem to get in and lever the planks with the least amount of effort.

If you don't have a wood burner, make sure you have a place to dispose of the broken pallet pieces. In the past I've simply burnt them and dug the resulting wood ash into the soil. This raises the alkalinity of the soil, so should be done only sparingly and only if the soil needs it.

ROTTEN WOOD

With all the will in the world some projects never get completed and instead you may end up with a pile of rotting old wood. There is unfortunately very little you can do about this, but what is your loss is the compost heap's gain. A healthy compost heap requires a 4:1 ratio of carbon-rich or brown waste (such as old dry leaves, cardboard or paper) to nitrogen-rich green waste (such as fresh lawn clippings and garden trimmings). The 'brown' or carbon-rich woody material is often the hardest to find. If you can, break up the wood into chips using a garden chipper or shredder, or if it is rotten enough you may be able to do this by hand. Sprinkle the chipped wood on the compost heap each time you add the green material.

PART 2

SPRING

As the slow hand of winter retreats, birds are busy raising their young, beekeepers see a rise in hive activity and the self-employed busy themselves into the new tax year. And spring is, of course, a very busy time for the gardener. You have to keep your eye on the ball in spring – it is far too easy to miss the short window of opportunity and fall behind.

It is true that things will quite often catch up: even if a seed packet says 'sow by end of May' you can usually squeeze in a few seeds at the beginning of June. However, for a staggered harvest rather than a glut, planting at the right time and in succession will mean there is more on the table in the coming months.

This is a time for real money saving: plants raised from seed come at a fraction of the cost of seedlings from a garden centre. A tray of cabbage seedlings might cost the same as fully grown cabbages from a grocer. This makes no financial sense whatsoever – buying seedlings is only worth it if you have really fallen behind and they are being sold cheaply.

If you're buying your seeds, modules, pots, potting compost and plant labels, costs

can really begin to mount up – and usually at a time (with winter fuel bills and the expense of Christmas starting to take its toll) when most of us can least afford it.

There are also environmental issues to consider when buying in new rather than recycling, adapting or making do with what you have. Pots and plant labels are

usually made of plastic, adding to landfill waste; propagators and greenhouses may be heated by non-renewable energy; and many potting composts contain peat – a wildlife-depleting, non-renewable resource.

The best approach is to work out what you actually need for each job, rather than what a garden catalogue tells you you need.

JOBS FOR SPRING

- Acquire seeds
- Protect from the cold
- Buy or make seed/potting compost
- Make plant labels
- Raise new plants
- Plant out or grow in containers
- Gather 'wild' extras

Chapter 9

ACQUIRING SEEDS

The most economical and traditional method of acquiring seeds is to save them from your own plants – this is covered in Chapter 24. Failing that, there are various other methods of getting seeds for the coming season.

BUYING SEEDS

It is very easy to go a little mad when buying seeds. You can completely lose sight of how much room you actually have in the garden and be tempted to buy up an entire seed catalogue. Try to make a plan of your beds first (see Chapter 2) and decide what is going to go where, and *then* buy your seed.

A plan will also help decide:
- exactly what you need
- how much room it will have / how much you can sow
- where it is going to be sown.

The plan can be a fluid one and you can have areas marked out as simply 'something interesting' so if some interesting seeds do come your way you will have room for them. The trick is to be realistic about how much space you have and the time you'll be able to devote to your seedlings. Seeds are really only of use if they are allowed to germinate – some have a limited shelf life and a year of storing can be enough to make them unviable for the following year.

Also, don't get drawn in by offers that may seem appealing but are really not worth it; quite often you will see mixes such as 'easy vegetable mix' or 'patio herbs'. These can be a real bargain – but only if the answer to the first of these questions is yes, and the answer to the second is no:
- Do I want to grow all seeds contained in the packets?
- Do I have any of the seeds already?

It's easy to go overboard when you are buying seeds.
Photo: Lou Brown

Start looking out for seed swaps from January onwards. *Photo: Lou Brown*

What type of seed?

If you want to save your seed for next year then you should choose open-pollinated (sometimes labelled as OP) varieties over F1 hybrids. F1s are the product of two known parent plants to give known results in the next generation. The offspring of F1 plants never come true to form, making them useless for seed saving.

You should also consider buying organic seed: organic seed plants don't pose as much of a risk to wildlife and human health as non-organic seed plants, which may have been sprayed. Organic seeds may also be from smaller companies that need help staying in business. If you intend to save seed year after year then think of the purchase in your first year as a one-off investment and spend a little more, choosing the seed company you buy from wisely.

Clubbing together

Most seed packets will give you far more seeds than you will ever use in one year, and it makes little sense to buy packets of 200 seeds when you may need only 50 or 10. The initial investment can be far smaller and you'll get a much broader range of crops if you club together with friends to buy seed. Those 200 seeds can be shared between four of you, giving you all 50 each at a quarter of the cost.

Extend this to raising seedlings and one person could raise all the tomato seedlings, another courgettes, another herbs, brassicas, lettuces, etc., until, after a few weeks, you can organise a plant swap (it could be a good excuse for a springtime party).

Seed swaps

Organised seed swaps can be an ideal opportunity to exchange your unwanted extra seeds for someone else's. Check out notice-boards in your area from the end of January to see what seed swaps are going on, and if you can't find any in your area why not organise your own?

I seem to find fellow gardeners who are swapping seeds and seedlings every year, and I've found that choosing a mix of unusual crops and heritage varieties alongside the more traditional crops means I have plenty to offer in return.

The 'classic' crops such as parsley and tomatoes can be slightly over-represented at seed swaps. Yet you can quite often find hidden horticultural gems at these events. I've come across some quite rare seeds at seed swaps, including locally saved seed, which should be well adapted to the local environment. You have to be careful with some saved seeds and be prepared for a surprise – many can be incorrectly labelled, or correctly labelled but contain seeds that have cross-pollinated with nearby varieties. French beans, squashes and brassicas all cross-pollinate within their species.

Most seed swaps are quite small local affairs and it can be possible to speak to the gardener who donated the seed. So, if you can, ask whether he or she put in measures to protect from cross-pollination (see Chapter 21, pages 174-5) or grew only one variety that year.

Try not to use a seed swap to just offload all your crummy out-of-date seed – this only makes for a crummy seed swap and means there is less chance of it happening the following year. Instead, take what you need from seed packets and donate the rest.

SEED FROM SHOP-BOUGHT FRUIT AND VEGETABLES

It might be tempting to simply buy a vegetable in a shop or supermarket, take out the seeds, sow them and see what happens. Yet shop-bought produce may be:

- bred in a climate vastly different to yours (e.g. grown in Kenya) and not adapted to your local conditions
- bred not to be resistant to pests as it relies on being sprayed
- genetically modified (mainly a problem outside the UK – at the time of writing)
- hybrids, which won't come true
- bred to be grown hydroponically rather than in soil
- lacking in flavour
- bred to give high yields from weak plants.

You might still see no harm in putting a few plants in, yet these weak, tasteless hybrids will take up room that could otherwise serve stronger, healthier plants.

Exceptions to the rule

There some exceptions to this rule. Organically grown produce from farmers' markets or small-scale grocers can be a worthwhile and cheap source of seed. If you can talk to the grower, you could ask if there is a risk of cross-pollination or if the produce is from hybrid/F1 plants.

Tomatoes, peppers and chillis are generally self-pollinated, so the seed should come true and is worth saving. You can plant up sprouting onions, leaving them to flower and set seed – it is a long process but two or three bulbs can yield a lot seeds and this makes use of onions bound for the compost heap.

Seed potatoes generally give better yields than shop-bought ones.
Photo: Lou Brown

Another exception to the rule (and one which should appeal to the experimental gardener) is concerning seeds or other propagules impossible to find in seed catalogues. 'Ethnic' supermarkets or market stalls with exotic fruit and vegetables can provide all kinds of propagating material, such as taro corms or chayotes ready to sprout.

Also, goji berries can be grown from the seed of the dried fruit and pea plants from dried peas. If you have the room and time, why not experiment? The results may be unpredictable, but isn't gardening a little like that anyway?

SEED POTATOES

Seed potatoes are screened for diseases and should produce good yields without the need for agrichemicals. Shop-bought potatoes *can*

produce a reasonable yield, and when money has been really tight I have put a couple in the ground to see what happens. However, I've always been disappointed with the results and have come to the conclusion that bought seed potatoes are the key to a good yield.

FREE SEEDS IN MAGAZINES

As I make some of my income writing for gardening magazines I'm on tricky ground here. The truth is, and I'm sure you don't need me to tell you this, magazines have free seeds only to entice you to buy that magazine. If you were going to buy a magazine anyway then it is worth buying one with free seeds; they usually have varieties of seed in season and will contain well-written and informative articles (that should secure me some more work!).

Chapter 10

....

PROTECTING FROM THE COLD

Living, as I do, towards the top of this spherical rock on its journey through space, in the early part of the year I experience the planet just beginning to tilt toward the sun. This physicality means the days get longer, the nights get shorter and the likelihood of needing a warm coat, hat and scarf when stepping outside gets less and less with each passing week. With these celestial changes also come changes back down on Earth, as the increased light and heat causes many of our plants to break their winter dormancy and grow more quickly. The further north we go, the colder it is for longer, so at latitudes such as those of the UK, northern Europe and north America, things warm up quite slowly. We can give nature a little bit of a helping hand by protecting our plants from extremes of cold, allowing them to believe the season is rather less inclement than it really is.

This is where both the garden inventor and the recycler in you should really take centre stage. Almost anything that will let in light but provide a barrier to the cold can act as protection. Such things come in all shapes and sizes and can be improvised from many everyday items.

CLOCHES

Cloches act like mini greenhouses, raising the temperature just enough to protect plants from a harsh frost.

Plastic bottle cloches

The simplest cloche to make is one from a plastic drinks bottle – the only specialist piece

Plastic bottles make perfect makeshift cloches.

Pros of plastic bottle cloches
- ✅ Very cheap and easy to make
- ✅ Double up as pest protection
- ✅ Useful and cheap solution for small gardens

Cons of plastic bottle cloches
- ❌ Can be limited in size; only really useful for the initial stages of a seedling
- ❌ You'll need many for a large number of plants
- ❌ Can be difficult to water
- ❌ Only provide limited protection
- ❌ May need to replace after each season

of equipment you'll need to make one is a pair of sharp scissors. Cut off the base of the bottle (this can be used as a plant pot) and place the top over tender young plants. These cloches are ideal for early lettuces and can double up as slug protection. The lids should be removed for ventilation (they can be replaced at night if a hard frost is forecast). You can reuse bottle cloches year after year or you could consider making new ones every couple of years. They do last a while, especially if stored away properly, but if left to the elements for too long they will begin to crack and crumble and leave plastic debris in your soil.

Corrugated plastic cloches

Sometimes it is far simpler to protect an entire row at once rather than individual plants. A quick, cheap and easy cloche can be made from a piece of discarded clear corrugated plastic, the sort usually used for roofing. It can be secured at each end with a series of sticks dug into the earth and simply bent into shape, or it can be shaped around wire loops. The two ends should be left uncovered for ventilation but should not be laid facing an oncoming wind as otherwise the cloche may act as a wind tunnel! For added protection at night, block the ends with something flat (a piece of wood will do) and remove it in the day.

You may need to cut the plastic to size, which will need to be done with a fine-toothed saw or circular power saw to avoid cracking or shattering. No matter how tempting it might

Pros of corrugated plastic cloches
- ✅ Cheap (if not free)
- ✅ Protect whole rows at once
- ✅ Easy to put up
- ✅ Easy to water

Cons of corrugated plastic cloches
- ❌ Can crack and shatter if worked in cold weather
- ❌ Limited lifespan as they are not UV (ultraviolet)-stable – keep somewhere out of direct light when not in use

be, avoid using secateurs, shears or a sharp knife as it will crack the plastic (I know from first-hand experience!). Also, cold weather will make the plastic far more prone to cracking, so try to keep it somewhere warm for a while before working it.

Glass cloches

Glass cloches are the ultimate in reusable protection and if looked after they can last a lifetime. They can look very stylish and add that professional look to a plot, but they are expensive to buy. You could either drop hints to rich relatives about antique Victorian frames or try to make your own from a second-hand demijohn or a large glass bottle (see box below).

HOW TO MAKE YOUR OWN DEMIJOHN CLOCHE

There are two methods used for cutting the base from a demijohn.

1 Use a glass cutter and carefully cut around the base of the demijohn.

2 Place a demijohn in cold water up to where you want the break. Then pour boiling water inside, using a funnel so the water doesn't splash on the sides. The difference between heat and cold will cause the glass to shatter right where you want it.

This second method has accidently worked for me whilst home-brewing, but when researching for this book, try as I might, the glass wouldn't shatter. It doesn't take long to try, so give it a go if you have a spare demijohn – it's a lot less fiddly and straightforward than using glass cutters!

FLEECE

Horticultural fleece can be a very low-cost way to protect your crops from low temperatures. Fleece is sold by the metre, cut off the roll in a garden centre, or in pre-cut lengths. All fleece should be UV-stable but check the label first. Most are petroleum-based and therefore will not biodegrade, and they are difficult to recycle, so you'll have to make your own decision on whether you want to use them given the environmental 'footprint'. Biodegradable fleece is slowly coming on to the market but, as you may expect, it costs around twice the price of its non-biodegradable counterparts.

Fleece can tear quite easily, so those requiring large unbroken sheets, such as growers and farmers, may have shorter lengths that they are willing to part with. Fleece also acts

Fleece can be suspended on hoops.

Pros of fleece

⊘ Cheap
⊘ Very easy to install

Cons of fleece

⊗ Rarely recycled, and hard to recycle
⊗ Can rip and tear very easily

as a protection against pests such as flea beetles and birds.

To put down, simply lay over your plants and place mounds of earth along the sides, or weigh down with stones or bricks.

COLD FRAMES

A cold frame is one of those garden essentials that is very simple to construct from recycled materials. It can be made from nothing more than an old window placed on top of a wooden or brick frame. I have seen old plastic packing crates with an old window on top work just as well as lovingly crafted cold frames – as long as there is light and protection from the elements they can be made from anything!

Cold frames can be used as:
- a place to start off crops in the spring
- somewhere to harden off seedlings before planting them out
- a protected environment throughout the growing season
- somewhere to protect cuttings.

Ideally they should be placed against a south-facing wall (in the northern hemisphere) of a building such as a garden shed. Failing that, aim to have the window part of the frame angled to face south.

A simple cold frame can easily be made with recycled materials.

COVERED PROPAGATING SHELVES

Mini plastic greenhouses or covered plastic propagating shelves seem to have grown in popularity over the last few years, yet the quality seems to be inversely proportional to their increased sales. At best they last one or two seasons, after which the plastic covers shrink, the zips break and in some cases even the plastic supports shatter. Rather than pay good money for what ends up being a temporary structure, you can use old metal shelving or make shelves out of pallets and cover them in UV-stable clear plastic (see box overleaf). It helps if the shelves contain large perforations (metal) or slats (wood), to prevent water building up and to allow air to circulate. They can get top-heavy, so either try to tie the whole thing in place to a large stone, post or breeze block, or weigh down the bottom shelf with heavy items such as bags of potting compost.

Growing vertically this way is a great way to cram a lot of plants into a small space such as a balcony or a back yard. Balcony growers may find that they have to keep the cover over the shelves permanently or cover them with netting to prevent birds tearing their plants to shreds – I've found that birds seem to be more active at this raised level.

UV-stable plastic sheeting

Certain types of plastic sheeting are stable in sunlight and (unsurprisingly) are usually labelled 'UV-stable'. Cling film, cellophane and thin polythene coverings, such as those on new mattresses, are examples of plastic which is by and large *not* UV-stable. You can get away with using this type of low-grade plastic for about one season but it will start to disintegrate very quickly, sending out plastic shreds and tiny particles of plastic into the environment as it does so. If you are on a limited budget and this is all you have to hand, by all means use it, but take it down the second it starts to fall apart or you will be clearing bits of it from the land for years to come. Even seemingly thicker plastic, such as builders' polythene, can disintegrate after a season.

Try to find plastic of at least 125 microns or 500 gauge, or preferably higher. eBay and Freecycle are likely sources for second-hand UV-stable plastic. Garden furniture is sometimes packaged in this more stable plastic but this may be prone to shrinking over time.

To buy new, ask your local hardware / DIY / farming supply shop and the counter staff should point you in the right direction. If possible, bring the plastic indoors when not in use and store in a dark place as this will prolong its life. Also try to keep the integrity of the plastic – holes and tears can grow so don't use tent pegs!

Squeeze a lot into a small space by using the vertical plane.

Pros of covered shelves
- ✅ Lots of plants in a small space
- ✅ Perfect for hardening off plants

Cons of covered shelves
- ❌ Need to be secured in place as liable to topple
- ❌ Can be difficult to remove the plastic
- ❌ You may need to buy the shelves

POLYTUNNELS

The basic frame of a polytunnel can be improvised with what you have to hand. The biggest mistake people make is to put one up in the middle of a cold spell – plastic expands in the heat and contracts in the cold, so pick a warm, sunny day to put up your polytunnel.

Mini polytunnels (essentially a large cloche) are best made on a warm spring day and consist of a clear plastic sheet stretched over a series of hoops, spread across the length of the bed. Larger versions can be made by scaling up the method shown overleaf, using scaffolding poles instead of bamboo canes to hold up the hoops.

Before you start, you need to think about what you wish to grow underneath the cloche/polytunnel.

Short plants: do you intend it to house short plants such as lettuces and salad greens? If so the tunnel can be quite small – around 30cm (1ft) tall at its tallest point.

Tall plants: if you wish to grow taller plants such as peppers, tomatoes and aubergines,

A bamboo cane is enough to support the hoops of a small polytunnel.

then it will have to stand around 1.2m (4ft) tall if not more.

Once you have decided your tunnel size you will need to find something for the hoops. Lengths of flexible pipe such as alkathene pipe (plastic blue piping used for water pipes) are ideal, or you could use PVC piping. Alternatively, you can use fencing wire (4mm).

OTHER MEASURES

You could, of course, put off sowing and planting until the ground heats up, although in the UK climate this does mean a fairly substantial delay to the growing season, which could leave you falling behind.

Alternatively, you can:
- lay down black plastic, e.g. Mypex (see page 210) to warm up the soil and plant through it
- mulch around tender plants with straw – this will be more effective if you fluff up the straw to trap air.

Pros of mini polytunnels

- ✅ Cheaper than glass
- ✅ Protect whole rows at once
- ✅ Easy to put up
- ✅ Cheap to fix (gaffa tape)

Cons of mini polytunnels

- ❌ Can get torn easily
- ❌ Won't protect plants from hard frosts
- ❌ Can be costly if buying new materials (especially plastic sheeting)

HOW TO MAKE YOUR OWN MINI POLYTUNNEL

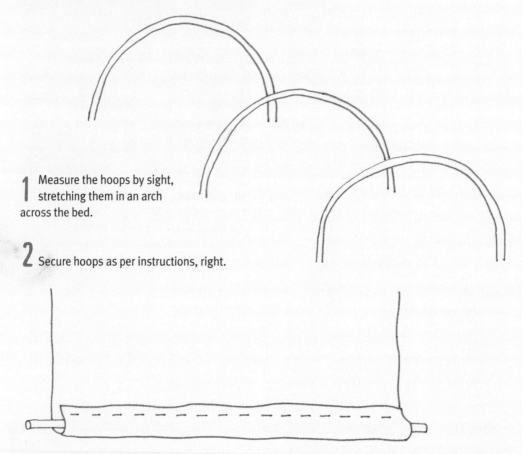

1 Measure the hoops by sight, stretching them in an arch across the bed.

2 Secure hoops as per instructions, right.

3 Cut the plastic sheet to the length of the bed.

4 Measure the width against the pipe, allowing extra room each side to secure in place.

5 Instead of cutting the sheet to the exact width, twist each side around a plank, cane or strong piping, then staple or nail into place. This should help with watering and ventilation as the plastic can be rolled up.

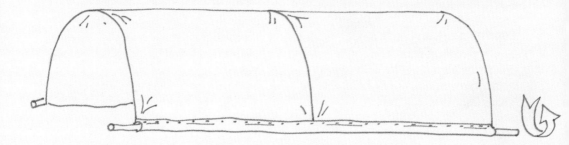

SECURING THE HOOPS

Hoops can be secured in any of the following ways.

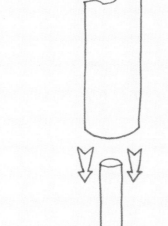

Slot the pipe over wooden or metal dowelling of 25-35cm (10-14") in length, pushed halfway into the ground. A bamboo cane will do the trick.

Use a flat colorail fitting (a hollow cylinder protruding from a flat bracket, used to secure curtains) or flagpole brackets screwed on top of the wooden edges of a raised bed. Or use brackets to secure the pipes to the bed edges.

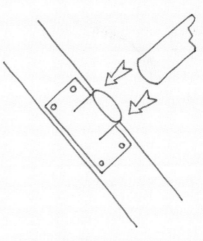

Dig a hollow metal pipe wider than the alkathene pipe into the ground, then slot the alkathene pipe in.

Chapter 11

∙∙∙∙∙∙∙∙∙∙∙∙∙∙∙∙∙∙

SEED AND POTTING COMPOST

The received wisdom is that there is no other substance like peat for retaining moisture and providing a low-nutrient potting compost for raising seeds. Like a lot of received wisdom, this has been passed on through gardening books without really being questioned. This misguided notion is so embedded in the public consciousness that even a major UK organic vegetable grower still uses this unsustainable resource for raising its vegetable seedlings – it seems the words 'organic' and 'sustainable' aren't always synonymous. Carnivorous plants, mosses and acid-loving plants naturally grow in peat bogs. Yet within this moist landscape you'd be hard pressed to find germinating vegetable seedlings and bedding plants!

Peat is useful to gardeners only because it is weed-free, light in texture and low in nutrients. The energy needed for a plant to emerge from a seed is present in the seed itself and not in the seed compost. All a plant really needs to emerge is something that will retain moisture.

Lots of other mediums are low in nutrients and retain water and can act as ideal compost for seedlings without causing the destruction of fragile landscapes. There are many types of

compost on the market that outperform peat-based composts, so it is worth doing your research beforehand. With an ever-increasing market for peat-free compost and constantly improving products is there really any need to devastate a pristine natural landscape to grow a few tomatoes?

Sieved leaf mould makes good seed compost, although you may have to pick out the odd stray weed.

The problem with peat

The lion's share of the world's harvested peat is used by amateur gardeners in the form of growbags and compost and with potted plants. According to the Wildlife Trusts, the UK has already lost around 94 per cent of its lowland raised peat bogs in little over 100 years. On the other side of the Atlantic they seem to be catching up, extracting peat at a rate of over 1 million tonnes a year from Canadian bogs, mainly for sale to the US horticultural market.

This represents a huge loss in biodiversity and further fragments an already fragile country-side. Moreover, peat bogs act as a valuable carbon store. The Irish Peatland Conservation Council claims that peat bogs hold more carbon than all of the world's rainforests. Peat moss filters around 10 per cent of the world's fresh drinking water and is renewed at only around 1mm a year. So the question has to be asked, why use it in the garden at all?

SEED, POTTING AND ALL-PURPOSE COMPOST: THE BASICS

Compost can be a confusing business. What do you need and what can you make yourself? First, there are various different types.

- **Seed compost** Generally a free-draining, low-nutrient compost for seeds.
- **Potting compost** Could more accurately be called 'potting on compost'. A generally more rich mix providing a growing plant with the nutrients it needs.
- **All-purpose compost** As the name suggests, a compost that can be used for most things – good for seeds and good for potting on.
- **Garden compost** The stuff you make at home in a compost bin. Can be used in potting mixes but never on its own as it is far too rich and can cause moulds.
- **Ericaceous compost** An acidic compost for acid-loving plants such as blueberries (add oak leaf mould and coffee grounds to mixes to make acidic compost).

CLUBBING TOGETHER

For those who wish to grow just a handful of vegetables each year, buying a big bag of compost can be a false economy. Quite often you may use only a half or a quarter of a bag and the rest will be left for a year to dry out or to harbour moulds and fungi. Some fungi can cause damping off, where your seedlings either never emerge or the stems become so badly damaged the young plants die.

Rather than waste money, time and plants this way, work out how much you might need and either make it yourself (see below) or club together with friends to buy a bag or a few bags between you. There are normally discounts for buying in bulk, so the more the merrier. The same of course goes for seed compost and potting composts.

MAKING YOUR OWN SEED COMPOST

At times I use straight leaf mould as seed compost, which I get free from a nearby formal garden. Big institutions such as this often have an abundance of resources and it's always worth asking for a bag or two. I use any excess to mulch my beds.

Two- or three-year-old (if not older) sieved leaf mould is perfect for most seed compost

A simple seed compost mix

- Two parts molehill soil.
- One part sharp sand.
- One part sieved leaf mould.
- If you have the money, a little vermiculite can aid moisture retention and is used in the place of sharp sand.

Some simple potting compost mixes

The following are some ideas for potting compost mixes.
- Equal parts garden compost, leaf mould and loam.
- 3 parts leaf mould, 1 part worm compost.
- Leaf mould and one teaspoon (no more) of concentrated chicken manure per 15cm (6") pot.
- 1 part loam, 1 part coir or leaf mould, 2 parts garden compost.

uses – see Chapter 27 for making your own leaf mould. If leaf mould is in short supply, or to assist with drainage, you can mix it with other growing mediums such as sharp sand, vermiculite or molehill soil.

If you don't have access to leaf mould you could experiment with 50:50 sieved garden soil and garden compost. I've tried this with good results. One major drawback to using soil is that you end up potting up in whatever soil type you have – heavy clay, for example, should be dried a little before it is mixed to avoid pots full of lumpy clay. Ideally you would use a lighter, more free-draining soil if you can get your hands on it. Make sure your garden compost is well-rotted if you use it, as it is too rich for most emerging seeds.

MAKING YOUR OWN POTTING COMPOST

Once they have grown to a sufficient size you'll have prick out your seedlings into a more nutrient-rich compost, as all the seed's energy will now be used up and the plants will begin to

get a little hungrier. Prick out once the plant has reached its first two true leaves.

One way of providing more nutrients at this stage is to add a liquid feed such as nettle and/or comfrey or seaweed (see Chapter 18). Alternatively, for future years you can use leaf mould that has been enriched by adding layers of comfrey and nettles at regular intervals as you stack the leaves (a bit like a lasagne).

Many commercial types of compost used for potting on will contain a mix of sand, peat and loam along with fertilisers such as hoof and horn or superphosphate. These fertilisers are really unnecessary if the potting medium is already fertile.

Molehills can be a welcome find for once, if you're making a potting mix.

There is no secret formula for the perfect potting mix, but the main requirements are:

- something that will retain moisture, e.g. leaf mould or coir
- something containing nutrients, e.g. well-rotted (not fresh and active) garden compost, worm casts or small amounts of concentrated chicken manure / chicken manure pellets (not too much!).

Chicken manure and worm compost can make for quite rich mixes for 'hungry' plants such as squashes or brassicas. If plants still seem to lag behind then a liquid feed can be added. Less hungry, quick-growing plants such as salad leaves can be grown in far less rich mixes.

You can have too much of a good thing: I carried out a test planting of corn salad (lamb's lettuce) in various mixes – it did really badly in pure horse manure and even worse in a pot with three teaspoons of concentrated chicken manure. However, there didn't seem to be much difference in results between using mixes of leaf mould and sand and using mixes with commercial potting compost,

Weeds in compost

Leaf mould, compost and soil can all contain weed seeds. You can 'pasteurise' the soil yourself by placing it in the microwave. This should eliminate all weed seeds and soil-borne pests. Garden organic (formally HDRA) suggests putting 900g (32oz) of soil in a microwave for around 2 1/2 minutes – it should first be sieved and *all* stones removed as these can explode, damaging your microwave – mineral soils may also do the same. Allow the soil to cool before you use it.

Alternatively, bake the soil in a clay (outdoor oven, not a clay kiln) or domestic oven (note that for health and safety standards a soil oven should not be used for food and vice versa). 'Cook' for around half an hour on a moderately high temperature.

including peat-based compost. Mixes with just one teaspoon of concentrated chicken manure per pot also fared quite well.

Sieving compost

Leaf mould and compost should be sieved to remove large particles before use in seed or potting compost mixes. Garden sieves come in different grades, allowing different-sized particles through.

In the absence of a garden sieve you can use any of the following.

- A length of chicken wire over a wheelbarrow or held by two people and loaded by a third.
- A small-holed shopping basket.
- The grate of a throwaway barbecue.
- A plastic mushroom crate.

Sieve your leaf mould and compost to get rid of clumps and other debris.

Chapter 12

RAISING NEW PLANTS

Just like a newborn child, a seedling will need more attention than at any other time of its life. Pot-grown seedlings grown under cover will need to be watered and kept warm and outdoor crops, such as carrots, will in addition need weeding to give them a good chance at life.

Growing indoors will provide warmth and protection from predators, but direct-sown plants will always be stronger and require less maintenance.

SOWING DIRECT

Sowing direct into the soil can be very cost effective as there's no need for pots, potting compost or propagators. It can also produce much stronger plants, as they don't suffer from any transplant shock, sometimes known as 'transplant check'. Although direct-sown plants may have to be sown later when the soil warms up, the lack of transplant check sometimes means they can catch up with pot-sown plants.

Direct-sown crops are more prone to damage from extremes of weather and predators such as birds and slugs. I've found to my cost that birds of the crow family (magpies, jays and crows) are intelligent enough to watch you planting bean and pea seeds and recognise them as food. I've had zero germination on

The sight of newly emerged seedlings is always a joy.

unprotected bean seed as magpies have watched my every move before swooping down and swiping the lot. I now shield the seeds with plastic half bottles or use a net for the first couple of weeks until the dicot or seed leaf appears.

Sowing peas and beans

✽ Peas and beans can both be sown when the weather is still quite cool, but they should never be sown in waterlogged or compacted soil.

Pros of direct sowing	Cons of direct sowing
✓ Makes for a more robust plant	✗ You have to wait for the soil to warm up
✓ Roots can head straight down rather than round and round	✗ More prone to pest damage (especially slugs)
✓ No need to harden off your seedlings	✗ Unfamiliar plants can be confused with weeds
✓ Little risk of pets, children or even yourself knocking the plants over	✗ Can be slow-germinating leading to confusion and double-sown beds
✓ Less prone to drying out	✗ Seeds can rot in wet soil
✓ Less maintenance	✗ Not suitable for tender crops such as tomatoes in cold climates
	✗ Difficult to manage if plot is away from home

When to sow direct

The table overleaf gives general guidelines for sowing seeds direct into the soil outdoors. These lists are by no means definitive and are mainly for the UK climate and day length.

SOWING INTO POTS, SEED TRAYS AND MODULES

Having weighed up the pros and cons, you may choose to avoid direct sowing altogether or choose to spread your bets and mix it with crops started in pots and seed trays. There are many advantages to sowing in pots, including starting off tender crops under cover and providing a weed-free environment.

Acquiring pots and other growing containers

If you are determined to buy containers to start off your seedlings it is worth investing in sturdy ones. In the case of modules (divided trays), for example, the cheaper flimsy ones are a false economy, tending to last only a season. You can reuse the more flimsy ones for a second year but they can crack, taking a few casualties with them. When buying modules (or large pots), check the depth of your windowsill or potting bench and make sure they don't have any overhang. A couple of inches sticking out is just enough to make

them an easy target for getting knocked over or generally bashed around. You can't always blame spillages on the dog!

However, the canny vegetable grower seldom has to buy modules, pots or seed trays. In any one year I can guarantee there are more

Direct-sown plants, such as these broad beans, can be stronger than those started in pots.

When and if to sow direct			
Seeds to sow direct in cold weather (but not if there's a ground frost)	Seeds to sow direct under cloches (before the end of the frost)	Seeds to sow direct after the risk of frosts	Seeds not suitable for direct sowing in cool climates
Broad beans Lettuce Parsnips Peas Sweet cicely (may even be beneficial to cold stratify in the freezer first!)	Broad beans (can also sow in autumn or spring) Carrots Radishes	All beans Beetroot Brassicas Leeks Onion sets (can also sow in autumn for spring) Radishes Squash Sweetcorn	Aubergines Chillis Peppers Tomatoes

pots hidden in sheds, recycling centres, skips and around the back of gardening businesses/charities than can ever be used that season. The flowerpot mountain we had at Eastside Roots, a Bristol-based garden charity I worked for, grew so tall one year we had to employ Sherpas to retrieve pots from its peak. I would advise anyone coming to take them to brush off the snow before giving them a quick clean with soapy water to avoid the build-up of plant diseases. They went away with a good pot and we got to remove some of the plastic foothills of the plant-pot Himalaya.

If there is a choice, always look for the best pots but also be gracious with what you are

Flowerpot mountain ranges are found all over the world.

given. A small donation will also help if taking from a garden charity.

Making your own pots

Anything that can hold compost yet allows excess water to drain can act as a plant pot.

- Old yoghurt pots with a hole cut in the bottom are ideal for starting off tomatoes.
- Plastic takeaway cartons with holes punched in them are great for starting herbs, onions and salad leaves.
- Or use old cottage-cheese tubs, mushroom trays, margarine tubs . . .

. . . I think you get the idea.

To avoid cracking plastic pots when puncturing them, heat a darning needle or skewer under a candle and melt them into the plastic. Or, if you've just gasped at the thought of melting plastic, just work very carefully with a sharp object, such as a penknife, moving in a slow circular motion, digging the holes from the inside to the outside of the pot. The holes can be enlarged by a Phillips screwdriver once the initial cut has been made. Try to cut through the thinnest layers and avoid any areas of double thickness. Around five or six drainage holes around the size of a pencil should do, or if you are using a darning needle cut lots of little ones.

Toilet rolls

Most seedlings don't like having their roots disturbed when they are transplanted. You can buy organic pots, which rot away when planting into a bigger container or into the ground, or you can improvise your own by planting into old toilet rolls placed on a seed tray (good for peas and leeks).

Paper pots

You can also make paper pots out of newspaper (see overleaf). These work well for a wide range of plants grown from seed and are completely biodegradable. On the downside, if they get too wet they can start to 'biodegrade' long before you get a chance to plant out your seedlings. The trick is to water little and often rather than apply floods of water irregularly.

PROPAGATION WITH ADDED HEAT

Late in the spring you can quite often find tomato and chilli plants for sale which seem to be weeks ahead of anything you may have growing at home. In some years you may even begrudgingly buy a couple in the hope of getting some early tomatoes. I've done exactly that in an attempt to get a head start, yet somehow the tomatoes never taste quite as sweet as the ones I grow myself from seed.

There really are a million uses for old toilet-roll tubes!

HOW TO MAKE A PAPER POT

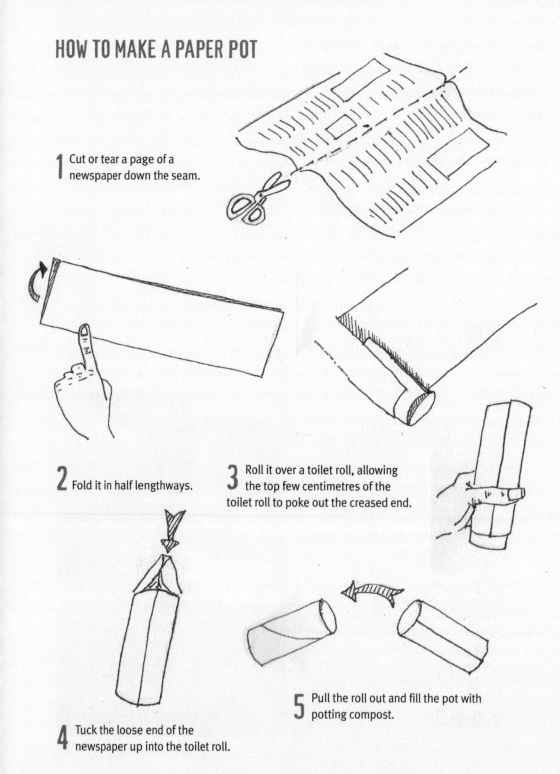

1 Cut or tear a page of a newspaper down the seam.

2 Fold it in half lengthways.

3 Roll it over a toilet roll, allowing the top few centimetres of the toilet roll to poke out the creased end.

4 Tuck the loose end of the newspaper up into the toilet roll.

5 Pull the roll out and fill the pot with potting compost.

The secret to this botanic miracle is heated propagation early in the season, sometimes as early as February or even January. Professionally this is done by sowing either in a heated greenhouse or, more commonly, on a heated propagation bench.

Propagation benches

A heated propagation bench usually has some form of capillary matting with a heated unit placed underneath. The whole thing can be covered or left open in a 'cold head and warm feet' method, which encourages plants to send out strong roots as they push down towards the heat.

A capillary mat is essentially just an absorbent piece of material laid out across a propagating bench. The downside to them is that they can attract flies and develop mould, but on the whole they are very effective in keeping pots hydrated. You can have some success with an old wool blanket, a cotton towel or even a nappy placed underneath emerging seedlings. If using a towel or blanket, to prevent mould growth this can be boil-washed, bleached or microwaved at the end of the season – or, if no longer required, and made from natural material, torn up and composted.

Heated matting

It is possible to improvise the heated mat using an electric blanket or a heated home-brewing mat, but these do rely on electricity to run and can be quite power hungry. Before you decide to raise all your seedlings this way, try to measure the power consumption of your chosen device using either a plug-in power meter or by noting down how much more your electricity meter records whilst it is on. You may decide they are too costly to run and instead choose another method.

Radiators as propagators

Many homes now have central heating with wall-fitted radiators on during the winter; these artificially heat your home to the temperature of a warm summer's morning. The radiator can act as under-heating for growing plants. They can either rest straight on top of a warm but not too hot radiator in pots, or you could make a shelf for the pots to rest on.

Propagating without added heat

Added heat is only ever needed to get things going that little bit earlier – usually for tomatoes, peppers and related plants, which need a long growing season and warm conditions. A little later in the season, a sunny windowsill can be a perfect spot for starting off other seedlings such as squashes and courgettes, maize and brassicas – a warm sunny spot is always going to be best, and even better is to have a source of light from above, such as a skylight, as the seedlings won't become etiolated (tall and leggy). Some important things to consider:

Radiator propagation in practice

Bill Herring, Head of Horticulture at Duchy College, Cornwall, uses the heat from a radiator to start off large seeds such as beans or those of the cucumber family. He writes:

"I start off seeds such as cucumbers, marrows and courgettes in a small propagator such as a margarine tub with damp kitchen tissue in the base. Place the naked seed on the tissue and then seal with cling film and leave on the radiator. Within three or four days a white root will appear. With care this is then placed into a 7.5cm (3") pot of potting compost, about 1cm (1/2") deep."

- South- or west-facing windows will work best.
- Turn the plants regularly to avoid the plant growing too much in one direction.
- Raise the plant up to the level of the window to minimise its stretching towards the light and becoming etiolated.
- Protect your windowsill from damp with old tiles or newspaper (especially in rented houses!).

PLANTING OUT

Once your seedlings have reached a sufficient size you will need to plant them out, either direct into the soil or into a container (see Chapter 14). There is little expense needed for this stage – you may be convinced you need to buy a dibber but this can be improvised with a large stick.

Hardening off

Imagine if you suddenly went from sleeping in a warm cosy house to a cold ditch in the middle of a cold spring. You wouldn't like it much and no doubt you would suffer as a result. Plants are no different; they have to get used to a change in temperature – and putting them straight outside after being in a warm house or propagator will shock them. To get around this, put your seedlings out in the day and bring them in at night for around two weeks before putting them into their final positions. Alternatively, you could put them in a cold frame as a 'halfway house'.

Cunning tricks in an unheated greenhouse

There are various methods you can use to protect pots from cold in a greenhouse.
- Tie a clear plastic bag over each pot
- Cover them with a cloche
- Hang shower curtains over your bench, pulling them to at night to retain the heat in a smaller area
- Tape bubble wrap to the inside of windows

CROPS FOR TENANTS, STARTING IN SPRING

No matter how short a time you may be in a property for, it is well worth starting a few crops off in the spring. Even a short let from this time will give you ample opportunity to get things in the ground and have at least one harvest before you move out. The chart below should give you some ideas.

Average growing times for common crops		
Crops for 1-2 months	**Crops for 3-4 months**	**Crops for 5-6 months**
Lettuces	Beetroot	Cabbages
Quick-growing herbs	Broad beans	Carrots
Radishes	French beans	Maincrop potatoes
Spinach	New potatoes	Onion
Turnips	Spring onion	Pumpkin
	Summer squash (incl. courgettes)	Runner beans (can be less)
		Sweetcorn

LAYERING

If you can bend a branch or vine to the ground you will be able to propagate it by layering. Nature often propagates this way by itself: next time you are near a bramble bush just take a look at any runner that has touched the ground – it may well be anchored, having sent down its own root system. Cut away that runner and you have a new plant.

Ground layering is best done in the spring, as the plant will be ready to put on its new growth for the coming year. Simply take a year-old vine or branch (one that is still flexible) and peg it down to the ground. Now cover that pegged branch with soil and wait for a year before cutting away from the parent plant and planting up somewhere else.

With longer vines such as kiwis you can snake-layer them. Peg down two or three sections of the vine and cover them each with soil. Each section should root, and at each point it does you will have a new plant.

In both cases the branches will need to be left for a year (or at least until winter), so this should be done somewhere in the garden where they won't get disturbed.

Layering is a simple way to propagate new plants.

Although for many plants spring is the ideal time to propagate by layering, some may lack the flexible growth needed for the stems to be moved down to the soil. If this is the case, wait until summer or early autumn to layer your plants, especially ones that die back and become very woody. If a branch looks or sounds as though it is going to snap, leave it alone.

Examples of plants for ground layering

- Kiwi fruit
- Blackberries
- Dwarf fruit trees
- Grapes

Cheap fruit trees

Sometimes it is easier to let someone else raise new plants for you, especially when it comes to larger plants such as trees and bushes. Be on the lookout for fruit trees, fruit bushes and fruit canes on sale during early spring, as nurseries often sell them off cheap in a bid to clear winter stock. Making regular trips can pay off, as they will slash prices before they discard old stock. Ask for bare-rooted trees or bushes, as they are always cheaper than the potted equivalent, and be prepared to haggle.

It is possible to bin dive / skip raid for fruit trees, but be aware that with all bin diving or raiding from commercial properties, you do run the risk of prosecution. As with all skipped goods, the contents of the bin are technically the property of the nursery or garden centre, even if they have been thrown away! A quick getaway may be hampered by a 12ft fruit tree, and if caught don't say I encouraged you!

If bargain-hunting or bin-diving your trees you should be careful to bring home disease-free stock. Look out for canker in trees or big bud in fruit bushes; if you see it, cut away infected branches or even bring a trunk right down to below a canker, leaving it to regrow new branches. Try to negotiate the price right down for infected stock, but beware – a half-price fruit bush is not a bargain if it infects all your existing fruit bushes.

A cheap fruit tree can be a real bargain.

Chapter 13

PLANT LABELS

Wherever you sow your seeds it is important to label them, as things can easily get confused or forgotten – it can be all too easy to sow two separate crops in a bed earmarked for one! Gardening tricks such as a quick-germinating row of radishes to mark a row of parsnips will help, but a simple plant label will help even more.

Labels can be used to record all kinds of important information, such as the variety and the date of sowing. These are important considerations, as you may find that certain varieties will do much better than others or sowing times greatly alter plants' performance.

A label will mean you are able to trace a sowing date back – to find, for example, if a struggling row of veggies were tender young shoots around the time of an unseasonably late frost. Armed with this kind of information you can eliminate other possible problems and next time sow once the risk of frost has gone or with frost protection.

LOLLY STICKS

Wooden lolly sticks make ideal plant labels as they are biodegradable, around the right size and, by and large, free. I learned a very valuable trick for finding lolly sticks from a couple in Bristol: they would find an ice-cream

Plant labels can be made from all kinds of things – like this section of yoghurt pot.

van and then in turn follow each path leading away from it. After they'd found at least two or three sticks in a similar place they would scour that particular area for more. It seems that there is an optimum number of paces which a person is likely to take whilst eating an iced lolly. Once the lolly eater has gone sufficiently far from the ice-cream van they tend to drop the stick.

Making it stick

✽ You will need to use a permanent marker pen to write the plant names on the sticks: CD writing pens work quite well. To be doubly sure the pen doesn't run you can always wrap the label in a plastic bag.

PLASTIC POTS / CARTONS

Plastic pots, especially large yoghurt pots, make ideal plant labels. Any plain white plastic carton is suitable and you can reuse them following a growing season by scrubbing the labels with a soapy cloth.

GET CREATIVE

At their wedding, my friends Leila and Matt (they wanted a mention) put stones with the names of all their guests around the reception room tables so we all knew where we were sitting and we had something to take home. A year later and our names are still as clear on the stones as they were that day. Using weatherproof paint you could easily use the same method to mark out rows of vegetables: I have seen similar things used for house numbers and they seem to last for some time.

Anything that can be painted on can be used, including:
- pieces of driftwood, for a more natural look
- bricks, for the industrial minimalists
- Tibetan prayer flags adorned with pictures of the vegetables hanging over the plot, for the more spiritually inclined
- small flags made from rags, for the sporty.

For fabric, use acrylic paint mixed with PVA glue to prevent the paint from running in wet weather.

HOW TO MAKE PLASTIC-POT PLANT LABELS

1 Avoid using transparent plastic pots as it is hard to see what is written on them on a sunny day (or a gloomy one for that matter); instead use plain white pots if you can get them.

2 Cut the pot lengthways with sharp scissors into strips 2cm (1") in width and around 10-12cm (4-5") in length.

3 As with the lolly sticks, write on them with a permanent marker pen.

Plant labels for the spiritually inclined.

Chapter 14

GROWING IN CONTAINERS

Container growing has become more popular in recent years and seed companies have cottoned on to this by selling 'patio' varieties of our favourite vegetables. Some of these, such as the patio salads, can be a bit of a false economy, as most plants only grow to the size they are allowed to. I've found that conventional varieties of salads actually do better in containers than specific container seed, usually for half the price.

There are exceptions to this rule, and growing compact dwarf beans as opposed to climbing French beans makes perfect sense if space is limited. Consider each seed on its own merits and go for specialist 'container' varieties only if they really do look like they are worth the money.

POTATOES

Large 'tonne' or 'dumpy' bags (builder's bags) make perfect planters for potatoes and are near-identical to bags on sale doing exactly the same job! Alternatively, a large plant pot will work just as well. Plant three to four seed potatoes in each dumpy bag or pot and cover with soil. As the plant grows, cover the foliage with soil leaving some of the leaves to poke out from the surface. Keep repeating this step as the potatoes grow until the bag is full. To harvest, roll the bag down.

A hanging basket doesn't have to be just for flowers.

WHAT TYPE OF CONTAINER?

The choice of container is really limited only by what you can find. They need to be big enough to accommodate the plant and its roots, so a 5-litre (1-gallon) tub is never going to be big enough for a courgette plant but a chilli plant will be perfectly at home in one.

Tired advice

For some time tyres have been recommended by some to grow potatoes in, but this is no longer advised as there are issues with toxic compounds leaching from the tyres into your potatoes.

Suitable containers and where to get them

Type of container	Where to get it from	Examples of what to use it for and extra instructions
Baby baths	Freecycle, parents of no-longer-small children.	Courgettes, dwarf beans. Drill holes in base.
Builders'/dumpy/tonne bags (woven sacks)	Builders, landscape gardeners.	Potatoes.
Old bathtubs	Skips, recycling centres.	Almost anything – including tomatoes, cabbages and grapes. You will need to add a layer of free-draining material such as straw to the base. *NB Be prepared to take it with you when you move if you have an allotment or live in a rented house, as the next owner might not want it there!*
Olive oil tins, 3 litre (0.6 gallon) or 5 litre (1 gallon).	Home, small restaurants and cafes.	Chillies, tomatoes, peppers. Wash thoroughly before use.
Plastic catering pot (mango chutney, mayonnaise, ice cream, etc.)	Restaurants, residential institutions (e.g. old people's homes, catering colleges).	Tomatoes, peppers, aubergines.
Sack (hessian or woven plastic)	Pet shops (old feed bags), hardware shops, restaurants and shops (rice sacks), greengrocers (potato sacks).	Lettuces, cabbages, strawberries (in holes cut in sides – see opposite).
Shoes	Home.	Basil, lettuces (i.e. small plants). Line with plastic first and drill holes in sole for drainage.
Trugs	Gardeners, recycling centres.	Blueberries, currant bushes, dwarf beans. Drill holes in base.

Plants in a sack

The rooftops of urban Kenya show signs of the innovation of the gardenless occupants. In order to have a supply of fresh vegetables, many of the women of Nairobi have taken to growing much of their daily vegetables in hessian sacks. The sacks are filled with earth and seedlings are slotted in through holes cut into the sack. If you wish to try this method on your patio or on a flat rooftop, a mix of leaf mould, compost and topsoil is an ideal growing medium, with additional nutrition supplied from liquid feeds.

Cabbages naturally grow on clifftops and cliff faces and are perfectly adapted to growing this way; other suitable plants could include salad greens, strawberries and tomatoes.

Make the most of limited space by growing in a sack.

Soils for pots and containers

Tony Kendle, Foundation Director, Eden Project

Plants in pots have to get all of their water and nutrient needs from soil that is tens or even hundreds of times smaller in volume than their roots would reach if planted out. The containers have to be watered on such a regular basis that it puts the structure of the soil under great pressure and this structure can start to break down. A normal soil maintains a healthy structure thanks to natural activity such as worms burrowing, which isn't as effective in containers. All of this means that for best results you have to be careful what soils to use – any old stuff won't do.

To get the best yields you need container soils with the right pH, the right fertility and the right structure. But pH and nutrition can be fixed if you need to, while structure is something you need to get right at the beginning.

Clay-rich soils can be very fertile in the garden but they rely on worm channels and the formation of clods and airways to stay healthy. In containers this structure collapses and they can become airless and toxic.

Sandy soils have a totally different structure; they are more uniform and not dependent on clods and pores. These work best in containers.

You can make heavy soils more sandy but you need lots of sand to do it – maybe twice the volume of the clay. If you scrounge sand to do this you have to rinse it thoroughly before using it, in case it's coated in lime or salt or something else the roots won't like.

Organic matter is great to add to pots because it helps hold water and nutrients. But not all compost is the same. Compost made from soft material such as leaves will break down quickly and before you know it the pot will be half empty – this is a useful material for containers for annuals or short-lived crops. For perennials you need a proportion of tougher material such as composted bark and twigs. This can last for years but won't release many nutrients, so will need more feeding.

Containers don't need drainage layers such as broken pots at the bottom. You will never find these in the millions of plants grown in pots in commercial nurseries. But it is crucial that they drain well or the root zone will become stagnant and the roots will die. Roughly speaking, soils hold water in micropores and air in the larger pores that drain freely. Think of a bathroom sponge – when you lift it out of the water the big holes drain quickly, but the whole thing remains damp. But do the sponge test for real and look more carefully. You will see a saturated layer at the bottom that doesn't drain. This is where water is held even in large pores, by capillary action.

What you will find is that, whatever way up you hold the sponge, this layer is the same depth. This is how it works in containers too. The soils will have a layer of a few centimetres at the bottom that doesn't drain well and will risk being stagnant. This means that the shape of pots really matters – wide shallow pots hold more water and drain less well than tall narrow pots of the same volume. Matching the right pots, the right soils and the right plants gets the best results, but it matters most for plants that will be in the pot for a long time and where good rooting is needed.

Chapter 15

GATHERING 'WILD' EXTRAS

Often in a plot you'll find an uncultivated but nonetheless edible section: extra food plants you didn't put in yourself, which will go into the cooking pot along with cultivated vegetables. These really are food for free, as, be they weeds or hedgerow plants, they will happily grow without any input from you – financially or physically.

The first green leaves of many trees, such as this hawthorn, are edible.

Spring is an excellent time for wild food as you will undoubtedly not have to go far to find it. Start by just looking up, and see what is growing on the fringes of your plot.

EDIBLE TREE LEAVES

The very first leaves of many common trees can be eaten in salads. They should be eaten when they are still light green and have not had time to build up their natural defences in the form of tannins. With the exception of lime, most should be eaten only in small quantities as they can be a little astringent.

Tapping a birch tree.

Edible tree leaves include:

Hawthorn Fresh new leaves can be used in salads, sandwiches or in cous-cous to add colour and texture. The blossoms can also be eaten.

Lime Young lime leaves can make a refreshing snack straight from the tree or they can be added to sandwiches. They mellow out the flavours of more fiery spring salad leaves such as wintercress, rocket and mustards. Martin Crawford, the forest gardener, has a coppiced lime tree on his plot – bringing the canopy down makes the leaves much more accessible.

Beech There seems to be a short window of opportunity for beech leaves (only two or three weeks) before the tannins build up. There can be a second flush of beech leaves in the summer, but with any luck you'll have plenty of salad leaves growing by this point.

Birch Many animals, including *Homo sapiens*, will nibble on the young leaves of the birch tree. They're good in a mixed salad with dressing. Trees can also be tapped for their sap just before they come into leaf. Drill a hole just under the bark layer, until it starts to seep a clear liquid. Insert a tube into the hole (a 13cm [5"] piece of plastic tubing from a child's Wendy house works well). Hammer in the tube and collect over night. The sap can be drunk straight away, used to make birch sap wine or boiled and reduced (for ages!) to make birch syrup. Collecting sap will help reduce the growth of trees that are causing too much shade. Be sure to plug the drilled hole back up with a cork or stick of the same size as otherwise the tree could 'bleed' to death.

OTHER SPRINGTIME EDIBLES

Goosegrass / cleavers / sticky Willy When they are young, before they get a chance to develop the Velcro-like hairs, these leaves can be used as a salad leaf or added to stir-fries.

Jack-by-the-hedge is a real treat in the spring.

Hop shoots The fresh shoots of hops make a great addition to noodle soups or stir-fries, or can be wilted and put in a salad (drizzle with nut oil dressing). They need to be cooked straight away as they won't keep.

Jack-by-the-hedge / garlic mustard Garlic/mustard-flavoured leaves – a good salad leaf; can be cooked like cabbage/spinach.

Wild garlic / ransoms One of the choicest wild plants. Bulbs can be planted underneath established trees for an extra spring harvest. Use the leaves as garlic flavouring; good in pesto.

COMPANION SQUATTERS

Edible plants can and do find their way in to your vegetable beds. On the whole it is better to hoe before they become too much of a problem, picking out the edibles as you do so. I've found one or two edible squatters can be tolerated but if there is any sign that they are harbouring pests or robbing your veggies of valuable nutrients they should be composted straight away.

Chickweed This has a characteristic star-shaped flower, hence the Latin name 'stellaria'. Chickweed favours pots and planters

Young wild garlic buds can be pickled and later used in salads.

just as much as open ground. It is a very nutritious addition to salads and can act as a useful ground-cover plant.

Hairy bittercress A very, very common weed. I used to add this to my sandwiches whenever I did any gardening work. It tastes a little like watercress. Any long-term gardener will know this will self-seed like mad and you should never be tempted to cultivate it.

PART 3
SUMMER

Summer is that time of year when we realise just how helpless we've been in breeding our modern vegetable plants. Leave them just for a couple of days and they look up at us and say, "Help, I need water, it's too dry and I can't get it myself," or "I've fallen over, can you tie me up again?" or even "Help, help, the weeds are pushing in and stealing my lunch money!" At this point you have to ask yourself the question, who is really in control?

As a species we've spent millennia carefully selecting plants for very specific characteristics such as the taste of the fruit, high yields or longer immaturity so we can harvest the leaves before the plant goes to seed and turns bitter. In selecting out these traits we have done so at the expense of others. Taste a wild cabbage: it is so bitter it is almost inedible. But how many wild cabbages do you see torn to shreds by caterpillars like our unprotected domestic varieties?

It is a mistake to think the summer is a time when everything is doing well and we can sit back and enjoy the bounty. We do this at our own risk, as it's a time to feed, weed, tie in and generally take care of our helpless and inbred food plants.

JOBS FOR SUMMER

- Support crops
- Deal with weeds
- Feed your plants
- Deal with pests and diseases
- Propagate plants
- Manage the 'summer bolt'
- Gather 'wild' extras

Making the most of a summer exodus

When universities reach the end of the final term, most students leave town – and landlords tend to hire skips to chuck out everything they leave behind. This is a great time for the thrifty gardener. From the end of May to the beginning of September in the student areas of towns and cities you can find anything from old carpets to use as weed-suppressant material (don't take plastic-backed carpet though), net curtains for plant protection, plant pots, tools and all manner of items with horticultural uses.

Chapter 16

GROWING UPWARDS

Space can be limited in most suburban and urban environments, with small or non-existent growing beds. In these situations the vertical plane can be utilised – growing crops upward instead of across a bed should increase yields and frees up a lot of space to grow other things. Squashes, tomatoes, cucumbers and beans will grow happily up canes and strings or across fences.

CUCUMBERS AND SQUASHES ALONG FENCES

Most plants in the cucumber/squash family will either trail or climb. Wire fencing can be covered with the lush green foliage of these plants, saving room in the beds for other plants. Support may be needed for larger fruits such as melons or pumpkins. It may not be possible to grow very large fruits without taking the fence down with it!

TOMATOES ON STRINGS

Time and time again tomatoes are strung to a single bamboo cane, which often breaks before the end of the season. Commercially, tomato plants are tied to horizontal wires or beams running the length of the greenhouse. Although I've heard stories of old wooden greenhouses collapsing under the weight, most greenhouses only house up to six plants and these should be able to take the strain.

If you're lacking in horizontal beams you can erect a similar structure to those you would use for climbing French beans. It should resemble a ridge tent (without the tarpaulin) and can be used on an outside bed or inside a greenhouse/polytunnel.

To tie the plants to the horizontal, start at the stem near to the soil. Tie a loop around the stem, with a gap to allow the stem to grow – rather like a lasso. Then circle the string

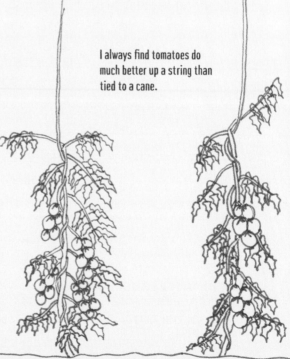

I always find tomatoes do much better up a string than tied to a cane.

clockwise up around the plant like a spiral staircase and tie into place with two slip knots so you can adjust the tension on the string.

Once the plants reach the beam the string can be moved left or right (as long as they're all in the same direction) to allow for more top growth. This will increase the yield of fruit as the plant can stay productive for longer.

BALCONY BEANS

French and runner beans will snake their way around just about any vertical structure. Successive sowings can be made in pots in the early summer, allowing them to grow up the metal supports of a balcony. A liquid feed should be added at flowering time about once every other week and the pots should be kept watered. If a metal pole is too smooth a bean may struggle to take hold, so twisting a piece of string along the length of the pole will give the plant something to grip.

BEAN SUPPORTS

If you don't happen to have a balcony you will need to build some sort of structure for your beans to climb up. The conventional approach is to buy bamboo canes, but this isn't the only option. Bamboo can, in fact, be grown in colder climates like the UK but unfortunately it seldom is – instead we usually rely on imported canes from China. Bamboo falls roughly into two groups, clumping and running. If you are considering growing bamboo, be aware that both types should have some kind of root barrier to stop them spreading. The clumping form is the easiest to manage for the novice grower.

All canes should be left to dry out for at least a year – I've found that green canes tend to bend and snap. The rafters of a garage or a shed are an ideal place to dry the canes as

Beanpoles waiting for the summer's growth.
Photo: Lou Brown

this will allow airflow around the poles in a low-moisture environment. Bamboo can also be a bonus food crop – the shoots should be peeled and boiled before using in stir-fries or noodle soups or as a vegetable on its own.

Hazel poles are a much more environmentally friendly alternative to bamboo, as coppiced hazel woods are wildlife-rich habitats. Hazel can be managed as coppice by cutting down to the base and harvesting the poles every few years. They take around seven years to grow and will last much longer than bamboo. See page 41 for more details.

Some allotment sites choose to grow a patch of communal hazel coppice on fallow plots for the benefit of all.

Metal pipes

Runner beans can pull down bamboo wigwam structures so benefit from something sturdier to grow up. A very traditional allotment keeper I once knew in Oxford would

A runner bean will climb up anything.

grow her runner beans year after year in the same spot over a large U-shaped construction she'd made from sturdy metal pipes. These were dug a few feet into the ground to avoid being blown over by strong winds.

There is no need to grow only beans up the pipes; the structure can be incorporated into a crop-rotation scheme. It could be used to support netting for cabbages or soft fruit such as strawberries, or to support tomatoes growing up strings or other climbing plants.

PEA SUPPORTS

Unlike beans, which rap around upright poles, peas attach their tendrils to horizontal

supports as if they were little hands climbing a ladder, holding the plant in place. Supports therefore need to have not only the height (anywhere between 60-120cm [2-4ft], depending on the variety) but also a number of horizontals. Stretch netting or chicken wire between poles or use bamboo canes with string tied between them. However, a far cheaper and more environmentally friendly option is to dig pea sticks in the ground. These are twiggy branches which can be left as they are or woven into each other to form a rustic-looking pea 'fence' for the plants to grow up.

PLANT TIES

It's preferable to have the man-made string over plastic, and garden string is relatively cheap. However, plant ties can be improvised from many common plants. Martin Crawford, the eminent forest gardener, grows New Zealand flax to use as plant ties. If you have tried to compost this plant you will know the leaves are strong and durable. Martin tears strips off the leaves around 1cm ($1/2$") in width, running the length of the leaf. These are strong enough to last a season and will break down naturally afterwards. The leaves of the cabbage/Torbay palm can be used in the same way and there are no doubt other plants with similarly tough leaves that are also good for the job.

For an extremely temporary measure I've used grass as string – it lasted about a week, long enough for me to find an alternative. I achieved this by rubbing the grass between my hands and roughly plaiting it.

"When I were a lad most garden string was made from natural materials, such as 'emp or 'essian. Nowadays it's all your fancy man-made fibres which, strong as they may be, they won't be feeding any worms in a 'urry." Anon.

Chapter 17

....

DEALING WITH WEEDS

Leave a plot for a week or two during August and you could have an uphill struggle dealing with weeds for the rest of the season. Despite many common weeds being edible, I personally prefer a carrot cake made with home-grown carrots to a chickweed salad. Keeping weeds at bay means you won't have to pay for all your failures at the local fruit and vegetable shop.

WEEDKILLER

Never be tempted to reach for the weedkiller at this point. The only evidence that it harmlessly breaks down on contact with a plant seems to come from the manufacturers. Whilst foraging I've mistakenly eaten plants that have been sprayed, causing quite serious gastric upset. I'm a relatively large mammal and if it affects me in this way I can only imagine what it would do to smaller animal life such as mice and voles.

If you use weedkiller on a path you are not an organic gardener, just as if you eat fish you are not a vegetarian and if you only smoke the odd cigarette you are still a smoker. We are all given to these self-delusions from time to time, it is part of being human, but using sprays is a habit most of us should be able to kick.

Rather than spray, the main ways to control weeds are to pull them, hoe them, exclude light from them, eat them or plant in such a way that they don't have a chance to grow in the first place.

NO-DIG AND WEEDS

There is a lot to be said for not disturbing weed seeds by digging year after year, instead letting them stay dormant deep in the soil. The no-dig system requires a plot to be rid of perennial weeds prior to cultivation. One way to do this is to double-dig or thoroughly dig a plot but some choose to forgo this approach and instead use mulches such as cardboard, left for a season, to deprive the weeds of light (see Chapter 5, page 80).

Weigh down cardboard mulch with stones.

A generous layer of compost can be added in the first and subsequent years to plant into and improve the soil. Weeds should be kept to a minimum with this method and what does come up can be simply hoed off.

MULCHES

I go into more detail about mulches in Chapter 6 (pages 96-8), but, in summary, a thick layer of compost or leaf mould will improve the look of a garden, improve the soil and help suppress weeds.

HOT WATER

The water left over from boiling the kettle or boiling an egg can be poured over troublesome weeds. This will damage the cell structure and after a few applications they will die.

GROUND COVER

Fast-growing and large-leaved plants can act as a ground cover, leaving little room for competitive weeds. I grow corn underpinned with squash most years, as squash plants tend to trail amongst the corn, shading out any would-be competitors.

Beans can also be planted to grow up the corn and have the advantage that they fix nitrogen. This can be difficult to get right, but I have found 'Cherokee trail of tears' to be one of the best varieties of French bean to grow up the corn stalks.

Thick sowings of salad leaves can be made around deeper-rooted plants such as cabbages, kale and cauliflowers to provide a ground cover in the same way. Dwarf or bush beans can also be planted in the same bed.

This style of planting is sometimes called polycropping or polyculture, as many different plants can be grown together in one place. The yields of each plant may be lower than if it were grown on its own, but overall you should get a lot more than you would from planting each crop separately.

Corn, squash and beans (and a stray amaranth).

Chapter 18

FEEDING PLANTS

If you fed a dog or a cat on nothing but cardboard and water you'd pretty soon be accused of neglect. Yet, without realising it, people treat their plants this way all the time.

MAKING LIQUID FEEDS

Ideally, all a plant's nutrients would come from the soil it grows in. However, the ideal situation is rare to find in horticulture. Plants grown in pots, greenhouses, polytunnels, on land that is newly cultivated or on certain soils may need a helping hand.

Comfrey — a miracle plant.

A liquid feed gives plants a dose of nutrients in a form they can easily absorb and it can be a way of controlling how much nutrition a plant receives. Liquid feeds can also give an extra boost around fruiting time.

Two of the best plants for liquid feeds are nettle and comfrey. Feeds can also be made with many other very common plants (see below) and from other high-nutrient organic material such as farmyard manure. See overleaf for how to make liquid feeds.

MINERAL ACCUMULATORS

Look at a well-maintained herbaceous border, mature woodland or forest garden and you'll see plants filling every level. Tall architectural plants and trees will occupy the top layer, followed by shrubs and plants in ever-decreasing size at lower levels. This structure is echoed below the surface of the soil, as plant roots, including those of common weeds, have evolved to inhabit different layers. Some roots, such as nettle, will stretch out just under the surface while others, such as comfrey, reach far down into the subsoil. In this way, plants take in different minerals present in the different layers of soil and hold them in their foliage.

Some plants – the 'mineral accumulators' – will take in and accumulate more of these

Making liquid feeds

Bag method Half- or quarter-fill a hessian or porous bag with manure or your chosen plant material, tie a rope around the top and drop it into a water container, with the rope hanging outside for easy retrieval. There may not be any need to dilute the feed if the bag is steeped in a large container full of water, but you will need to if water levels are low during dunking.

Holes in the bottom of a bucket will allow rotting comfrey liquid to drip through – with no smell!

Wet method Half-fill an average-sized bucket with comfrey and top up with water. This should be left for a week or two until it smells absolutely foul. Water down by a ratio of around 8:1. You can also add nettles (or use just nettles) for added nitrogen, to use on leafy plants, or other plant material with a high nutrient content.

Dry method Cut holes in the bottom of a plastic bucket and half-fill it with comfrey. Place the bucket into another bucket and weigh down the leaves with stones. A concentrated liquid feed will slowly drip from the top bucket into the bottom one, and should be watered down by around 8:1 or 10:1. Again, you can also add nettles or other high-nutrient plants.

minerals than others. They can be dug in as a green manure, used as a plant feed or added to the compost heap for extra nourishment. They should be used before they go to seed as their nutrients will be 'locked' up in the seeds to ensure the next generation.

The two most commonly used mineral accumulators are comfrey and nettle. A mix of the two will make a very well-balanced feed suitable for pouring on your tomatoes and courgettes to encourage fruit. Even added to a compost heap, many of these mineral accumulators can provide added minerals and trace elements to your compost, which in turn will be added to your soil to be taken up by your growing plants and eventually included in your and your family's diet.

Other common mineral accumulators include borage, carrot, cleavers, plantain, chicory, mint, lemon balm, yarrow and strawberry.

IDENTIFYING NUTRIENT DEFICIENCIES

The two charts opposite detail possible nutrient-deficiency symptoms, the role of each mineral and the plants you could apply as a liquid feed to deal with the deficiencies.

Adding plenty of compost and organic matter should deal with deficiencies in many minor nutrients such as copper and zinc. Towards the end of the season plants start to naturally look a little nutrient deficient – most notably, tomatoes will show signs of magnesium deficiency. Adding a liquid feed may help a little but usually it is an indication that the season is coming to an end and the plant has given you all the fruit it is capable of that year.

URINE AS FEED

Green leafy crops like a lot of nitrogen, and human urine contains ammonia, which breaks down into nitrogen. Once you get over the 'yuck' factor, using urine as a plant feed makes a lot of sense. Farmers spend huge amounts of money on nitrogen fertilisers and sewage companies spend huge amounts of money removing nitrogen from the water supply.

You can 'harvest' urine in a good old-fashioned piss pot or in a plastic bottle with a funnel in the top. Water it down by around 8:1 for leafy crops or around 20:1 for non-leafy crops, and use about once a fortnight. Nitrogen aids leaf growth, so this is a good feed for salad leaves and cabbages. Urine also makes a great compost activator, breaking down carbon-rich 'browns' such as cardboard, sticks and stems.

Major nutrients		
	Nitrogen (N)	Phosphorous (P)	Potassium (K) (sometimes called potash)
Needed for	Leaf growth / photosynthesis.	Roots, stems, germination.	Flowers and fruit, disease resistance.
Deficiency symptoms	Yellow leaves, stunted growth, premature leaf drop.	Stunted growth, purpling of plant, small crops lacking in flavour.	Scorching on edge of leaves.
Suggested weed/ herb feed	Chickweed, clovers, dandelion, nettle, vetches.	Comfrey, dock, sheep's sorrel, clovers, lemon balm, goosefoot family (incl. fat hen).	Chickweed, comfrey (good source), tansy, dock, borage.
Alternative feeds	Urine, chicken poo, worm casts, farmyard manure.	Chicken poo, rock dust, worm casts, farmyard manure.	Wood ash*, worm casts, farmyard manure.

* Limit to 1-2 applications a year and don't use on acid-loving crops.

Other important nutrients		
	Magnesium (Mg)	Calcium (Ca)	Sulphur (S)
Needed for	Photosynthesis, making chlorophyll.	Cell structure, growth, enzyme activity.	Growth, photosynthesis.
Deficiency symptoms	Interveinal chlorosis.	Blossom end rot, black hearts in celery.	Stunted growth, young leaves mottled yellow and green with yellowish veins.
Suggested weed/ herb feed	Carrot leaves, comfrey, dandelion.	Cleavers/goosegrass, comfrey, dock.	Nettle, plantain.
Other sources/ tips	Organic matter, including liquid animal-manure feed, seaweed.	Egg shells, wood ash*.	Air pollution – deficiency rare especially in cities. Add compost to balance soil.

* Limit to 1-2 applications a year and don't use on acid-loving crops.

Chapter 19

DEALING WITH PESTS AND DISEASES

Many creatures have adapted to find ways of feeding their young. We mammals produce milk, bees make honey, birds gather insects, and caterpillars like to go for the nice row of cabbage seedlings you've just planted out. Unless you wish to start farming caterpillars, or slugs, aphids, etc., then something will have to be done about them.

FINDING A BALANCE

Some forms of pest control, including organic ones, are expensive and short lived, needing investment year after year. One alternative is to try to attract certain beneficial insects to prey on pests by planting flowers such as marigolds and nasturtiums. Aiming to balance

Dreaded caterpillars!

a plot in this way will certainly help – consider it as much for wildlife as it is for crops.

I was once told by a salad grower that prevention is better than cure: he concentrates on 'wellness' rather than dealing with disease. This is all well and good, but it is a little like being told by someone that they never get toothache because they avoid sugar, whilst you are writhing in agony before a root canal operation. I imagine that most people are probably reading this section because there is something wrong with their crops, not because they want advice on what they should have done months before to prevent it.

That said, there are simple measures you can employ to avoid future problems and keep your plants well, such as providing:

- good drainage
- good air circulation
- a healthy soil (even in containers)
- a clean environment (e.g. cleaning away fallen tomatoes, removing pots that may harbour pests)
- the right location (does that plant need to be in full sun – is it more suited to a different climate?).

You can also avoid practices such as watering from above or watering in the midday sun, which can scorch plants' leaves, and make sure a plant is adequately fed and watered.

However, you may be doing all of these things right yet find that pests and diseases still get the better of your fruit and veggies. Something will need to be done to deal with the problem in hand and prevent it from getting any worse.

BIOLOGICAL CONTROLS

One of the mainstays of organic gardening, biological control, is basically an artificially introduced way of keeping down pests naturally. These controls usually take the form of a living organism that preys on another living organism, such as a nematode for slugs, a tiny wasp that lays its eggs in whitefly larvae, or just something with a big appetite, like a ladybird.

Gather your own biological controls

It's a little-known fact that ladybirds (or ladybugs) have one of the most active sex lives of any insect. They rival any touring rock musician, with sessions lasting up to 8 or 9 hours and up to 30 different partners in a year! What is perhaps more impressive is the knock-on effect of this high libido on the local pest population. If you consider that the females can lay up to 1,000 eggs in a season and the resulting offspring can eat around 5,000 aphids during their short lives, then that is potentially 5 million fewer aphids every year from one female!

Gathering up and introducing these hungry, highly sexed, insect Elvis Presleys to your crops can make a huge dent in the aphid population.

Buying biological controls

Most biological controls are very effective but cost an arm and a leg. You have to weigh up the pros and cons of using them. A bad infestation of greenhouse whitefly can adversely affect an entire crop of tomatoes. One biological control of, say, *Encarsia formosa* (a type of wasp) may be all that's needed to save the crop. The control may well be expensive but should work out less than the cost of a season's worth of tomatoes if you were to buy them in a shop.

The prohibitive costs of biological controls can be combated somewhat by clubbing together with friends. However, although it might be tempting to share one treatment between four you could end up with a quarter of what you need. Instead, bulk-buy between you as this will bring the cost right down, and do your sums beforehand to work out precisely what you need. Always use the control as soon as you get it – they are living things and they do best going about their business and not sitting in a padded envelope in a warm room.

BARRIER METHODS

If you can stop a pest getting its teeth into or laying its eggs on your crops then you may not need to provide any other form of control. A barrier method is something that stands in the way of the bug and its dinner (or nursery).

Net curtains

Nut curtains are a perfect barrier against egg-laying insects such as the cabbage white. They can get heavy, especially when wet, and cause growing seedlings to distort under their weight. However, hoops, sticks or even an upturned hanging basket can be used to give a little support and keep the sagging nets from damaging crops.

A pair of second-hand net curtains bought in a charity shop / thrift store can cost around the same as a specialist horticultural net or mesh, so from a purely financial perspective there may not seem to be much advantage. From an environmental point of view, however, it is always better to reuse materials rather than invest in new goods made from unsustainable materials such as plastic.

Enviromesh

This is an ultra-fine meshed net, useful for allowing light in and keeping pests out. The fineness of the mesh means pests such as aphids are kept at bay, along with birds and butterflies. It also acts as an effective barrier

against carrot root fly, which in some parts of the country can be devastating to a carrot crop. Enviromesh is lightweight and can be used as a floating cloche or supported with canes/hoops. It comes at a price and is man-made but is a very effective barrier.

Fleece will provide the same protection as enviromesh, and commercially this is used for protection against carrot root fly. However, in hot weather plants will 'sweat' with the extra heat trapped by the fleece.

Some garden centres or online retailers will sell enviromesh by the metre; this works out a lot cheaper than buying a ready-cut pack. When buying, make sure you take into account how you are going to weigh it down and add around 15cm (6") either side to allow for burying the edges or pegging them down with stones/planks of wood.

Horticultural nets

Nets keep off birds and, if the weave is thin enough, butterflies too. You can buy plastic

---

Second-hand nets

- **Mosquito netting** Perhaps you only used this once in India or Thailand; isn't it time it had a new lease of life?
- **Sports netting** Cricket nets or tennis nets can be used but may be heavy and will need a lot of support. Schools and sports clubs are likely places to find second-hand sports nets.
- **Fishing nets** Sometimes these will wash up in coastal regions, or local fishermen may know of second-hand or scrap sources of old nets.
- **Protective netting** for car windscreens, although only if it is discarded, as these are quite expensive.

netting by the metre in most garden centres or improvise with what you have at home. At one time horticultural nets were made from natural materials but now these are like gold dust as they've been phased out in favour of much cheaper plastic ones. To prolong the life of your nets you'll need to keep them weed-free, removing bindweed and brambles, which will weave their way into the mesh.

Fixing an old net

With all the care in the world, a horticultural net will still get ripped and torn. I've been alerted to this by seeing small birds happily flying into my fruit cage and even more happily fly off with a beak full of fruit! The simple way to fix the hole is to just place an additional piece of netting over the gap and tie it into place with garden twine. For small holes you should be able to bunch up the net and stitch it back together.

Weeds, sticks and grass can all get caught in a net and will have to be carefully removed. I remove small patches of grass with a garden knife (cutting the grass, not the net) or with a pair of shears if it's really grown through. Once you've freed the netting it can be hung on a piece of rope tied between two trees or on a washing line, which will make removing additional debris a little easier.

Cabbage root fly barrier

Cabbage root fly will cause a plant's leaves to droop and turn bluish in colour. It affects all members of the cabbage family, including broccoli and cauliflowers. It's a particularly nasty pest but thankfully quite easy to prevent.

A barrier between the root of the plant and the soil surface should be enough to prevent the adult burrowing down and laying its eggs (it is the maggot that does all the damage). To make one you need a piece of flexible material cut into a disc of around 15cm (6") in

This clever home–made device will prevent the cabbage root fly laying its eggs.

diameter. The material can be rubber matting, hessian-backed carpet, weed-suppressant material such as Mypex or even roofing felt – just whatever you have to hand. Cut a line to the centre of the disk then cut a hole in the centre big enough to fit around the stalk of the plant (see picture above).

Cotton

Geoff Hamilton (no relation, before you ask) would use a length of cotton thread as crop protection. He would dig two sticks into the soil at angles to make a triangle (with the ground as the base) at both ends of a row of vegetables. He would then wrap the cotton around them until there was no room for a bird to fly in between the threads.

Caribbean-style defences

In my allotments in both Bristol and Oxford I noticed a trend amongst Caribbean plot holders. They would push countless sticks into the ground around their crops. At first I thought they were supports for beans, as many had beans growing up them. However, a Jamaican on a neighbouring plot told me he dug them in to stop birds. He placed the sticks no more than 30cm (12") apart, posing a problem for any bird wishing to swoop down and peck off tender leaves from his vegetables.

ENEMY NUMBER ONE AND TWO: THE SLUG AND THE SNAIL!

I'm glad that chickens, frogs and birds eat slugs and snails, as it would otherwise seem that the only place in the ecosystem for these molluscs was to eat their way through the world's supply of salad leaves. I've planted out rows of lettuce seedlings only to see them disappear overnight having fallen prey to ever-hungry population of slugs and snails. Thankfully, a number of measures can be taken to prevent slug damage, all with their own virtues and vices.

Pellets

You can now buy an organic slug pellet, which has been approved by the Soil Association. It is by far the most effective measure I have ever come across. They are best used in the spring but you will need to deal with slugs throughout the growing season. These pellets are made with ferric phosphate, which breaks down to iron and phosphate, which can actually be beneficial to your soil as opposed to harming wildlife. The older, non-ferric types are dangerous to animals and children and should not be used.

Beer traps

Slugs and snails can't resist the smell of beer and will slither out of their hidey holes all over the garden if they smell it. If you bury a plastic container such as a yoghurt pot up to its neck amongst your veggie beds, then pour in 5cm (2") of beer, they will pay it a visit only to drown in a boozy grave. Emptying these can be quite unpleasant, but more so if you don't do it regularly. I would dispose of them on a bird table, though I often wondered if this led to inebriated birds from marinated molluscs. You could also put the slugs on the compost heap.

The beer doesn't have to be of top quality – the slops bucket from a pub or the dregs of cans following a party would do. The website www.slugoff.co.uk claims it is the yeasty

Snail looking for a tasty salad.

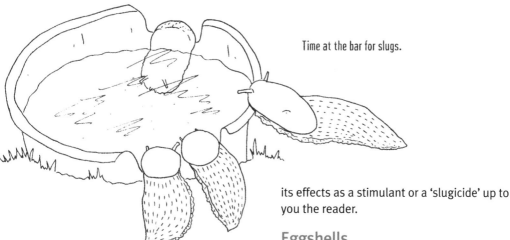

Time at the bar for slugs.

smell the slugs are after and advises mixing the following ingredients well and using in traps in place of beer:

- 2 cups of warm water
- 2 tablespoons of flour
- 1 teaspoon of sugar
- 1/2 teaspoon of yeast.

Plastic bottles

Collars made from plastic bottles are good for protecting plants from slugs.

Coffee grounds

I have never found coffee grounds to be particularly effective but I know gardeners who swear by them. I'm ready to admit I may be missing something here, so if you are a devoted coffee drinker then there is no harm in giving them a go. The theory goes you should sprinkle the grounds around your plants, just as you would do with slug pellets, and that the caffeine inhibits certain enzymes and the slugs keel over and die. Opposing theories claim it just keeps them awake all day and all night, giving them more time to munch away all your veggies in a caffeine-induced feeding frenzy.

Caffeine is an appetite suppressant in humans, so I will leave any deductions as to its effects as a stimulant or a 'slugicide' up to you the reader.

Eggshells

I've observed many first-year allotment holders using eggshells as a slug deterrent, but they never seemed to continue this practice into their second year.

Bran and bread

Birds like to eat bread and will return to the same spot to eat if they know it to be a good source of food. Slugs will eat bran but it will

Nowhere to hide!

Slugs like to hide somewhere dark and moist during the day: this can be under stones, under pieces of wood or even down the sides of a raised bed. Taking away these habitats will decrease the number of slugs as they will have nowhere to run (well, slither) and nowhere to hide. Sprinkling sharp sand around the edge of a raised bed will create a scratchy surface they won't want to crawl over. Removing the wooden surrounds of a raised bed and making more of a deep bed system (where the bed is raised into a mound and the edges are cut with a spade) seems to work well for salad beds, as it deprives the breeding slugs of a home.

kill them. Some birds will also eat slugs! Throwing out a mix of bran and stale bread will kill off the slugs, feed the local birdlife and use up your stale bread all in one go.

Farming supply shops or wholesalers will sell 25kg (55lb) bags of bran for very little, and this should last you the season.

Bran is effective only in dry weather – as soon as a shower of rain comes down you will have to reapply it. Remember too that birds will also go for berries and leaves if they are not netted, so if you do experiment with this method make sure you protect susceptible plants.

APHIDS

There are many different kinds of aphid and they are one of the worst pests a food grower will encounter. They can be born pregnant and can give birth ten days after being born themselves, making them a formidable foe. They are often referred to as 'plant lice', as they act in the same way that fleas do to mammals, although instead of sucking blood they suck the plants' sap.

Blackfly, greenfly and pea aphids are among the different types of aphid you may encounter; all are slightly different, but all cause similar damage and all are dealt with in similar ways (including using biological controls – see page 161).

Aphid sprays

Aphids love nothing more than to tuck into the fresh sap of growing plants. In doing so, they leave open wounds, allowing further pests and diseases to attack growing crops. A simple way of controlling them is with a home-made soap or rhubarb spray. You can pick up plastic spray bottles quite cheaply these days, or use an empty kitchen/ bathroom spray bottle that you've thoroughly washed out.

The soap spray is simple to make: add a few squirts of environmentally friendly washing-up liquid to a spray bottle and top up with water. Use about as much as you would for a full bowl of washing up (ask someone who regularly washes up if you don't know how much this is) for a 50/75ml (1.8/2.6 fl oz) spray. You can rub off the aphids once you have sprayed them, which should kill off any you've missed. Soap flakes can be used instead of washing-up liquid – add a spoonful for 50ml and dissolve well.

Alternatively, leave around five or six rhubarb leaves in a bucket of water for around a week before adding the liquid to a spray bottle. This method is unfortunately very indiscriminate: it will kill anything on the plants, including beneficial insects such as ladybirds.

Aphids and ants

Ants can 'farm' aphids, 'milking' them for a sticky secretion they exude. Providing an alternative sticky substance can be enough to divert their attention. The last scrapings of a jar of jam can be placed below your plants and the ants will go for this instead, leaving you to deal with the aphids.

Woolly aphids or mealy bugs

Fruit trees are often prone to infestations of woolly aphids, which appear as little white puffs of cotton all over the tree. These can be removed with just a sponge and some soapy water; however, it is difficult to remove all of them and the tree can become reinfected. I've found that a mix of methods works best with this pest, so in addition to using the soapy water, attach a bug hotel (see pages 48-51) to the branches, tie up bird feeders to attract blue tits (which feed on woolly aphids) and prune out any weak or damaged branches to

The lowdown on nasties – methods of control			
Pest	**Control**	**Pros**	**Cons**
Aphids	Soap spray	Very cheap.	Can be a mucky job cleaning off dead aphids.
	Ladybirds	Free.	Time-consuming to gather.
Birds	Net	Can use repeatedly.	Weeds can get tangled in the net.
	Net curtain	Cheap or free.	Will need support as can crush plants, especially when wet.
Cabbage root fly	Home-made collars	Free.	Very little.
	Crop rotation	Free.	Need four beds to rotate effectively.
Carrot root fly	Fleece	Cheap and easy to use.	Carrots can 'sweat' in hot weather.
	Crop rotation	Free.	Need four beds to rotate effectively.
Caterpillars	Enviromesh	Creates an effective barrier.	Non-biodegradable. Can be costly.
	Net curtain	Cheap or free.	Needs support as can be heavy and damage plants, especially when wet. Non-biodegradable.
	Fleece	Can double up as frost protection.	Non-biodegradable.
Mice and rats	Cat	You get a pet in the process!	Expensive to keep and will go for the local birdlife.
	Spring mouse trap	Cheap. Can bait with anything you have to hand (e.g. peanut butter).	Unpleasant to clear out. Mice can still be alive when you find them.
	Humane mouse/ rat trap	Culprits can be set free. Trap can be bought and shared collectively.	Have to find somewhere to release the animal, and it may well die in unfamiliar surroundings anyway.
Slugs	Organic pellets	Very effective.	Costly.
	Nematodes	Very effective over small areas.	High-cost measure. Needs to be in enclosed beds not open ground.
	Beer traps	Cheap – especially if using pub slop tray.	Traps need to be emptied regularly. Not for the faint-hearted.
	Head torch and hands	Free.	Time-consuming.

reduce the risk of further reinfection. You may have to tolerate a low level of infestation but it's worth being vigilant.

BLIGHT

Wet weather towards the end of the summer provides the perfect opportunity for potato blight to sweep in, destroying entire harvests of both tomatoes and potatoes. Allotment sites are notorious for this, as I found to my cost during my first year of growing tomatoes. In mild cases I found that the infected leaves and fruits can be removed and the plants will, to an extent, recover. Alternatively I've pulled the entire plant and ripened the uninfected fruits on a windowsill or in a drawer with a banana (bananas give off ethylene gas, which will help ripen many fruits, including tomatoes).

Spays made from horsetail / mare's tail can go some way towards preventing the disease, but in a bad year this will ward it off for only a short time. Another way to avoid blight is to avoid the blight season altogether – early potatoes can be grown in place of maincrop ones and some Eastern European varieties of tomatoes will fruit a month earlier than their Western counterparts.

Watering the base of a tomato or potato plant and avoiding the leaves (good practice for all plants) can help reduce the risk, as can growing the plants under cover. To illustrate this point, one year I covered my plants with a clear sheet of plastic stretched over the top like an A-frame tent. Most of my allotment site was hit by the infection but only the plants at the two uncovered ends of my tent succumbed to the blight, and only on leaves growing outside the tent. Similarly, I've observed only tomatoes growing under open windows or vents in greenhouses being infected, with neighbouring plants looking completely untouched.

The potato blight fungus is a water-borne mould that needs warm – but not hot – and wet conditions to survive. Despite popular misconception it can't survive the heat of a large compost heap. As long as infected tubers are not allowed to regrow, composted infected plant material shouldn't harbour the disease until the following year. This may not be appropriate for very small heaps that don't reach a suitably high heat, however; consider it only for bins of 1m (3ft) square or more.

Attracting beneficial insects

In the summer there is still time to sow herbs such as parsley and coriander around the edges of your beds (or in the entrance to greenhouses or polytunnels) to attract beneficial insects. Allowed to flower, these plants will attract predators such as hoverflies.

Marigolds can be sown at the start of summer to flower that season, or sown at the end to flower the following year. If you are not worried about how they look, bedding plants past their best are quite cheap (if not free) over the summer months – these can be left to seed, giving you a bonus crop the following year. Look out for seeds to collect from friends' gardens as the summer comes to a close.

Chapter 20

PROPAGATING PLANTS

Each season offers opportunities to generate new plants from old ones, ensuring a new stock for the future. The summer is no exception: for example, herbs can be propagated from semi-ripe cuttings and strawberries can be propagated from runners.

STRAWBERRIES FROM RUNNERS

Strawberries propagate by seed or by sending out runners. Runners will provide a mature plant much quicker than can be grown from seed and, as the plants are clones of the parents, they can be selected for beneficial characteristics such as prolific fruiting or adaptation to local conditions. If you have ever propagated a spider plant indoors then you'll be familiar with the methods used for propagating from runners.

The simplest way of getting new plants is to ask a willing neighbour if he or she has spare plants that could be dug up for you. Runners will plant themselves just about anywhere and grow like a weed when they do, which means that spare ones are quite likely. Discard any diseased-looking plants and pot or plant up only the healthy ones. A little comfrey and nettle feed should help them root.

If taking from your own runners you can afford to be more selective, rather than just

Propagate strawberries from runners.

getting what you are given. Again, choose healthy-looking, disease-free strawberry plants and select runners that have put on a lot of leaf and root growth. Bury a 7.5cm (3") pot into the soil underneath the runner and fill with potting compost (ideally a compost/sand mix). I've used just soil in the past and, although not ideal, the strawberry plant will still set root. Peg the runner down with either a U-shaped fencing pin or a 5cm (2") twist of metal wire, or place a rock on the runner stem. After a month or so the plant will have rooted and it can be cut from the parent plant. The new plants can then be put out in their final positions or even potted up and sold on for an bit of extra cash.

HERBS FROM SEMI-RIPE CUTTINGS

Semi-ripe cuttings are useful for propagating herbs such as sage, rosemary and lavender. The names of most methods of taking cuttings are self-explanatory. Softwood cuttings are taken from the softer wood in the spring, usually with soft herbaceous growth; hardwood cuttings are taken from harder older wood, usually after leaf fall. Semi-ripe cuttings sit somewhere in between. This is not as complicated as it sounds. Think of a rosemary sprig in the summer – it is no longer completely soft and springy but is beginning to turn brown and harden up. It is, in other words, partially matured or 'semi-ripe'.

HOW TO TAKE A SEMI-RIPE CUTTING

1 Cut a piece of this year's growth around 6cm (2 1/2") in length just below a node (the buddy bit a leaf comes out from). Place straight into a polythene bag.

2 Take off all but the top few leaves.

3 Place in a free-draining compost or compost mix,* pushing around a third of the stem into the potting medium. If the stem is not firm enough to go in by itself, use a pencil to make a hole.

4 Water from the bottom up (place in a tray and add water to the tray).

5 Put no more than three cuttings to a pot and cover with a plastic bag.

6 Cuttings benefit from some bottom heat, so place in a propagator, on a radiator (keep an eye on it so it doesn't scorch) or near a similar low-level source of heat.

7 Leave for four to eight weeks. Don't be tempted to wiggle the plant or pull it out to see if it has any roots!

8 Pot on when ready.

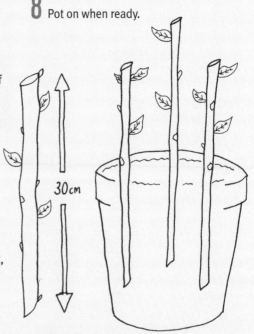

30cm

* In an ideal world the cutting should be placed in a 50:50 mix of perlite or vermiculite and potting compost. However, for the sake of one or two cuttings it is not worth buying a big bag of special material that you will never use again. The important thing is that the cutting is placed in a free-draining environment so it doesn't rot away. Sand or coir could be used, mixed with sieved compost.

Chapter 21

MAKING THE MOST OF YOUR CROPS

Food economy represents possibly the most tangible saving you may make in a household – minimising waste and making full use of all parts of edible plants can help with your budget no end. This is especially true for the home grower, as many plants may not be harvested to their full potential, and parts of other edibles may be needlessly wasted.

USING THE WHOLE OF THE VEGETABLE

We are used to buying our vegetables in a supermarket or from a greengrocer, so are more familiar with a vegetable in isolation, away from its parent plant. For example, beet-root is sold leafless, pickled and peeled; Brussels sprouts are removed from their stem; and courgettes come deprived of their flowers. Unaccustomed to the plant as a whole, you may not be aware of all its edible parts.

Nasturtiums are edible, and also act as a decoy for predators, a pollinator attractant and a ground cover.

Nasturtiums

The flowers and leaves can be eaten in salads or put in vinegar or oil for flavour and colour. The buds can be blanched and pickled and then used like capers, and the cooked stems can be used in soups. (Old stems can get a little chewy so the soup is better blended.)

Courgette flowers

Prized by some chefs more than the courgette itself, courgette flowers are best stuffed, battered and deep fried. Suggested fillings include soft cheese, such as ricotta, mixed with herbs. For something more substantial, stuff with seasoned couscous or rice. Try not to over-fill the flowers; refrigerating them before applying the batter should help them keep their integrity. Both male and female flowers of the courgette can be eaten.

Broad beans and peas

Young broad beans can be eaten like mange tout, early in the season. This encourages the plant to produce more pods. To prevent both beans and peas from growing upwards, the tops are usually pinched out – on both plants these tops are quite edible and can be lightly fried or used in salads.

Brussels sprouts tops

The tops of Brussels sprouts can be eaten like cabbage or spring greens. Taking the tops before the sprouts have been harvested will reduce yields but it will encourage the plant to produce sprouts faster. If you missed the harvest and sprouts begin to uncurl, they can eventually be harvested like broccoli – I find the taste superior to the actual sprout.

Turnip tops

The young leaves of the turnip can be eaten and are even seen as a delicacy in some parts of the world.

Purple sprouting broccoli

You can harvest the leaves of broccoli plants as they are growing. One or two from each plant every now and then shouldn't impede growth, but taking too many will rob them of the energy needed to produce good florets.

Beetroot

Beetroot is related to chard and perpetual spinach, and all have edible leaves. The younger leaves can be used in salads and the older leaves can be cooked. You can also eat the leaf stems; chop them up finely and add them to a warm salad, soup, stew or casserole.

Vegetable tops and tails as stock

Leek tops and other, otherwise discarded parts of a vegetable (or even some weeds) can be boiled up to make a vegetable stock. Water-soluble vitamins and some trace minerals will leach into the stock pot, making highly nutritious 'green water'. You could add:

- leek tops
- onion peel (will cause stock to go brown, useful for making gravy)
- tough stalks and ribs of cabbages
- weeds such as goose grass, fat hen and nettle
- tops of root vegetables such as carrot and parsnip.

Bring to a steady simmer on a low heat and add strong, robust herbs such as rosemary, thyme and bay. I sometimes add yeast extract or soy sauce for extra B vitamins, salt and colour. The stock can be reduced down and frozen as individual 'portions' in an ice-cube tray ready for use.

DRYING HERBS

A supply of dried herbs is a worthwhile addition to the kitchen cupboard, for culinary use and for making teas. Drying is a very simple process and doesn't require any specialist equipment (other than some string).

On a dry day, cut a handful of healthy stalks or branches, remove any diseased or damaged leaves, bunch them up and tie them at the base. They will need both heat and airflow to dry well, so can be dried anywhere you may dry clothes – above a radiator, in an airing cupboard or even on a washing line. I tie herbs to the handle of a top window as this seems to provide both steady heat and airflow.

Herbs can be dry within 24 hours of putting them up, but in places with restricted airflow, such as an airing cupboard, you may need an

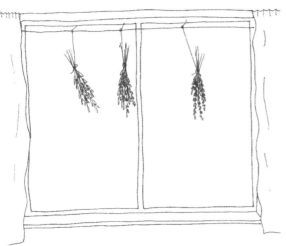

Herbs can be dried by hanging them in a window.

increased drying time. They will start to crumble to the touch when ready. If left in the window for too long they start to fade and lose their potency.

Most herbs, including mint, lemon balm, oregano/marjoram, nettle and sage, can be dried this way. You can also dry evergreen herbs such as rosemary, but there seems little point if you have a fresh winter's supply.

If you require herbs for teas, simply rub the dry leaves off on to a folded newspaper and decant into a storage jar. For finer culinary herbs, transfer into a plastic bag and agitate until they crumble into the desired size, or use a coffee grinder. Transfer into smaller jars and use in cooking.

Herbs should be stored away from direct sunlight.

THE SUMMER BOLT

The bulk of seed saving comes in the autumn, as plants ensure their survival for the coming year. But in the summer plants can also set seed, often through a process known as 'bolting' – when the plant sends up a stem, which bears flowers, which eventually turn to seed. This seems to happen almost overnight (hence the term). Most plants go to seed when they are under some form of pressure, making them feel the need to produce the next generation. If lettuces dry out they can react to this lack of resources by bolting, so you may have to resign yourself to plenty of watering in the summer. Direct sun can also encourage plants to bolt, so plant lettuces in dappled shade.

If you don't manage to deter plants from bolting, you can always make the most of it by saving the seed for the following year, or even use it this year with successive sowing.

Harvesting the summer bolt

I would often leave beet spinach (sometimes called leaf beet or perpetual spinach) to self-seed across my allotment, as it produced bonus free plants away from the main beds. The downside to this method is that bolting plants can harbour pests, especially aphids, and I found that if the plant was creating more work than necessary it was seldom worth keeping. Chard, beetroot and sorrel are among some of the plants that will bolt and self-seed, but you will need to monitor for pests.

Lettuce seed can be very easily saved from bolted plants; lettuce can cross-pollinate but most of the time you don't need to isolate them. Don't choose the first ones to bolt as you will be selecting for this trait. Instead select your favourite for flavour and pest resistance – in short your healthiest-looking plant. After it has bolted it will begin to produce a yellow, dandelion-like flower and start to resemble wild lettuce, a common weed. The seeds, like dandelions, are dispersed by the wind and the yellow flowers give way to seeds with a white feathery coating. A rough 'sowing' can be made that year by simply shaking the plant on to bare soil. This will produce seedlings which can then be transferred to their final growing positions. Alternatively, to save for next year or have a little control over where it is sown, you will have to separate the 'feather' from the seed. This is a fairly lengthy but simple process – see box below.

Isolating plants for seed saving

Seed saving is described in more detail in Chapter 24, but during the summer, as your vegetable plants are flowering, you should be aware of the possibility of cross-fertilisation. If you are selecting for specific traits you might want to prevent this from happening.

- **Cucurbits – squash, courgette, marrow, pumpkin, cucumber and melon** will all cross with close relations. So courgettes, for example, may cross with other summer squashes such as petty pan or acorn squash. To avoid this always keep the female flowers (those attached to the fruit) covered with a bag and pollinate by hand with a cotton bud / Q-tip or brush. Grow only one cultivar of melons or cucumbers at a time under cloches or in a greenhouse, as they will cross with any similar relations within half a mile.
- For **aubergines and peppers** you will need an isolation cage (see opposite) or grow only one variety at a time in a greenhouse.
- Close relations within the **cabbage family** will cross, so grow only one kind at a time (e.g. just broccoli or just cauliflower) if you want to save seed.

Cross-pollination with **French beans** is unlikely, but to be sure, try to grow around 10m (33ft) from other French beans.

Tomatoes are usually self-pollinating (though sometimes need help) so should be fine.
Peas are self-pollinating, so are not a problem.

HOW TO SAVE LETTUCE SEED

1 Let the flower/seedhead mature in a bag for four to six weeks or until the stalk becomes brittle.

2 Rub the dried flowerheads between your fingers or palms over a sheet of newspaper.

3 Separate as much of the unwanted material from the seed as possible.

4 The seed can be 'cleaned' further by rubbing against a sieve to separate the feathery plumes and other debris.

5 Store the seed in a marked envelope.

USE UP YOUR SEED

Seeds have only a limited life, and there is little point in holding on to old packets of seed if they will expire before next spring. If you have a lot of some seed that is not very fresh and you're not confident that it will last till next year, it's worth using it up. Many vegetables can be sown successively through-out the season, increasing the amount grown on the plot and allowing for later harvests.

Many salad leaves can be sown quite late as they offer a quick return, especially if you wish to harvest the leaves and not, for example, the whole head of lettuce. Beetroot, radishes and some varieties of carrot can be sown right through the summer, and summer squashes sown in July in the UK will give you a bonus crop just as the spring-sown ones have come to an end.

HOW TO MAKE AN ISOLATION CAGE

SIDES | TOP

1m (3ft)

1m (3ft)

1 Use an old mosquito net or old net curtain.

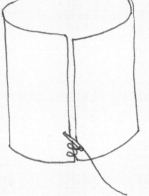

2 Cut a 1m² (3ft²) section for the top.

3 Sew the top to a 4m (13ft) round of the netting fabric.

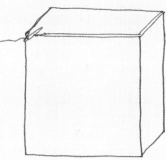

4 Dig four canes into the ground in a square, a metre apart, and run some string around the top and middle of the canes.

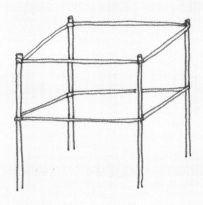

5 Cover the netting over the canes and weigh it down with stones or dig some earth around the base.

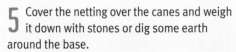

Chapter 22

GATHERING 'WILD' EXTRAS

Weeds can be a valuable extra crop, especially in years of unpredictable weather and subsequent unpredictable crops. During the summer, weeds are growing at their best and can be harvested along with conventional crops. The summer rains can bring with them the fruiting bodies of fungi (or mushrooms, to you and I). There is a lot of fear surrounding the picking of mushrooms, but careful study or the advice of an expert will aid the recognition of these protein-rich extras that can appear in your garden. As with all wild food, just be sure you know what you are picking.

A rare treat — blackcurrants in the wild.

FRUIT FOR FREE

At times nature can do a better job than we can, and our hedgerows and gardens often boast a real abundance of fruit without any input from humans.

Blackberries
These need no introduction; just don't let them get out of hand. The first to ripen are always the sweetest, so eat these raw and save the rest for jams and pies.

Blackcurrants
These can sometimes be found in hedgerows. A handful of foraged berries can be made into individual portions of jam by microwaving for around a minute, adding an equal amount of sugar, stirring, then microwaving again for another two to three minutes.

Wild cherries
Often planted for their blossoms by town planners, wild cherries can pop up in the most unlikely places, often overhanging gardens and allotments. Wild cherries shouldn't be eaten in abundance and lend themselves much more to being made into wild cherry vodka or wild cherry brandy.

Fill a bottle with wild cherries (there is no need to stone them), top with sugar (use around 100g [4oz] of sugar to every 500g [1lb] 2oz of fruit), then pour on your chosen spirit,i.e. brandy, vodka, gin or whisky (use cheap brands as it makes no sense to mask the flavour of quality spirits). Store the bottle in a cool dark place and shake it from time to time. You can do the same with almost any soft fruit, but raspberries, mulberries and sloes work particularly well.

MORE COMPANION SQUATTERS

It is a shame that not all weeds are edible, especially in the summer when you can get overrun with them. Thankfully, however, some of the most common ones are edible, and can make welcome additions to the kitchen table.

Goosefoot family (including fat hen)

Fat hen and other chenopods (members of the goosefoot family) can pop up quite uninvited on a plot but may be welcomed none the less. They are quite distinctive – grey/green in colour with leaves resembling a goose's foot in shape. The leaves can be eaten and the seeds are an excellent, if not fiddly, source of protein. They quite often grow with potatoes and can be cooked alongside them as a spinach substitute in saag aloo (spicy potatoes with spinach). The downside of these plants is they do suck up both pollution and nitrates, so should not be eaten if you are not growing using organic methods in that bed, or if they are growing next to a busy road.

Dock and dandelion

Docks and dandelions both have edible uses but they come with very deep taproots so can compete with other plants, and the leaves can host pests. Although I've known gardeners to actively cultivate them, my opinion is they should seldom be tolerated in a garden as there are much better plants that will take up their niche (sorrel and goat's beard spring to mind). Dandelion leaves can be eaten, and the flowers made into a cough syrup (cover with water and boil with 500g [1lb 2oz] sugar for every 25 flowerheads – once the mixture is thick and syrupy, strain the flowers and

The zinc in a dandelion flower makes it the perfect ingredient for a cough syrup.

store in a sterilised jar; use in moderation). The roots can be roasted or cooked with spices as a vegetable. Dock leaves can be boiled in a few changes of water (boil and discard the water) and used as a vine leaf or spinach substitute.

ESCAPEES

Plants such as leaf beet / perpetual spinach, sorrel and rocket can all self-seed and spread quite freely around a garden. Depending on where they pop up (and what they are), you could leave them or even begin to cultivate them. I've seen rocket go to seed in one area and soon populate the entire neighbourhood. Look out for blackfly on bolted leaf beet and give it a squirt with soap spray (see page 166) if it becomes a problem.

SUMMER HERBS AND TEAS

It's not just the food cupboard that can be replenished during the summer: medicinal and culinary herbs and herbal teas can be restocked.

Lime flowers

Lime blossoms can be gathered, dried on a windowsill on top of some newspaper and stored until needed. I have a cup of lime flower and lemon balm tea when I'm having trouble sleeping, and within half an hour I'm usually off in the land of nod.

Wild herbs

Many herbs self-seed easily or spread and grow wild on an allotment or in a garden, and some also occur naturally in the wild. If your plot is lacking, ask friends and neighbours for rampant herbs such as marjoram/oregano, mint and chives, as they will no doubt have more than enough to spare. Try to contain rampant herbs using submerged planks or sunken pots.

Wild herbs, for example thyme, marjoram, mint and lemon balm, are no different from their domesticated counterparts and should be used in the same way.

Yarrow

Yarrow is a small feathery herb commonly found in grassland. It can be used in a tea and there is some evidence to suggest it can help staunch bleeding if you have a minor cut. It will self-seed if allowed to flower.

SUMMER MUSHROOMS

From early summer onwards mushrooms really start to appear in abundance in UK gardens, parks and fields. Many are edible and, if correctly identified, make a valuable additional source of protein. Get a good guide to identify mushrooms correctly (an excellent one is *Mushrooms* by Roger Phillips – see Resources), and always cross-reference with another guide to be absolutely sure.

Puffballs

The giant puffball, *Calvatia gigantea*, is a prize find in the summer – look on grassland for this football-sized fungus. Don't pick if there is only one on its own, and try to leave at least one to spore and reproduce.

The puffball is a distinctive summer mushroom.

Other smaller puffballs are edible when they are young. These include the stump puffball, *Lycoperdon pyriforme*, found in woods on decomposing logs, and the brown puffball, *Bovista nigrescens*, found in grasslands and fields. To avoid misidentification, when you cut a puffball in two it should have a solid block of pure white in the middle, not grey or brown, and should *not* have the appearance of a smaller mushroom inside.

Field mushrooms
(Agaricus campestris)
Be particularly careful in identifying this as it can look like the yellow stainer, *Agaricus xanthoderma*, which will cause a serious stomach upset, if not worse. A yellow stainer will stain chrome yellow when cut or bruised and will have an unpleasant inky smell, which can become more pronounced on cooking.

Wood ear / jelly ear *(Auricularia auricula-judae)*
This looks like a brown ear and has the texture of one, but despite this it is rather good in soups. It will spit if you try to fry it. It grows mainly on elder and there is little else that looks like it.

Wood ear, or jelly ear, grows all year round.

Wild food 'dos and don'ts'

- Do pick few plants from a wide area rather than lots from one place.
- Do make sure you are 100-per-cent certain what you are picking.
- Do ask for permission to pick on protected sites and sites of special scientific interest (SSSIs) – it is best practice to ask, wherever you are picking.

- Don't spread invasive plants – Japanese knotweed can be spread from as little as 1g of plant matter and Himalayan balsam sends out lots of seeds.
- Don't uproot plants – including plants without roots, e.g. fungi – without the landowner's permission.
- Don't pick any more than you need – remember you are sharing with the local wildlife!

Honey fungus *(Armillaria spp.)*
The name 'honey fungus' can be used to describe many different species in the *Armillaria* genus, the main one being *Armillaria mellea*, which itself has many subspecies. It is a mild stomach irritant and should be boiled and the water discarded before cooking thoroughly, and even then it can make some people (a minority) ill. It can be confused with the inedible sulphur tuft (*Hypholoma fasciculare*), so be careful with identification. Honey fungus can be a serious pest in the garden so don't bring home any logs with it on them.

To some this may all be more trouble than it is worth, but honey fungus is quite tasty and very, very common towards the end of summer and early autumn.

PART 4

AUTUMN

In some urban areas it is difficult to mark the seasons by anything more than the clothes that people are wearing. But for food growers time can be marked in a much more real way – by what goes on the table and at the plot.

Autumn is my favourite time of year food-wise – it's a time of pumpkin soup, corn on the cob and apple pie. It is also when work on the plot eases off to a more manageable pace.

AS THE COLD COMES IN

As the nights draw in, most low-lying plants, including salad crops, can be covered with a fleece or cloche to protect them from extreme low temperatures. This will often give only 1-2°C (2-3°F) of protection, but it can be enough to stop the plant's cells freezing. Warm-season crops such as peppers and aubergines will certainly need wrapping up towards the end of the season. See Chapter 10 for more on protection from cold.

END-OF-SEASON BARGAINS

Herbaceous perennials can be picked up for pennies at the end of summer. If the leaves have all but died, check the root system: if there are still fresh white roots, rather than brittle brown ones, there is a good chance that the plant will bounce back next spring. It's always worth haggling – many of these plants will end up in the bin, so you can offer even less than the reduced sticker. If the plant looks dead you may even be able to get it for free.

Cut-price seeds may also be available at the end of the season. Check the sow-by date on the packet and, if they are still in date, try making an offer for much less than the marked price. If the retailer won't move on the ticket price then the seeds are not worth buying now – wait until spring for new seed, which will last longer. Cheap isn't cheap if it's a false economy.

JOBS FOR AUTUMN

- Harvest crops
- Save seed
- Propagate plants
- Store crops
- Make leaf mould
- Gather 'wild' extras

Chapter 23

HARVESTING

Even though the light intensity has diminished and plant growth begins to slow down at this time of year, there are still plenty of jobs to be done as summer gives way to autumn. Harvesting continues, plant debris are composted and containers emptied. We also try to get that little bit extra from our plants as the main growing season comes to a close.

CONTAINERS FOR YOUR PRODUCE

How many times have you arrived at your plot only to find you haven't got anything to put your harvested fruit or veggies into? Or how often have you been out walking and realise you have no way of harvesting the copious amounts of fresh, plump blackberries hanging from the hedgerow?

At the start of my wild food walks I teach people to get over this problem by making a paper bag from a daily newspaper (see opposite). Many cities now offer a free daily paper, so finding one shouldn't be a problem.

MAKING A FRUIT PICKER

The best fruit on any tree is always slightly out of reach, at the very top where it will get the most sun. This is good news for our feathered friends but not so much for us. It is good to share a certain amount with the

birds but there is no reason why they should take all the high-grade fruit and leave you with bruised, misshapen and rotten apples! Long-armed pruners can be useful for taking

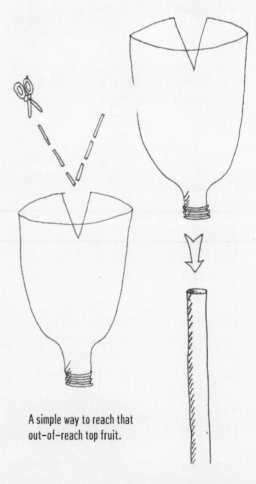

A simple way to reach that out-of-reach top fruit.

HOW TO MAKE AN ORIGAMI BAG

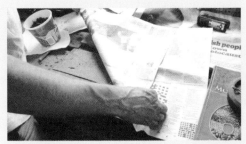

1 Fold the bottom corner to the top edge to form a triangle.

2 Fold the rectangular part over to the edge of the triangle.

3 Open up the triangle and tuck in the rectangle part – you should now have a triangle shape.

4 Fold the right-hand corner to the long edge.

5 ... and repeat with the left-hand corner.

6 Fold down the front flap.

7 Fill with produce.

down fruit at the top of a tree, but the fruit can still fall bruised.

Fruit pickers can be made by cutting the top off a plastic bottle. A small 'v' is cut in the side and the bottle top is attached to a long pole. Old-fashioned ridge-tent poles or children's Wendy houses seem to have the right girth of pole to fit into the bottle top; bamboo will work but it can snap if extended too far. To further prevent bruising you can place padding in the bottom of the picker.

GETTING AN EXTRA HARVEST

Like a runner sprinting at the end of a marathon, crops have a little energy left to go just that little bit further towards the close of the year. They might need a bit of encouragement to do so, and we can also use different techniques to harvest or harvest parts we would normally not consider. The following are a few examples.

Lie tomatoes down

Carefully remove the upright supports of a tomato plant and lay it down on some straw. Cover this with a long cloche to ripen those last few green tomatoes.

Or, harvest the last green tomatoes and put them in a drawer with a ripe banana. Bananas release ethylene gas, which signals the ripening process in the tomatoes. (Peppers respond in a similar way.) Alternatively, pick them green and store (without the banana) in a cool dry place. The odd one or two may go mouldy but the fruits will slowly ripen, spreading the harvest out. I've eaten tomatoes and peppers stored this way right up until early December.

Cut cabbage stalks

The roots of a cabbage plant are still intact once you have cut off the cabbage. Cut a

Ripen the last few fruits under protection.

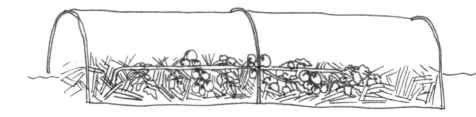

cross in the stem and, if you're lucky, four small cabbages will miraculously sprout up from it.

Harvest sweetcorn stalks

Sweetcorn is a grass and, like many grasses (including sugar cane), it has a pithy carbohydrate-rich centre. Whilst still green the stalks can be crushed with a hammer or put through an old-fashioned mangle to produce a green sweet liquid. This liquid increases in sweetness as it is reduced by boiling. It can then be drunk as a cordial or used in cooking.

Reuse spent compost

Container growers know all too well that at the end of the season, once everything is harvested, they can be left with piles of spent compost. This can be rejuvenated in an ordinary compost bin.

- Discard any compost and plants that have exhibited the signs of any nasty soil-borne pests or diseases.
- Break up any large stalks or roots left in the pot and sprinkle a layer of spent compost and plant matter into the compost bin.
- Add layers of 'greens' and 'browns' (see Chapter 5, i.e. kitchen waste and grass clippings along with torn cardboard and woody material).
- Repeat this layering process until the bin is full.
- Leave to compost.
- Sieve before use.

Growbags may still contain sufficient nutrients to be used the following year to grow less hungry crops such as lettuce.

Make use of sunflower seeds

You can leave the heads of sunflowers where they grew to feed the passing bird population. However, if you need to use the bed or have a problem with squirrels, or if you just want a tidy garden, this isn't always practical. Instead, make a feeding perch by removing the head and placing it in between four lengths of string.

HOW TO MAKE A SUNFLOWER FEEDING PERCH

1 Take two lengths of string around 2m (6ft) in length.

2 Fold them in half and tie them in a cross at the centre of each half.

3 Take the four lengths at the other end and tie into one large knot.

4 Slide a large sunflower head into the bottom of this 'harness' and hang from a tree.

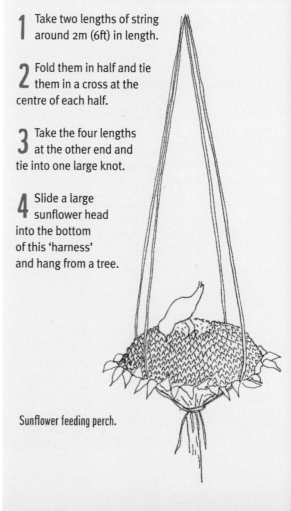

Sunflower feeding perch.

Chapter 24

SAVING SEED

Seed saving will not represent the biggest financial saving on a productive plot, but in terms of food security and biodiversity it is the most important thing you can ever do.

SAVING COMMON SEEDS

For a vegetable garden adapted to conditions in your part of the world you should save seeds from the widest range of vegetables you can. Some are easier to save than others, but it really isn't rocket science – apart from some time and a little growing space you have very little to lose by giving it a go. Some common vegetable seeds are covered below; others are discussed in the box opposite.

Remember to label your seeds before storing, with the date, variety and any additional relevant information such as sowing time.

Tomato

The jelly-like coating around the seeds of a tomato can make this a slightly more difficult seed to gather than some. To get around this, old greenhouse growers would simply stamp a few fruits into the ground at the end of the season and they would grow the following year. Alternatively, you can try the following approach.

1. Scoop out the seeds of a good-quality tomato from a disease-free, strong plant.

Beans – an easy seed to save.

2. Put the seeds in a jar and top with water.
3. Place somewhere warm and leave to ferment for three to four days.
4. Run the seeds under a tap in a sieve to remove the unwanted fermented 'goo'.
5. Put the seeds on a porcelain plate to dry.

Carrot

Like parsnips, carrots are biennial. In areas with mild winters they can be mulched in the autumn and left to resprout in the spring. In colder areas they should be dug up in autumn and replanted in spring.

Carrots can cross with wild carrots, producing a thin spindly white root. It can be hard to avoid this, but watch out for these roots in the offspring and weed them out.

Seed saving

Pippa Rosen, owner of the organic seed company Beans and Herbs

There are many good reasons for saving seed. Vegetable varieties can suddenly be taken off a commercial grower's catalogue list, effectively becoming extinct if home gardeners do not choose to save the seed. Many worthwhile varieties have been lost in this way, especially over the last 70 years!

You can save the seed of vegetable varieties that have particular desirable characteristics: for instance, you may wish to grow tall peas, like those grown in Victorian times, to give a long harvest over the summer. Over the decades most peas have been bred short to make them all mature at the same time so they can be harvested mechanically for commercial packing. These are the varieties now most often for sale in seed packets and it is no longer very easy to find the tall varieties.

Other desirable characteristics to look out for include taste; tolerance to cold, wind, wet and dry conditions; early or late harvesting; and disease resistance.

Growing your own vegetables and saving your own seed year on year also gives plants an opportunity to evolve. This is important, as it gives us our best chance of having the right plant varieties for future climatic conditions. Here are a few examples of what you can start with if you are new to seed saving.

- **French beans,** either climbing or dwarf, are ideal. If you are growing more than one variety, make sure you keep the varieties 10m (33ft) apart from each other. Grow them for eating as on the seed packet instructions, but leave a few plants at the

end of the row for your seed crop. Do not pick pods to eat; instead, leave them to go completely dry on the plants. Collect the dry seed pods by mid-October, before the first frosts. Shell out the bean seeds and spread them out on plates to dry out in an airy place indoors for another three weeks, shaking or turning them every few days. Pack into envelopes and label with the bean variety and the year of harvest. Store in a cool, dry, mouse-free place until sowing time the following year.

- **Peas** are sown early in the year so have every good chance of maturing and going to seed, whatever kind of season we get. Peas are mostly self-pollinating and will give you lots of seeds for sowing the

Beans dry well in the pods left on the plant.

(Cont'd)

(Cont'd)

following year. Leave a few plants just for your seed crop. Dry, label and store as for French beans.

- **Parsnip** seed has to be fresh to germinate well, so this is another good seed to save. Grow your parsnips as you would for cropping the roots. In the autumn, out of your whole crop choose about 12 to 16 good-quality roots, dig them up and check them over. Replant these, 40cm (16") apart in November. Like many root crops, parsnips are biennials. This means that they will flower and set seed in their second season. Tall and lime green in colour, they are very attractive in flower. Wait for the seed to completely dry on the plants and then collect, dry out further, pack, label and store.

Open-pollinated (not F1) varieties are the ones to save seed from, as the plants will generally stand up to a wider range of growing conditions. Avoid saving seed from any F1 variety – the vegetables from these seeds, although edible, would not be reliably the same as their parents.

In the first half of the twentieth century there were many small seed companies, which between them offered a huge number of vegetable varieties for customers to choose from. Now a few large seed companies determine what you grow, by having comparatively fewer choices. However, you can seek out less-common varieties that are not available for sale and these can often be hardier, of far superior flavour, and well suited to growing on a small scale. One way of finding these is to attend a seed swap (see page 118); there are also some seed companies that specialise in more unusual and 'heritage' varieties (see Resources).

Seed saving is for everyone – from those who just save a few coriander seeds when their plants bolt to those who take it up so enthusiastically they never need to purchase seed again. As well as saving you money, your own saved seed will not have had any chemical treatment in the packet, as is too frequently the case with bought seed. You will also have the satisfaction of having some control over what you produce to eat, and of taking your part in a time-honoured tradition.

A carrot poised to flower.

1. Cut the flowerheads once they begin to dry and turn brown.
2. Place them in a paper bag and hang to dry further.
3. Once dry, rub the seeds from their casing on to a sheet of paper. They will have a little chaff still attached and this can be left on or removed.

Squash, pumpkin, courgette and cucumber

Squashes can cross-pollinate very readily with each other (see page 174). Seeds should be saved only if the plants have been grown in an isolation cage (see Chapter 21) or the flowers have been pollinated by hand and tied to prevent crosses with nearby plants of the same family. They should be grown to full maturity, which will mean a fat cucumber or a courgette left to become a marrow, with large seeds inside.

- Scoop out the centre containing the seeds.
- Wash off the vegetable matter.
- Dry on a dish on a windowsill.

Cabbage family

Plants in the cabbage family will cross with other cultivars in the same species, forming unpredictable offspring. It is quite easy to avoid cross-pollination by allowing only one plant in each species to go to seed each year. The seed will keep for quite a number of years, so stocks can be built up.

When growing plants for seed they should be allowed to build up the energy to produce viable seeds. The odd leaf can be harvested, but on the whole the plants should be left alone. Some of the *Brassica oleracea* species will need to overwinter before coming into seed in the spring, so allow room in your planting scheme for this long process.

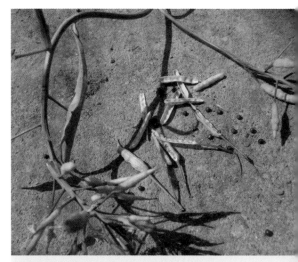

Seeds in a long thin 'pod' are very characteristic of the cabbage family.

The seeds of all brassicas form in small 'pods', which should be left to dry out on the plant. Once fully dry, rub the pods inside a bag, then decant as many seeds as you can without the chaff, later winnowing out any further chaff or removing it by hand.

Onions, leeks and garlic

Like other bulbs, onions will flower if left to overwinter. Likewise, leeks and garlic can be

Cultivars of species within the cabbage family	
Cabbage species (*Brassica oleracea*)	Broccoli, cabbage, cauliflower, kale, kohlrabi, Brussels sprouts.
Radish species (*Raphanus sativus*)	Radish, mooli.
Swede/rapeseed Species (*Brassica napus*)	Rapeseed, Swedish turnip, rutabaga.
Turnip species (*Brassica rapa*)	Turnip, Chinese cabbage, pak choi, mizuna.
Other species	Horseradish, rocket, mustard, watercress and wintercress: these are all genetically different enough from each other and from other cabbage family plants to be grown without the risk of cross-pollination.

left in the ground to form their large decorative flowers. They will not look out of place in a flowerbed rather than a vegetable bed if you are short of room. Dry the seeds on the plant and tap on to a piece of newspaper.

STORING SAVED SEED

Seeds should be kept in dry, dark, cool conditions, such as in an envelope in a box at the back of a seldom-used cupboard. It is important to maintain a constant temperature.

Different seeds will remain viable for different lengths of time.

Average length of time seed remains viable	
Type of vegetable	**Years**
Beans	3
Cabbage family	5
Carrot	3
Coriander	5
Cucumber	5
Leek	3
Lettuce*	5
Maize	2
Melon	5
Onion	1-2
Parsley	1-2
Parsnip	1-2
Squash, pumpkin, marrow, etc.	4**
Tomato	4

* See Chapter 21.
** 4 years under perfect conditions, but squash seeds are notoriously difficult to save.

Sprouting old seed

Sprouting seeds is a useful way of using up seeds close to (or past) their sow-by date. Alfalfa is perhaps the most well-known sprouted seed, but radishes, broccoli and mustard can all be sprouted in the same way. If the seed is particularly old you may not get full germination, but the sprouts can be bulked out with sunflower seed, lentils, chick peas or anything 'sproutable' you may have stored in the back of your kitchen cupboard.

How to sprout seeds

- Soak the seeds in a jar in a dark place, such as a kitchen cupboard.
- Either put the seeds in a sprouter (these come up very regularly in charity shops / thrift stores, etc.), or carefully rinse the jar (with the seeds inside) and reuse this (the jar should be no more than a quarter full of seed if using this method). If using the jar, tie a piece of permeable cloth around the top of it.
- Return the jar/sprouter to the dark cupboard and rinse daily, pouring away the old water as you do so (it will ferment and pong otherwise).
- Depending on what seeds you are using, the sprouts will have grown noticeably in around three to five days (possibly longer in cold rooms).
- Once they have really developed a 'tail' of around 2.5cm (1") they can be greened off for a couple of days on a windowsill to improve the flavour and to increase the amount of nutrients.

Sprouted seeds can be grown right through the winter and spring and provide valuable vitamins and minerals, which can be a struggle to find from the plot at that time of the year.

Chapter 25

PROPAGATING PLANTS

I once dug up a blackthorn tree that had grown as a weed right where I wanted to put a pond and left it to dry for firewood. Three or four months later I decided I liked the form of the tree so painted it blue and replanted it on the corner of my plot as an *objet d'art*. To my surprise it regrew new branches! Despite months of neglect and a paint job, the tree was still alive. It is these amazing regenerative powers of nature that makes it possible to pull up and chop up a rhubarb crown or simply poke a stick in the ground to gain new plant material.

HARDWOOD CUTTINGS

Figs, gooseberries, currants, mulberries and elder, along with many other edible and ornamental plants, can be propagated from hardwood cuttings in the autumn once their leaves have fallen.

Cut pencil-thick pieces 15cm (6") long for small shrubs and up to 30cm (12") long for larger shrubs and trees, such as elder. The cuts should be above a bud on the top and below a bud on the bottom. The top cut should be slightly slanted away from the bud to allow rainwater to run off.

The cutting can then be placed at two-thirds of its depth into any of the following.
- A pot of gritty compost or a sand/compost or perlite/compost mix. The pot should be big enough to accommodate three cuttings.
- A cold-frame bed.
- A shaded spot in a hedgerow.
- A trench lined with sand to a depth of two-thirds the size of the cutting.

Hardwood cuttings can be left to root in pots — just be sure they don't dry out.

PRUNING AND PLANTING

For most fruit bushes pruning should take place once the leaves have fallen – often around the same time as you might take a hardwood cutting. As long as you are not pruning out diseased wood there is no reason not to combine the two jobs, planting up your cut wood around the edge of your plot to produce an edible hedgerow.

There's no need to throw away your prunings if you have space to create an edible hedge.

DIVISION

Division is the easiest way to propagate new plants from old. As the name suggests, you simply divide up the plant's roots when it is dormant. Rhubarb is the best example of an edible plant that can be divided. It is a tough old thing: its large root ball acts as an energy store, enabling it to withstand harsh winters before popping up before most other crops are even awake. It is this large root ball, or 'crown', that makes it one of the easiest things to propagate by division.

The plant should be well established, giving thick stems each year, and the older and larger the plant is the better. Here's what to do.

1. Wait until most (if not all) of the leaves have died off and dig up the crown.
2. Split it in two with a spade, ensuring you have at least one bud or growing tip on each piece (you can split it into four if you have a very big crown).
3. Replant in a weed-free area, preferably in a bed prepared with well-rotted manure.

And that's it!

Don't take too much stem off in the first year as it will need to put some energy down into the root ball.

LAYERING

Generally, layering is best done in spring – see Chapter 12, page 139, for details. Some plants, however, aren't flexible enough in spring to be bent down to the soil, so for those that are very woody at that time of year, such as kiwis, layering is best done in autumn.

Chapter 26

....

STORING CROPS

Just as squirrels bury nuts and bees make honey, we also need to find ways to store our food throughout the winter. In food science, methods of food preservation can be described with something known as 'hurdle technology'. Micro-organisms need certain conditions to survive, and foods that present a number of 'hurdles' to them will last longer than those with none. A highly acidic or a high-sugar environment can be such hurdles, such as in pickles or jam. Salting, drying and canning all present further hurdles, along with more technical methods difficult (or impossible) to replicate at home, such as freeze-drying and atmospheric packaging. Some vegetables, on the other hand, are quite easy to store without processing: just keep them in the right conditions and they will last for months.

DRYING

Drying is one of the oldest and most effective methods of food preservation and one that needs very little financial input.

Apple rings

When I first met my partner she had the whole of a lean-to at the back of her shared house festooned with strings of apple rings. The other members of her shared house thought she was a bit of a nutter, but it was one of the things that first endeared her to me.

HOW TO MAKE DRIED APPLE RINGS

1 Core and peel the apples, brushing with a layer of lemon juice to prevent browning.

2 With a sharp knife, cut the cored pieces as thin as you can: around 0.5cm ($1/2$") thickness should do.

3 Thread the apples through their cores on to string and hang in a warm airy place such as above a radiator, in an airing cupboard or on the wall next to a fireplace.

4 Alternatively, they can be dried on bamboo canes cut to fit the width of an oven. Repeatedly dry the apple rings on the residual heat after baking for a number of days. They can be air-dried in between if the oven is not on much.

5 When ready, the apple rings should have shrunk to around half their size and be slightly bendy.

6 They can be stored in a tin, a jar or in a plastic bag sealed with the air squeezed out. They will keep for anything from six months to a year.

String mushrooms up to dry.

Plums, apricots and grapes

These fruits should be kept whole – bruised or damaged fruit should be put to one side for alternative recipes or for composting. They can be dried in any of the following ways.

- **Layered on a baking tray** and pre-severed in the same way as for apple rings, e.g. by repeated drying in the residual heat of an oven.
- **Dried in an airing cupboard** for anything up to a week (or more).
- **Put on a wire rack** suspended above a radiator or storage heater.

They should shrivel up and darken in colour once they are completely dried; this can take anything up to a week depending on your method – for this reason cover with a cheese cloth, muslin cloth or tea towel. Once fully dry store in an airtight container and use within three months.

Mushrooms

A simple yet effective way to dry a large quantity of mushrooms is to suspend a wire rack above a radiator using string and drawing pins – the back end of the rack rests on the radiator and the string is tied to the front and the other end pinned around 30cm (12") above the radiator, forming a secure triangle. The heat of the radiator rises up through the rack, leaching the moisture as it does so.

Another method, just as effective, is to string mushrooms up using a needle to thread a piece of cotton through their centre, and hang in a cool, dry place with plenty of airflow.

Beans

Beans for storing and beans for seed are dried in the same way. As long as the autumn weather is not too wet, beans can be left in their pods, on the plant where they grew, to dry. However, during prolonged wet weather you will have to bring them indoors to dry to stop them going mouldy.

Use a large darning needle to thread the bean pods together. This works best if the pods are spread out on a string rather than in bunches. Hang them up somewhere light and airy. My old flat had a beam near to a light window (see picture), which was perfect for drying strings of beans.

Important: Dried beans contain a toxin in the skin and should be soaked and boiled until soft before consumed. Usually the results of eating uncooked beans are nothing worse

Dry beans inside during wet weather.

STRING-DRYING VEGETABLES

1 Moist vegetables such as aubergine may benefit from first being dipped into coarse salt to draw out excess liquid before being strung up.

2 Cut your chosen vegetable into thin slices, around 3mm (1/8") if possible. Dry for anything from three days to over two weeks in a window or airing cupboard or above a radiator, or make use of the residual heat of an oven (see apple rings, page 193).

3 Cover with a netting or cloth if insects are a problem.

than bad wind, but there have been fatalities from this practice.

String-drying vegetables

Peppers, turnips, courgettes and aubergines, along with many other vegetables, can be cut into small rounds and strung up to dry in the same way as for mushrooms (see left).

FRUIT LEATHERS

A fruit leather is essentially a flat strip of dehydrated fruit. Leathers can be made with any soft fruit (e.g. blackcurrants, raspberries or strawberries), tree fruit (e.g. apples, pears) or wild fruit (e.g. hawthorn berries). Mixtures seem to work really well, for example, using a sweet fruit to balance out a less sweet one – I really like haw, rosehip and apple. They make excellent lunchbox fillers and contain much of the nutritional qualities of hydrated fruit.

- Puree the fruit. If it looks necessary to add liquid, add no more than one part water to eight parts fruit.
- Push the puree through a sieve to remove stones, pips, skin, etc. Check the taste: if it is too sour, add sugar.
- Spread the liquid on a tray in a very thin layer (about 3-6mm (1/8-1/4"). You will need to put something on the base of the tray to prevent the leather from sticking. What you use will depend on the method of drying – see table below for options.
- Dry – see table below.

It is very difficult to give exact times for drying as there are so many variables in drying a fruit leather, including its thickness, how hot the sun is and the moisture content of the fruit.

Drying methods for fruit leathers	
Method	**What to use for a non-stick sheet**
Oven on lowest possible heat for 8-12 hours	Microwave-proof plastic sheet
Above a radiator or storage heater	Cling film or microwave-proof plastic sheet
Dehydrator for around 8 hours	Greaseproof paper or microwave-proof plastic sheet
Car window on a hot day	Plastic sheet – cover with cloth or mosquito net to protect from flies
Outdoors in sun	Plastic sheet – cover with cloth or mosquito net to protect from flies

The leathers are ready when they are no longer sticky but smooth on the surface. If one method doesn't seem to be working (remember it can take a few days in some cases), then try in combination with another.

Making a food dehydrator

A dehydrator is a very effective way of drying fruit and vegetables, but is expensive to buy. However, a makeshift dehydrator can be made using items you may have lying around.

Home-made dehydrators take longer than bought ones to dehydrate food. It is important that they should not be left unattended, as there is a slight fire risk.

FERMENTING

In some parts of the world fermentation is a common way to preserve foods. One example is sauerkraut, popular in Germany and the US; it is made from a mix of vegetables and spices and based on cabbage.

Sauerkraut

You may think you don't like sauerkraut as, let's face it, fermented cabbage really doesn't sound like a treat! Yet each time I have it I wonder why I don't eat it more often – the mix of spices, mild acid bite and soft leaves transforms the humble cabbage into a worthy addition to any meal.

Preparing sauerkraut is very straightforward and the ingredients can be as simple or complex as you choose to make them. It is best made with firm cabbage hearts rather than loose-leaf varieties, and the tough stalks should be removed (unless you are grating the cabbage), along with the first loose outer leaves.

HOW TO MAKE A FOOD DEHYDRATOR

1 Coat the inside of a cardboard box with tin foil (shiny side out), using double-sided sticky tape or glue to secure the foil in place.

2 Cut a hole and push in the head of an old table lamp.

3 Put an extra layer of foil behind where the bulb will be.

4 Screw in an old-fashioned halogen (non-energy-saving) bulb.

5 Cut a slot in each side of the box wide enough for an old fridge or freezer shelf.

6 Slide the fridge/freezer shelf into the slots.

7 Cut your fruit/vegetables into small slices and place on the fridge/freezer shelf.

8 Close up the box and turn the lamp on.

Inside a home-made dehydrator.

HOW TO MAKE SAUERKRAUT

1 Finely chop or grate the cabbage.

2 Pack into a large bowl, mixing in generous amounts of salt as you do so. In total you should use around a tablespoon of coarse salt per large jar; quantities will vary and you'll need to use more in warm weather and less in cold.

3 Add a few good-sized pinches of spices – ginger, juniper berries, thyme, chilli, clovers, sage and cumin are all used in sauerkraut recipes.

4 Strands of other vegetables, such as radish, carrot, mooli, spring onions, garlic and beets can all be added to a sauerkraut mix. Use what you have to hand and add flavours you like rather than sticking rigidly to a recipe.

5 Squeeze, push and cram the cabbage down in the bowl, mixing the ingredients up as you do so.

6 The salt helps to draw the liquid from the cabbage and will form brine for the cabbage to sit in.

7 Place a plate on the mixture, weigh it down with a heavy object and leave until the liquid starts to cover the plate – usually a little less than 24 hours. If this hasn't happened, add a little home-made brine (15:1 water to salt).

8 Scald some jars with boiling water and fill them with sauerkraut mix. Don't put the lids on yet. Around 1-2.5cm (1/8-1") of liquid should form at the top of the jar. Squeeze the cabbage some more if this doesn't appear.

9 Leave at room temperature for three to four days, pushing down the cabbage if it starts to rise above the liquid line. You may need to add a little brine if the cabbage doesn't form enough liquid on its own to cover the solids in the jar.

10 After three or four days the cabbage will start to develop a smell a little like 'off' milk as the lactic acid fermentation starts to take place (see box below). Some surface mould may appear but this shouldn't harm the ingredients under the brine and can be scooped off. Sauerkraut can be stored in a cupboard or cellar and will keep for anything up to six months.

Fermentation smells

Because many fermented products, such as sauerkraut, are preserved using lactic acid (a smell we usually associate with rancid milk) they can smell quite bad when you first open them. This smell soon goes once you leave the jar open for a while and should not be taken as a sign that the contents have gone off. If you have left the jars for a long time, check for putrid flavours or signs of moulds, just as you would with a pickle or chutney.

STORING WITHOUT PROCESSING

Some foods can be stored with very little input from you. They don't need to be put into a jar or a bottle, just kept in the right environment or the right conditions.

Apples

If you've stored apples and found they have all rotted before December, it is quite often not to do with poor storage but the choice of an unsuitable variety. Some varieties of apple that ripen in the summer should be eaten more or less as soon as they ripen, as they will keep for only a few weeks, if not for just a few days. Others are more adapted to colder weather as they develop hard skins in the autumn, allowing them to be stored right across the winter. These are usually late-season apples, the last to ripen of any tree. As a rule of thumb, apples that ripen in October or November should last right through the winter.

Wrap each apple up in newspaper and place in a box out of sunlight. If possible the apples should not touch each other. Supermarkets, greengrocers, cafes and juice bars quite often throw out the indented separators they've had their fruit delivered in. As an ex-juice-bar owner I know full well that most are more than willing to let you take these boxes off their hands. Boxes can be stacked on top of one another to save room, and they should be stored in a cool dry place such as a shed, garage or damp-proof cellar. Depending on how much room you have, stacked pallets may make a suitable storage unit.

Squashes

You should try to leave squashes outside for as long as you can: they will naturally develop hard skins as they dry in the sun, allowing them to be stored over winter.

Pumpkins drying naturally.

If a frost is forecast, bring in any which haven't fully ripened and place on a windowsill to dry. Some squash plants – especially, it seems, the butternut squash – will send out lots of small fruit towards the end of the season. Most of these smaller fruits simply won't have time to ripen before the season ends and should be removed, leaving one or two larger ones to receive all the plant's energy and ripen fully.

Once they have dried, either outside or on your windowsill, if unblemished or cracked they will store right through until January. They should not be stored anywhere too cold or damp – a kitchen is ideal, or you could arrange them decoratively around the house.

If you are really pushed for space indoors and need to store them in a garage or shed, use boxes insulated with screwed-up newspaper.

Roots

Root crops, such as carrots and turnips, can be stored in a cool environment, deprived of light. Typically this is a box filled with sand or dry spent potting compost. The sand box mimics conditions in the winter, holding the root in suspended animation rather than allowing it to rot or resprout (although a small amount of resprouting and rotting may occur).

To make a sand/spent-compost box put a 2.5cm (1") layer of sand or compost into the base of any of the following:

- a discarded drawer
- a plastic packing crate
- an old wine crate
- an old fridge with the door taken off.

Place the roots in the sand/compost, ensuring they are touching as little as possible. Cover with sand/compost so no part of the root is in contact with the outside air. The process can be repeated with more layers of sand and vegetables.

Storing roots and potatoes in a clamp

I normally eat most of my potatoes as they come out of the ground and store any excess in a large hessian sack I once found outside an ethnic supermarket. Occasionally I will come across a squashy one at the bottom of the sack, but on the whole this is an effective method of storing small quantities of spuds.

NEWSPAPER

SAND

Vegetables stored in spent compost or sand.

HOW TO MAKE A ROOT CLAMP

1 Dig a square shallow hole about half a spade's depth and put down a layer of straw. The size of the hole will depend on how much you have to store, but a 1m (3ft) square should do the trick for most small-scale growers.

2 Pile the vegetables you wish to store on the straw before covering them again with a thick layer of straw (about a hand-span's depth) and then with around the same depth of earth. You'll need to make a ventilation hole from the vegetables to the outside world; this can be done with an old pipe stuffed with straw.

Friends of mine grow on a large scale and choose to 'clamp' all of their root vegetables (including their potatoes) for use in the winter.

Each time you retrieve any veggies from the clamp you should re-cover with straw and earth. After a time they may start to develop wispy white roots, but these don't harm the flavour of the vegetables and they can be brushed or peeled off.

FREEZING

In many houses, including my own, the refrigerator and the freezer cost more to run than any other appliance. The more that the fridge and freezer are filled, the more efficiently they work, so filling them with surplus produce can be a wise move. The space in large freezers can be shared out amongst friends and neighbours, as it is much cheaper to run one large freezer than five small ones. The cost of running the freezer can be worked out using a plug-in energy-efficiency meter.

Chop and blanch your vegetables before you freeze them; the harder the vegetables the longer you should blanch them. For example, a courgette may be blanched for one or two minutes; a carrot for nearer three or four.

Arrange the chopped, blanched vegetables on a baking tray, ensuring that none of the pieces are touching, and place in the freezer overnight. This will prevent your entire winter's supply of courgettes freezing in one solid lump. Remove the frozen pieces with a fish slice and place in a plastic bag or tub with greaseproof paper between each layer (this sometimes sticks to the vegetable pieces, so don't wedge them in too tight).

The cells of fruit such as apples, plums and tomatoes will rupture if frozen, turning them into mush when defrosted. They will benefit from being cooked into a pie filling (for apples or plums), a sauce (tomatoes or aubergines) or even soup (just about any vegetable) before being frozen and put into bags or tubs. Bags tend to mould to every contour of their filling, making the contents and the bag impossible to prize apart, so if you need to use bags rather than tubs they should be taken out of the freezer well before you need them and placed in a bowl to defrost.

Be sure to label the containers: very few people like parsnip pie and custard.

Chapter 27

······················

MAKING LEAF MOULD

A good supply of leaf mould in the garden is as good as money in the bank. Leaf mould is truly amazing stuff and will save you money on buying in compost for seedlings and/or potting on (although for this purpose it will need to be enriched), and will act as a good mulch in the autumn or spring. (See Chapter 11 for details of making seed and potting compost.)

If I work in private gardens I add a good layer of leaf mould to the beds after removing annual weeds. This not only suppresses further weed growth but also gives a beautiful black contrast to green foliage. This instant 'wow' factor can mean the difference between being asked back to a garden for further work or being given your marching orders.

Unlike compost, tree leaves take time to rot down.
- A rough mulch suitable for use on overwintering brassicas will take a year.
- Leaf mould suitable for seed or potting composts will take at least two years and should be sieved for best results.

Some autumn leaves look almost too good to make into leaf mould, but in a couple of years you will be thankful for it.

HOW TO MAKE A LEAF-MOULD CONTAINER

A CHICKEN-WIRE CONTAINER

1 Dig in four wooden posts roughly 60cm (2ft) apart in a square.

2 Stretch chicken wire around it in one continuous piece and nail to each post to make a box shape.

A CYLINDRICAL LEAF-MOULD CONTAINER

1 Take a length of wire around 30cm (12") long and form into a cylinder, securing the ends with cable ties.

2 Cut a series of flaps of equal length using wire clippers.

3 Fold the flaps into the middle and secure with cable ties.

4 Cut a new piece of wire to fill in the remaining gap and again secure with cable ties. The container can be tied or nailed to a single post.

GATHERING LEAVES

Leaves from conifers, laurels, eucalyptus or any other tree with a waxy leaf should *not* be gathered for leaf mould. Instead use broadleaf species and try to avoid anything badly infested with pests such as leaf miner.

Beech leaves are among the best to use for leaf mould, but they do take the longest to break down. However, these large trees seldom grow in small urban gardens. When I lived in Bristol I'd rake leaves up from nearby paths. Nine times out of ten this was fine, but occasionally amongst the leaves I've found broken glass or beer cans, along with signs of urban life I'd rather not mention. Since then I've always gathered leaves using a strong pair of gardening gloves.

Local authorities sometimes deliver autumn leaves to allotment sites and, depending on how they are managed, private parks or gardens may let you take their leaves away.

An enterprising friend of mine would rake the leaves of private gardens each autumn, charging the owners and making a tidy sum along with a huge batch of leaf mould.

MAKING LEAF MOULD

The process of leaves decomposing to leaf mould is not heat dependent, unlike compost. They can be left to break down in a wire cage or just tied up in a black bag with holes in it.

A stronger mix

✳ Adding layers of comfrey and nettle will create a more nutritious leaf mould, good for use in potting and growing on (see Chapter 11).

Chapter 28

GATHERING 'WILD' EXTRAS

The wild foods surrounding a garden or a vegetable plot really come into their own at this time of year. Bright red berries signal their presence to the birds – and to the gardener with a foraging eye. Haws, hips and nuts grow happily without any interference from us and their effortless yields can, at times, rival the cultivated part of a plot. Wild food does not need to be a main focus of a dish, but it can be a welcome added extra to home-grown produce.

WILD FRUITS

Some wild fruits come from very common plants but are very uncommon as food. Yet in times gone by they would have been eaten as much as we now eat imported food such as bananas and oranges. Wild fruit, like all wild food, comes with a zero food miles tag, and all have their own unique tastes and textures.

Haws

The berries of hawthorns are very high in pectin, making them useful for jellies, jams and sauces that refuse to set or thicken up. Quite simply, push a handful of haws through a sieve, adding a splash of apple juice if they don't seem to go through first time. Add this

mix to a jam, jelly or sauce that needs a bit of encouragement to set.

Apples

Because an apple grown from seed will never resemble its parent, wild-grown apples tend to vary drastically in size and flavour. They

Hawthorn berries make a lovely ketchup (see overleaf).

HOW TO MAKE A HAW KETCHUP

Hawthorn berry ketchup is one of those great old 'recipes', as it can be improvised with whatever weight of berries you pick. It can be surprising how much the fruit will reduce down once you begin cooking, so pick at least a carrier bag full to get a decent amount of ketchup.

1 Wash the fruit and remove big stalks and stems (you don't need to remove them all but too much will impair the flavour).

2 Place the prepared fruit into a pan and cover with one part water and one part spiced vinegar (such as pickling vinegar).

3 Bring to the boil, allow to cool slightly and push the mix through a sieve.

4 Return to the heat, adding a tenth of the fruit's weight in sugar.

5 Add salt to taste.

6 Check for flavour: it may be necessary to spice it up a little if the spiced vinegar isn't very strong; if so, add a pinch of cayenne pepper, a teaspoon each of coriander and cumin, return to the heat and try again. Once it is to your taste, use a funnel to pour into clean bottles sterilised with boiling water.

7 Seal and label.

8 A variation of this requires slightly more sugar and Chinese five-spice powder to make a 'haw-sin' sauce.

can range from a small sweet crab apple to a large sour apple, with everything in between. Larger apples can be made into cider and small crab apples made into chutney. The seeds and the tough casing of crab apples can be removed by pushing the fruit pulp through a sieve or a muslin bag once it is cooked.

Rowan / mountain ash berries

Rowans are usually grown as ornamentals or hedging trees, producing large crops of orange berries. These berries make good eating for birds or for us, cooked and made into a tart jelly. The berries are best after a frost, which can be mimicked by placing them in the freezer. If you can't find a recipe, use one for rosehip jelly or the haw jam recipe in

the box above. I've come across recipes for Rowan schnapps, adding the berries and sugar to vodka in the way you would for cherry brandy. Rowan berries are not to everyone's taste and they are pretty revolting unless plenty of sugar is added.

Elderberries

Elderberries can be made into a ketchup using a tomato ketchup recipe. These fruits are a perfect partner for apple and can be made into jams, pies and pickles. They also make very good wine.

WILD NUTS

The price alone of shop-bought nuts should be enough to encourage people to go out in

Wild chestnuts are often smaller than cultivated ones but still taste delicious roasted.

their local area in search of them. In my experience, shop-bought nuts simply can't compare with fresh ones.

Chestnuts

UK-grown chestnuts are a little smaller than imports from mainland Europe but are just as good to eat. Sweet chestnut trees are on the large side so you are unlikely to find one in your garden, but they are a common parkland tree. Don't confuse them with a horse chestnut, which has a tougher spiky shell and a rounded nut. Instead look for a pointed nut with a flat side – check in a tree identification book or online if you are unsure of the difference.

Chestnuts can be used in all kinds of ways but I like them best fresh in risottos, or scored (cut a cross in the flat side) and roasted on a fire.

They keep for up to a year if dried on a windowsill or above a radiator. Once dried they can be rehydrated in soups and stews or ground into a flour and added to cakes, muffins and pancakes.

Walnuts

Like wild chestnuts, wild walnuts can be a lot smaller than ones you may be used to. They will need to have the green skins removed before you can eat them. Lay them out on a newspaper-covered table somewhere warm and airy. The skins will begin to blacken and will eventually peel off very easily. I've stored them for over a year in a cool dry place; they will begin to shrink if stored for too long so are best eaten by Christmas. Be warned: the skin will stain your hands or whatever surface you dry them on.

Hazelnuts

Until I moved to Devon I only rarely found a worthwhile hoard of hazelnuts. In towns and cities where populations of squirrels are high you will seldom see more than one or two on a tree. They can sometimes surround a garden or be found in parks, but you may have to harvest them early to beat the squirrels to them. If you find enough to fill a small bowl you should be able to make hazelnut milk (see overleaf), which once tried is never forgotten.

HOW TO MAKE HAZELNUT MILK

Hazelnut milk makes a good alternative to dairy milk for anyone with allergies or concerns over animal welfare. The recipe is very simple, and the leftover nut pulp can be made into delicious nut burgers or nut roasts, or mixed with mushrooms to make a fantastic nut-and-mushroom burger.

Ingredients
Approx. 100g (4oz) shelled hazelnuts.
500ml (1 pint) water.

Method

1 Put the hazelnuts into a bowl that they will only half fill.

2 Top the bowl up with water and leave to soak overnight.

3 Discard the water (or use for a nut stock) and place the soft hazelnuts in a blender.

4 Top up with around 500ml of water.

5 Blend the mixture.

6 Pass it through a sieve or muslin bag and squeeze.

7 Bottle and refrigerate the juice.

WILD AND UNUSUAL SPICES

Growing your own spices can seem a little challenging in a temperate climate. It is not often you see a cinnamon tree in Newton Abbot or cardamom pods growing in your average Birmingham garden. However, there is a good chance that some of the flowers or even weeds you have growing in your back garden can be used as spices.

Hogweed seeds

As with many members of the carrot family, hogweed seeds contain aromatic compounds that give them a very distinctive flavour. The seeds can be used green or dried on the plant. The flavour is quite unique – slightly citrusy. I've used the green seeds with cucumbers and the dried seeds in a nettle risotto. As with all plants of this family (which includes the deadly poisonous hemlock), be sure you have identified it correctly.

Nigella seeds

Nigella flowers give way to soft, papery rattles containing small black seeds with a spicy kick. Either dry-fry them with other spices and use in curries, or add to cakes and biscuits.

Wood avens roots

Wood avens, or herb bennet, is a weed I remember strongly from my childhood as it grew all over the outskirts of my school playground. It generally grows in shaded places, especially under trees. Small yellow flowers give way to a bur-like head made up of a number of seed hooks. I remember my six-year-old self back in the early eighties thinking that these plants, with their spiky tops, looked like the punks I would see walking around my local streets.

It is beneath the surface that these plants now have most interest to me, as the roots contain eugenol, the same substance that gives cloves their flavour. Place the scrubbed roots in a small muslin bag and add to a pan of cooking apples for a clove-like flavour. The taste is rather mild and so it may be more of an interesting curiosity or a culinary experi-

Hogweed seeds make a surprisingly citrus–flavoured spice.

ment rather than a regular addition to your spice cupboard.

Horseradish roots

Horseradish is a much more common 'weed' than most people think – it has a real tendency to spread and should be contained if you find it growing in your garden. It looks a lot like dock but the larger leaves break up and become toothed as the plant matures. As it belongs to the cabbage family it has characteristic white brassica flowers and is prone to attacks from the cabbage white butterfly. The root is best dug up in the autumn and, as with all plants, you will need the landowner's permission if you are digging it up outside your own garden (see page 179). The root can be frozen whole and grated into meals as and when you need it. Or add a little grated root to some cream and parsley to make a horseradish sauce.

Jack-by-the-hedge roots and seeds

Jack-by-the-hedge is a common weed with edible leaves tasting a little like garlic and mustard – hence its alternative name, garlic mustard. Less well known are its seeds and roots, which can be used like mustard seeds and horseradish root respectively.

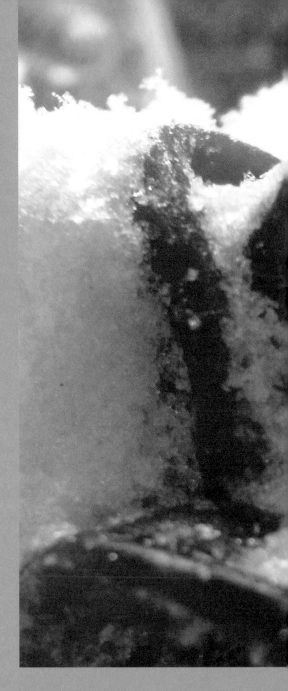

PART 5
WINTER

Winter draws the curtain of life closed on the productive plot. Like living statues, perennials and overwintered crops stay in suspended animation, waiting for the warmth of spring to rouse them back into growth. It's a time when everything stops, a time of stillness, a time of solitude, as none but the hardiest of gardener will

brave the chill winds. Each winter the canvas of the plot is wiped clean, leaving it ready to be painted anew with seeds and seedlings come spring.

This kind of clichéd rhetoric found in gardening books and magazines seems to indicate that there is nothing to do in the

winter, but on the contrary it can be a very industrious time of year if you want it to be. It's time to build, plan, protect, fix, prune and plant. It is a time to catch up and tidy up, and to lay the foundations ready for the coming spring.

JOBS FOR WINTER

- Protect your soil
- Build structures
- Acquire and maintain tools

Chapter 29

WINTER PROTECTION

A lot of our food plants now come from much warmer climes, typically the Mediterranean, so they can need a little help to see them through the winter. In addition, an exposed plot can be vulnerable to erosion by the wind and the leaching of nutrients as a result of persistent heavy winter rains.

COVERING YOUR PLOT

When you are faced with opposing theories such as 'roughly dig your ground to expose it to frost and break up heavy clay' against 'cover your plot during winter to prevent nutrient leaching', what do you do?

The answer is simple:
- Expose your soil to frosts only if it is heavy clay and needs breaking up. If you have worked it into a fine clay loam this won't have to be done every year. Any nutrients lost can be returned via well-rotted manure in the spring.
- Constant wind and rain on exposed soil will wash away any nutrients, and cold weather can kill some beneficial soil micro-organisms. So cover light soils with cardboard, green manure, sheet black plastic or woven black plastic during the winter. Black plastic will also help warm the soil up in the spring, allowing you to sow or plant a couple of weeks earlier than on an uncovered plot.

Rhubarb may reward you with harvest a few weeks early if protected by straw.

Using black plastic

The use of woven and sheet plastic mulches is quite a controversial one. Some swear by it, claiming it means the difference between using weedkillers or not. Others claim that cardboard not only does exactly the same job but is also free and has the added bonus of being incorporated into the soil as it begins to decompose.

If you do decide to use black plastic, it does need to be managed. If neglected, a thin layer of soil can build up on the surface of the plastic (especially woven types) and weeds will begin to grow on this new soil layer. Eventually the weeds will not only penetrate the plastic but will also secure it in place, making it near-impossible to remove without tearing.

To prevent this, carry out regular checks on the plastic. Remove any decomposing covering you may have on the surface, such as woodchip, and replace with a fresh layer if you prefer to keep it covered. Even uncovered plastic can be brushed clean from time to time and any weeds encroaching around the edges should be removed.

PROTECTING PLANTS

A lot of overwintering plants are adapted to the cold and don't need any further protection. Onions, parsnips, broad beans and brassicas can all stay in suspended animation through the winter, waiting for the sun to reappear and the nights to draw out.

Others, however, need a bit of mollycoddling. I go into detail about protecting plants from cold in Chapter 10, and many of the methods described there are equally relevant in winter. Fleece, cold frames and cloches can all give a crucial helping hand to plants in the cold and bitter months. Peas, winter salads and oriental salads can all be sown in the late summer or autumn and grown under protection through the winter for a late winter / early spring harvest.

Some plants can be convinced into thinking that spring has come early. If you mulch rhubarb with 30cm (12") of straw around its crown on a warm day in the late winter, much of the warm air will be trapped in air pockets.

This can encourage the rhubarb to emerge a few weeks earlier than usual.

PROTECTING THE GREENHOUSE AND POLYTUNNEL

The winter of 2010-11 was exceptionally cold across the UK, including where I was down in Devon. I found myself looking after a polytunnel, which got down to -8°C (18°F) at one point, yet we managed to keep most of our salads alive (including some tender crops such as coriander).

It didn't cost to protect the plants: they were simply covered over with a fleece and the doors of the polytunnel were kept closed.

Plants in a polytunnel can need extra protection when temperatures drop.

Chapter 30

SMALL-SCALE CONSTRUCTION

Small projects that can be done in a day or over a weekend can give you a great sense of accomplishment. Both of the projects described in this chapter can feasibly be accomplished over a weekend. What's more, in the case of the second one, once completed you will have a place to sit and relax for a well-earned rest.

BUILDING RAISED BEDS

New growing beds can be put in at any time of the year, but winter is ideal as there is generally less growing on the plot than in the

Raised beds provide structure (but also slug cover).

Pros of raised beds
- ⊘ Aid drainage for heavy soils and retain moisture on light soils
- ⊘ Easy to work
- ⊘ Prevent pernicious weeds such as couch grass becoming a problem
- ⊘ Can look appealing and will help define paths
- ⊘ Easy to attach hoops for cloches and fleecing
- ⊘ Can be used on concrete or gravel if there is no soil in your garden
- ⊘ Can be built high for those who have trouble bending or for wheelchair users

Cons of raised beds
- ⊘ Can be a breeding ground for slugs, especially in overshadowed areas
- ⊘ Not necessary if an existing deep bed or other system is working well – it will be making work for yourself and using up resources
- ⊘ Difficult to remove weeds if they are allowed to become a problem

summer months, so less to clear. If the beds are to go directly on to soil, the plot will have to be cleared of weeds. This means either double-digging, sieving the soil for roots of pernicious weeds such as couch grass and ground elder, or carefully going through with a fork, pulling out any weed roots. Laying down weed-suppressant material such as cardboard, black plastic or old carpet in the spring will get rid of all but the most persistent of weeds. However, this is no help if you are

facing clearing a new bed now, in the middle of winter.

See Chapter 8 for advice on what wood to use. Remember to use a thick layer of plastic sheeting between the soil and the bed if using wood that has been treated with potentially hazardous chemicals.

Are raised beds for you?

Contrary to popular belief, raised beds are

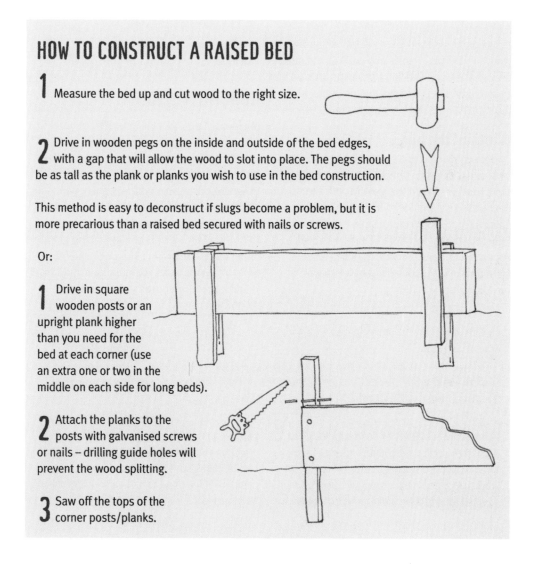

HOW TO CONSTRUCT A RAISED BED

1 Measure the bed up and cut wood to the right size.

2 Drive in wooden pegs on the inside and outside of the bed edges, with a gap that will allow the wood to slot into place. The pegs should be as tall as the plank or planks you wish to use in the bed construction.

This method is easy to deconstruct if slugs become a problem, but it is more precarious than a raised bed secured with nails or screws.

Or:

1 Drive in square wooden posts or an upright plank higher than you need for the bed at each corner (use an extra one or two in the middle on each side for long beds).

2 Attach the planks to the posts with galvanised screws or nails – drilling guide holes will prevent the wood splitting.

3 Saw off the tops of the corner posts/planks.

not ideal for every garden. There are pros and cons to be considered before investing time and effort in them.

Depth of the bed

If constructing a raised bed on soil, plants can work their roots below the level of the wooden bed. Therefore, unless the purpose of the raised bed is to improve waterlogged soil, its depth is not crucial.

Constructing a bed over a non-soil base layer will require the same considerations as with container growing (see Chapter 14). The depth of the bed will dictate what will grow well in it. Salads, onions and ball carrots need only shallow soil and will grow in as little as 15-20cm (6-8"). Brassicas and potatoes need more than twice this – 35-40cm (14-16").

Width of the bed

To determine the right size for your proposed bed, squat down on one side and stretch your arms forward. Touch the ground with the tips of your fingers and measure this distance. This will mark your comfortable reach into the bed and should therefore be taken its centre. For example, my comfortable reach is 60cm (2ft), so a bed of 120cm (4ft) in width would be the perfect size for me.

Other factors to take into account would be the width of any fleece, black plastic, netting or polythene cloches you may wish to use on the bed.

For beds on gravel gardens, you are essentially making a box with no base or lid. Use the same method as above – drilling or nailing planks to an upright. It is best to clear a space in the gravel so the bed sits on the weed-proof membrane.

Filling the bed

Your raised bed can be filled with a good mix of either topsoil, compost, manure or leaf mould. See Chapter 14 for more details.

MAKING A BENCH

My favourite old bench consisted of nothing more than a long flat, thick piece of wood with two thick wooden legs screwed to it – rather like a squat, miniature Stonehenge. I loved spending time on that bench, watching pollinators in the summer and my friendly robin in the winter. Many of us feel the need to put our feet up now and again and simply enjoy the garden rather than work all the time, and none more than one of my oldest friends, the former drummer Chris Eaves.

Take a seat

Chris Eaves, a partner of Eves and Lewis Landscape Design, designing gardens in the north-east of England.

There is always plenty to do in a garden, but there are times when you just need to take a moment and enjoy the products of your hard work. It is great to have somewhere to park yourself, and to have a permanent place to perch is a must – saving you the trouble of dragging chairs in and out of the shed. If you can identify a spot with a good view, sunny position or secluded feel, then consider this for your seat.

(Cont'd)

(Cont'd)

There are lots of different seats and benches available in all sorts of materials at all different prices, but putting together a bench for yourself can be a simple DIY job with the reward of a sit-down at the end. ("I'm just testing it out to make sure it's OK.")

There are a few basics to consider with a seat or bench, which can help with the design.

- **Height** The height of the seat from the ground is important. Too short and we will be sitting with our knees around our ears; too high and we'll be swinging our legs like a toddler in a swing. We are all different shapes and sizes so you can tailor your construction to yourself but as a general rule allow about 45cm (1ft 6") from floor to seat.
- **Depth** This will depend on how you want to use your bench, how often and for how long. A very simple plank seat will give you something to perch on but is not great if you fancy sitting for longer . A good depth of seat to aim for is 50cm (1ft 8") – this will give you balance and comfort.
- **Choice of material** In general, use whatever you have to hand, but for the seat I try to stick to using wood: this doesn't get as cold as stone or concrete and so is more pleasant to sit on in cold weather. Avoid old railway sleepers, which can contain all sorts of toxic material and can also stain your clothes – especially in warm weather if the tar and creosote with which they have been treated leaks out.

In our design projects we often use materials that we have recycled or saved from a skip. This dry-stone-style bench that we created for a client was built using stone and slate that had been part of a rockery which was dismantled.

Dry stone bench.

For another bench we used surplus offcuts from some paving construction to create plinths to support a decking seat. If you can make friends with a landscaper they will often have leftover material that they would usually just throw in a skip.

Plinth and decking bench.

Have a good search around for old timber – non-returnable pallets can be a good resource, although they do need some processing, taking apart, removing nails, sanding down, etc. We created a large lounging bench using inexpensive 75mm x 75mm (3" x 3") fence posts and an old pallet.

(Cont'd)

(Cont'd)

Fence-post and pallet bench.

Driftwood, if you are lucky enough to be near the sea, is another interesting material. The first bench I created was made from some washed-up lengths of timber, and it has lasted ten years untreated, due to the salt in it.

Driftwood bench.

If you are using softwood and you want it to last it may need treating with some form of preservative. I have sometimes seen people use creosote (now creosote substitute) to treat the timber of a bench, but this is not recommended as the leached oils can stain clothing and is generally not nice stuff. A clear preservative is far preferable and if possible it's best to obtain an eco-friendly one. Oils such as teak oil can be used to preserve timber, and these also bring out the natural wood colours.

Putting it all together

If you are working with stone you may need to cement things together, or, if you are feeling more adventurous, try some dry stone construction. The most common cement is made up of one part ordinary Portland cement mixed with four parts building sand.

Lime mortars can also be used, although they are not as widely available and take longer to set. All mortars can be quite caustic, so make sure you wear gloves.

When fixing your timber together it is best to use fixings that are galvanised or coated for use outside. If you use ordinary screws or nails they are likely to rust and will be the first thing to fall apart. Extra strength can be given to joints by using exterior-quality PVA wood glue.

As you become more experienced there are various other jointing methods for timber that can be explored, such as using dowels and tenon-and-mortise joints.

Whatever material you use, enjoy yourself and make sure you sit down and give the work a good test at the end of it all.

Chapter 31

BUILDING LARGE STRUCTURES

For some projects you really have to put the hours in to get results. No more so than with getting larger structures in place. Sheds, greenhouses and, to an extent, green roofs can all take time to make. However, they do offer much more long-term rewards – such as somewhere to put your tools, a refuge in inclement weather, a place to grow under cover and a haven for wildlife. If you can, put some time aside for these projects: I try to go with the little-and-often approach, putting in an afternoon or so every week until it's done.

PLANNING PERMISSION

Planning permission can be an irritating but necessary hoop to jump through before putting up any kind of structure. It varies from country to country and region to region and, as with any law, what you thought was law ten years ago may have changed considerably.

Allotments and community gardens usually have their own policy on structures; a quick call to the site representative should be enough to find out about this.

Nine times out of ten, putting up small structures in a garden should be fine,

especially if the structure doesn't over-shadow a neighbour's house or garden. Planning permission is not needed (in the UK at least) as long as your greenhouse or shed complies with the following rules.

- It is not at the side or front of the house but in the back garden (where it can't be seen).
- It is further than 2m (6 1/2 ft) from a

The author with his old home-made shed (and his old haircut).

HOW TO TAKE DOWN AND REASSEMBLE A SHED

TO TAKE DOWN A SHED

1 Sheds are best dismantled by at least two people – one to unscrew bolts and the other (or others) to hold the panels up.

2 Choose a day when no strong winds have been forecast.

3 Take photos of the shed with a digital camera to refer to when reassembling.

4 Remove any glass (if possible) – wrap each pane to protect it in the move.

5 Take the roof off first, and try to keep it in one piece rather than in two. If you do need to take it apart to move it, try to disturb the roofing felt as little as possible.

6 Unbolt one side at a time; use oil or other lubricant if the bolts have rusted in place. Keep the bolts in a safe place.

7 Take everything with you, including the foundation blocks if there are any.

TO REASSEMBLE A SHED

1 Make sure the area you wish to place your shed is completely level.

2 Put down blocks to raise the shed from the ground.

3 Work from the base up – again, with at least two people.

4 Refer to digital photos of the shed if necessary.

boundary fence (parts of it can be nearer but it must be further than 2m at the highest point).

- The centre of the roof and therefore the overall height is no higher than 4m (13ft), with an eave height of no more than 2.5m (8ft).
- It takes up a space no bigger than 50 per cent of the area around the original house. So no more than half of the garden can consist of buildings.

A quick call to your local planning authority is a good idea if you are in doubt, and is better than having to take down a greenhouse mid-growing season or being compelled to dismantle a shed. Always check first if you live in a listed building or within a national park.

SHEDS

A salvaged second-hand shed or one built from recycled materials will represent a huge saving to any gardener. What's more, it will breathe individuality into the plot and can be 'made to measure' for the gardener's requirements.

Salvaged sheds

The vast majority of sheds will be made up of four side panels, two roof panels and a base/floor. If you come across a dismantled shed, check that all the pieces are there before taking it away. If not, you may have to improvise the missing piece or pieces, or try to make one good shed out of the bits and pieces of two.

Unless you have the means to move it in one piece, a pre-assembled shed will have to be dismantled to take it to its destination.

Building a shed

The choice of materials for a home-made shed will depend on what you have around.

You could be lucky and have a stack of durable marine ply to hand, or you may have nothing but pallets. See Chapter 8 for more advice on what wood to use.

If you follow good basic building principles your shed will last as long, if not longer, than any shop-bought shed. Here are some simple guidelines.

The bare bones of a shed in progress.

Raise the base from the ground If the shed does not come into contact with wet ground it will be less likely to wick up water and rot. Use blocks to rest a flat floor plate on, or raise the shed on 'stilts' made from thick wooden legs.

Build a basic box shape and measure gaps big enough to fit whatever doors and windows you may be using.

Put in cross beams as you build – triangles are the strongest geometric shape. The more you put in, the stronger your shed will be (think of the eaves of Tudor buildings or the Eiffel tower – made of many triangles and very durable).

Green roof If you wish to put on a green roof (see pages 223-5), make sure the roof is strong enough to bear the extra weight.

Waterproofing Roofs will need to be waterproof – use roofing felt or lightweight wooden tiles, or put on a corrugated plastic or tin roof.

Measure your height Not a durability factor but important! It is essential that you can stand in your own shed comfortably. It is also important that your tools fit, so take into account the size of large tools such as rakes and wheelbarrows.

To put these basic theories to the test I asked James brown of Carpenter Oak, a leading timber-frame construction company, how he would tackle the problem of constructing a shed from pallets similar to the one I made (pictured on page 219).

BUILDING A GREENHOUSE

A new greenhouse can be expensive: they seem to come in a price range from quite a lot to downright extortionate. Unlike a polytunnel, however, which may need re-covering every five years, a greenhouse is a one-off cost (short of replacing the odd pane of glass), so it may be worth shopping around if you have the money, or trying to find a free or cheap second-hand one if you don't.

Structurally, greenhouses can be made in a very similar way to a shed, except that the panelling is replaced with clear plastic panels, acrylic panels or old windows, and the choice of base may require more thought.

Base

Whether you buy new, salvage your greenhouse or build it from scratch, it will need some kind of base to secure it. It is always going to be cheaper to prepare the base yourself before setting up your greenhouse. The base can be on an existing piece of flat concrete or hard-standing, in which case you will be raising plants on benches in the greenhouse. This has the advantage of minimising damage from pests and diseases that could build up in the soil. However, it does make watering an issue and will mean you have to bring in new compost every year for your plants.

Triangles are the strongest geometric shape, so are important for a sturdy shed.

Making a basic pallet shed

James Brown of Carpenter Oak, Devon

The average bought shed is expensive and often badly made, using poor-quality wood treated with chemicals. You can make your own shed for a fraction of the cost using mostly recycled materials. This can be done in numerous ways, but I would suggest using pallets as the basis of your construction.

You will need:

- Pallets
- Some old paving stones
- 50mm (2") galvanised nails
- 100mm (4") galvanised nails
- A few lengths of 4"x2" timber
- A door
- A window
- Roofing felt – for which you will probably need to buy 40mm (1 1/2 ")screws
- Claw hammer or crowbar
- Screwdriver (or better still, cordless drill . . .)

To make your shed

1. **Base** Make the ground flat. Put down slabs to stop the bottom of the shed rotting.
2. **Floor** Remove the slats from one side of sufficient pallets using the claw hammer or crowbar (see page 112) to create the desired 'footprint' for your shed. Then nail these slats and more back down to create a continuous floor. Try to overlap boards between pallets for stability.
   Top tip: To stop nails splitting boards, do not nail them too close to either end and try blunting off the point of each nail with your hammer, as this helps.
3. **Walls** Remove the slats from enough pallets to give you boards to clad your whole shed. Create your walls by nailing these pallets vertically to the floor and on top of each other to the desired height on each wall. Fix them well at the corners.

Leave a gap for the door (on a side that faces away from the prevailing weather) and window(a), which includes space to line the edges with a board. (NB Locate the pallets so that the supports run vertically, in order that the cladding boards can be nailed across them horizontally.)
Top tip: If the structure wobbles too much while you are making it, try nailing some lengths of wood diagonally across the walls to stiffen them.

4. **Door and window** Fix them in place flush with the edge of the structure. It is best to screw the window into place. To do this you will need to pre-drill a hole through the window frame to allow the screw to pass right through. Be careful not to hit the glass! Your reclaimed door should come with hinges attached. Screw your door hinges in place so that the door opens inwards. Your lining boards need to be solidly attached as they will carry the weight of the door.

5. **Roof** If your roof space is small enough, just lay some pallets across the gap, with a little overlap around each edge. If not, fix some lengths of 4"x2" across and rest the pallets on them. Lay the roofing felt across these so that it sheds water and lap it over the edges so that it covers the overhang. Fix boards over it and over the edges to help hold it down.

6. **Cladding** Starting at the bottom, nail boards horizontally across each wall and then work upwards, overlapping them by 20mm (1") or so until you reach the top. Overlap the edges of the boards over the window frame and the door to keep the rain out.

7. **Rainwater harvesting** Start to think about collecting all that useful water that falls on the roof! (See Chapter 6.)

Alternatively, you can build a wooden base (which will eventually rot, so might not be suitable for wet regions) or a small brick or block wall – both of these kinds of bases or foundations will allow you to put beds into the greenhouse. These bases can also increase the height of the overall growing area and provide insulation from outside temperatures. It might be possible to mount a greenhouse on railway sleepers, but there should be some kind of barrier between them and the soil to prevent leaching of chemicals (see Chapter 8, page 109).

The greenhouse needs to be attached firmly to the base. A masonry drill will come in handy at this point. Bolt the structure in with galvanised bolts and washers.

Second-hand greenhouses

People get rid of greenhouses all the time, and you can often find second-hand green-houses advertised for free, or very cheap, for anyone willing to take them down. Look in the usual places, but you could put up requests on community noticeboards.

- If you can, find out the dimensions before you pick it up, so you know whether you have room for it and can prepare a base in advance.
- Take pictures of the greenhouse when it's up and when you are taking it down, so you can refer to them when you are putting it back up.
- You could ask the owner if he or she has the original plans, or see if you can find them online.
- Bear in mind that if there are many panes of glass missing you will need to replace them, which can get very costly.
- Be very careful moving the glass: wrap it in towels, blankets and/or clothes – anything you have – to cushion it during the move.

Second-hand greenhouses are often given away free.

Where to grow in the greenhouse

- If you want a greenhouse for seedlings, you will be growing exclusively in pots and/or modules, so consider putting a bench in, as it will make life a lot easier. (An old table or half a pallet will do.)
- If you wish to grow plants (such as tomatoes and peppers) to their full size, then permanent beds will be more suitable than pots.
- Consider a wicking bed (see pages 93-5), especially in warmer regions.
- To prevent diseases building up, some greenhouse owners routinely change their soil every four or five years. To minimise the need for this, regularly rotate crops and make sure the soil in the beds is enriched and improved.

GREEN ROOFS

Every time a building is put up, an area of habitat can be lost. A green roof can redress this balance. Green roofs are good for all kinds of wildlife, providing an elevated refuge for birds and insects away from predators, and they can add an extra layer of biodiversity to your garden, not to mention looking great.

Another advantage of green roofs is a potential reduction of the risk of flash flooding, easing the pressure on your sewerage system. They act as a living sponge, holding on to rainwater and delaying the time it takes to be released into the sewer or storm drain system.

Building a green roof

The biggest mistake anyone makes when constructing a green roof is to forget quite how heavy a load it will be. A green roof can be anything up to two or three times heavier than a roof made with tiles, greatly increasing pressure on load-bearing structures.

For the DIY gardener this means using thick posts with triangular beams to spread the upper load as much as possible. When working on the construction of a free-standing green roof, I used large tree trunks as supports with triangulated beams leading off in both directions. The posts were buried to around a third of their height, which means considerable foundations needed to be dug.

Stand-alone green roofs can be used as a wood shelter, a place to escape from the rain or, as with one of the ones I built, a cover for a cob oven that was slowly dissolving in the rain.

A green roof on an existing building

Sheds should be reinforced to take the extra weight of a green roof. An extra layer of strong weatherproof wood such as marine ply will go a long way to help, but you may also need to add extra supports to cope with extra weight on the shed frame. Check that the shed is in a good state – any weak or rotten wood will be put under further pressure.

Sadly, warranties and home insurance can be affected by green roofs on summer houses, large sheds, homes and garages. That's not to say you can't put them on these buildings, but you should be aware of the worse-case scenario if you do. Again, reinforcing any structure will help hold the weight of a green roof, and it may keep your warranty and/or insurance intact (check with the manufacturer or your insurance company).

This green roof in Staverton, Devon, acts as a mini wildlife haven.

HOW TO BUILD A GREEN ROOF

These guidelines should help you build a green roof with a soil depth of around 5cm (2").

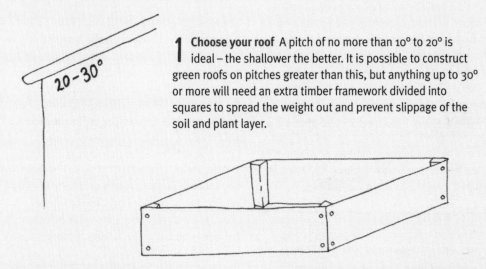

20–30°

1 **Choose your roof** A pitch of no more than 10° to 20° is ideal – the shallower the better. It is possible to construct green roofs on pitches greater than this, but anything up to 30° or more will need an extra timber framework divided into squares to spread the weight out and prevent slippage of the soil and plant layer.

2. **Enclose the sides of the roof**
- Build a raised-bed-like structure of dimensions to match the area of your chosen roof – this will enclose your soil and the various other layers of the roof. You will need to first decide what materials you wish to use and make sure the wood is the correct depth – 25cm (10") should be more than enough.

- Any screws should be covered with silicone sealant to prevent tearing of the waterproof layer that will cover them.
- Don't screw your wooden bed directly to the existing roofing felt but to an eave or other less important area.
- On all but the smallest sheds, on which you can reach the roof easily at ground level, build this enclosure on the ground and then put in place.

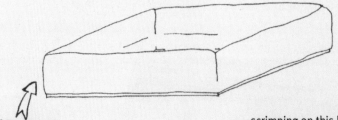

MEMBRANE

3 **Add the waterproof membrane** Pond or damp-proof liners will work best, but anything durable and waterproof will do. If using second-hand liners, make sure they are in good condition and all holes have been fixed

– scrimping on this layer could cost you your shed! As there shouldn't be any holes in the liner, fixing it in place can be problematic. You can wrap it over the sides and screw it in place on the outside of the planks, or use a sealant over the screws – the first option is less problematic in the long run.

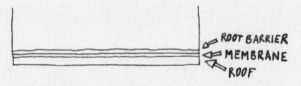

4 **Root barrier** This is not necessary for plants with shallow roots, such as sedums or mosses. A couple of layers of compost bags will do for smaller roofs, or you could use impermeable membrane or plastic sheeting.

5 **Drainage layer** Materials for the drainage layer can include foam, gravel, crushed rock/brick, crushed lava or expanded clay balls. For shallower roofs most of these can be mixed in with the soil layer. Larger materials such as the clay balls won't be suitable to be mixed with the soil layer, however, and should be used as a layer on their own.

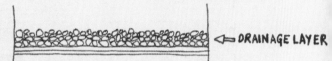

6 **Soil layer** Environmental concerns aside, it is really important not to use peat for the soil layer as it can be flammable!

- Fires are also possible when using foam for the drainage layer or a substrate high in organic matter for the soil layer. A layer of gravel around the edge will help contain fires.
- Clay soils will be too heavy to use on their own: perlite or sand can be mixed with topsoil (for any soil type) to lighten the load.
- The soil layer should be no deeper than 10cm (4") – any more will put a lot of stress on the roof.

Depth of soil:
- Wildflowers need around 7.5cm (3"). (They will thrive in nutrient-poor soil.)
- Sedums and mosses need 2-5cm (1-2").
- Grasses need around 10cm (4").
- Varying the depths of soil will increase the chances of biodiversity.

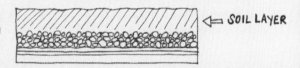

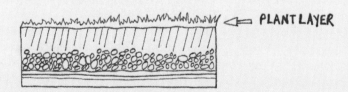

7 **Plant layer** Where possible, choose plants in keeping with the local ecology, although they may not always be appropriate for the scale of your roof.

- Sedums can be bought in rolls – as a natural product they will grow in time, so you don't

need enough to fill the roof in one go.
- Wildflowers can be sown, as can grass seed.
- Turf can be rolled across the roof.
- Weeds will come in from time to time: some you will welcome and some you won't, so you will need to keep an eye out for them.

Chapter 32

TOOLS

You may have read elsewhere that before you even think about gardening you need a good-quality fork and spade, a galvanised metal watering can with a brass watering rose, top-quality secateurs, a trowel, a hoe, a rake . . . the list goes on and on. It is true that many of these things will make life a lot easier, but rushing out and buying them all can mean a considerable investment. Farmers in many parts of the world tend quite large pieces of land with just a mattock or azada (a kind of ridging hoe) and a large knife or a machete. These tools have the benefit of being multifunctional: the mattock acts as a spade, a rake and a hoe, and the machete is used for cutting back scrub, for pruning and even cutting the grass!

A few pairs of nails can be all that's needed to hang a wide range of tools.

I'm not suggesting you run out and buy these two tools (although they do come in handy), but seek some middle ground between the Western way and that of a farmer in a developing country. A good spade and a fork are fairly necessary, but is an onion hoe or a dibber a vital piece of equipment? Can you make do with what you have and borrow less-vital things as and when you need them?

BUYING TOOLS

New tools vary hugely in price, and buying a brand-new hand fork or pair of secateurs for what seems like a tenth of the cost it should

be may seem like an absolute bargain. However, after weeks rather than years of use, when it buckles, bends or snaps, you will regret not having spent a little more on a decent tool. I've found that most really cheap new tools are cheap for a reason and a complete false economy. Good-quality tools, especially those with a guarantee, cost a little more at first but in the long run they are well worth it. Look for good solid iron or steel and good hardwood rather than pine handles and aluminium heads. More importantly, don't assume that a local garden megastore is your only option – that way you'll be out of pocket very quickly.

SECOND-HAND TOOLS

The cliché that things in the old days were built to last holds a lot of truth – it is not unheard of to work with tools over a hundred years after they were made. Some would have no doubt shifted thousands of tonnes (or tons when they were made) of muck and will be capable of shifting thousands more. When buying second-hand:

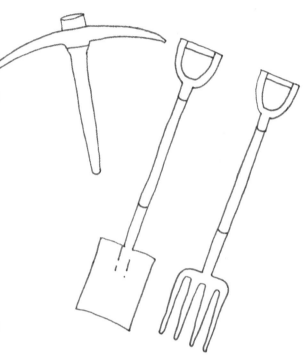

- Look for the same qualities as you would when buying a new tool – a good wood handle and a quality metal head.
- Think twice about buying anything you think you can't repair, such as forks and spades with moulded plastic handles.
- Look for signs of wear and tear: if it looks as though the head of a spade might fall off in the very near future, it probably will!

Old tools can be found in the usual places – eBay, Freecycle, local free papers, magazines and ads in shop windows. They will also pop up in reclamation yards and church jumble sales, and some tool shops will have a second-hand section.

BORROWING TOOLS

In some well-run shared spaces, such as allotment sites, there may be a central location where tools are lent out to those in need of them. This removes the burden of

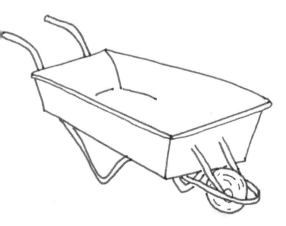

needing to buy everything at once and can make the difference between clearing a plot or letting the weeds grow for another year.

In many cities across the US and Australia, tool libraries lend out tools either free of charge or for a nominal yearly or monthly subscription. These include not only garden tools but tools for home repair and building work.

This service is sadly lacking in the UK, and I would like to think that some enterprising person reading this might consider setting one up. Many of the tool libraries in the US started with government funding, but in the absence of this a subscription-based system could make the whole project self-financing.

Informal tool borrowing

Aside from organised tool borrowing, most people are more than willing to lend their tools out. As an act of appreciation I've sharpened blades and cleaned tools before giving them back and/or offered a share of

On tool sharing and the Freeconomy

Mark Boyle, founder of The Freeconomy Community (www.justfortheloveofit.org) and author of *The Moneyless Man*

Normally the sound of a lawnmower revving on a peaceful summer's afternoon would be enough to ignite a belching "Just let it grow wild, mate!" or "Get yourself a scythe!" from me. Since the day I realised that beauty comes not from visual aesthetics but from what something represents I developed an unhealthy loathing of neatly trimmed lawns, and an intolerance for the destroyers of tranquillity which make them so. This time, however, I compassionately decided to put my patio rage to a slightly more positive use.

Something dawned on me that afternoon: I was living on a street of 45 houses, and never once – in three years – did I hear two lawnmowers going at the same. Yet over half of the residents owned one. Not only was this symbolic of our complete disregard for the world's precious resources and energy, it was also a waste of hard-earned cash. And all that was required to change it were two things: a slight change in societal culture and a little bit of simple organisation.

But I didn't just want to organise my street's tool pool; I wanted to organise it globally. Just a few days before my pathetic eureka moment, I'd launched a worldwide skill-sharing project called The Freeconomy Community, which now has local groups in over 100 countries around the world. Using some very clever software, it enables any member anywhere in the world to access free skills and labour from any other freeconomist within anything up to a 25-mile radius of his or her doorstep, all done on a 'pay-it-forward' philosophy. "If this could be done for skills, then why not tools also?" I thought. So two months later we launched Toolshare, allowing anyone anywhere in the world to share their tools efficiently with their neighbours.

Aside from all its other free services, Freeconomy is now the world's largest toolsharing project. When you sign up, you can choose to list any of the tools you own that you're willing to share with other members in your local neighbourhood. And even if you choose not to, you can still access the tool pool of all other members regardless. The terms on which members lend and borrow is up to the individuals involved, as long as no money changes hands. Freeconomy is based on the philosophy that by sharing what we've got, whether it be our skills, our tools or our knowledge, we can build bonds between people – and therefore more resilient communities – that would be unlikely to occur when the act is performed only for one's own benefit.

But a word of warning: even sharing our tools is not a long-term sustainable solution. The only way many modern tools can be produced, especially anywhere near as cheap as they currently are, is by utilising the economies of scale that arise from all of us hoarding what we've got. The infrastructure and factories required to produce one strimmer will cost millions to put in place, and it is only viable if the business sells a lot of them. Tool-sharing is, however, a fantastic transitional tool to be utilised given the economic and ecological crises we face.

A truly sustainable solution would be to re-design the way we live in order to not need so many (or any) noisy, high-embodied-energy tools to begin with, and find ways of meeting our needs in life by working in harmony with nature. In the meantime, however, sign up to your local Freeconomy toolshare scheme – or better still, go and say hello to your neighbour, tell them what tools you've got and get them interested in the whole idea.

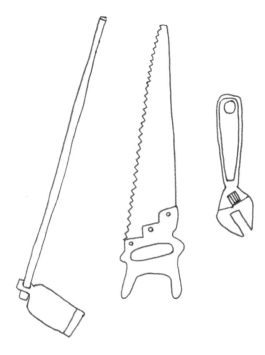

with the tools of a deceased friend or relative should see it as an honour.

DE-RUSTING AND FIXING OLD TOOLS

Just because a tool is rusty or broken doesn't mean it should instantly be thrown away and replaced with a new one. Here are just some ways of bringing back tools from the dustiest tool graveyard.

De-rusting tools

I've lost count of the number of times I've finished gardening for the day and put far fewer tools back in the shed than I took out. I've sometimes found them again months, if not years, later, inevitably in a much more rusty and weathered condition. Aside from self-archaeology it can be common to inherit a garden or allotment along with the rusty tools of the last owner. Unless they have become brittle and past the point of no return, most rusty tools are well worth saving.

There are two ways of cleaning the rust off tools. The first is to get some heavy-duty abrasive paper or wire wool and rub like mad until all the rust comes away. This is *really* hard work; it can take hours and leave you quite exhausted. It is a good solution for

my produce in exchange. If lending to you is rewarding then people will be more willing to lend again.

If you wish to enter into this kind of exchange remember that borrowing should be a two-way thing – if you need to borrow something from someone else you have to be willing to lend to them in turn. The kind of person who locks away all his or her tools but expects to borrow from everyone else tends to lose friends very quickly.

INHERITING TOOLS

I came by many of my tools from my grand-mother's second husband, a very keen gardener called Frank. Poor Frank had no immediate family, and my parents were left in charge of clearing his house and garden. As they knew I would put them to good use they were very keen for me to take his gardening tools and even encouraged me to do so. Frank was an excellent gardener and I feel proud to continue gardening with his tools. I believe anyone given the opportunity to work

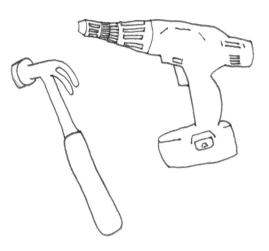

HOW TO REMOVE RUST FROM TOOLS

1 Put the tool you wish to de-rust into a vice.

2 De-rust one side at a time.

3 Remember that metal on metal will cause a spark, so wear protective goggles, gloves, etc. if you have them.

4 Finish off the job by dipping the tools in a bucked of oiled sand to prevent further oxidisation.

anyone quitting smoking who needs to take their aggression out on something, but otherwise there are easier options.

I prefer to use a wire brush fitting for an electric drill. It costs a similar amount as the abrasive paper but clears the rust in no time.

Replacing handles

Even if used with all the care in the world, tool handles will break from time to time and you will need to replace them. Look for matching handles amongst your own tools with broken heads, or ask friends and family whether they have any that might fit. (You could also try Freecycle.)

Failing that, take the head or handle to a hardware shop and see if they have one matching in size.

Removing a broken handle (with an intact tool head)

1. First remove the bolt/pin holding the old handle in place. Use a metal saw or an angle grinder to remove the 'head' of the bolt.

2. Once one side is removed it should be possible to knock the bolt/pin out with a nail and hammer.

3. If it is moulded in place, i.e. you can't tell where the bolt ends and the spade begins, skip this step and go straight to step 5.

4. Once the bolt/pin is removed it may be possible to pull out the broken handle; otherwise try opening up the seam with a hammer and chisel until the wood falls out.
5. If it won't pull out, put the tool head into the centre of a fire and burn out the wood. It should go without saying that this is not suitable for plastic-handled spades! Use gloves to remove the head and run under the tap or plunge into water once removed.

6. Bang out any charred bits of wood and remove the bolt/pin.

Removing a broken tool head (with an intact handle)

1. Remove the bolt/pin as above (steps 1 and 2).

2. Place the handle in a vice or on a workbench and hammer off the head.

Attaching a new handle to a tool head

- Slot the new handle on to the metal collar of the head (this is when you can really tell if the handle is too small!). If it is too big then use a wood file to get a perfect fit.
- Bang the handle in place. I use a hammer on the top part of the 'T' of a spade or fork, alternating sides to get a clear fit. Make sure there is no movement or wobbling of the new handle in the collar.
- Drill through the hole in the collar, through the new wood of the handle and out the other side. This bit is tricky – one slip and you've broken the drill bit. To avoid this, clamp the head in a vice or workbench.
- Insert a rivet or nut and bolt. Secure the nut or flatten the other side of the rivet.

FINAL WORDS

Over the years I have travelled down the country rather like a sock slips down inside a wellington boot. From the Midlands to the south-west of England I have gardened on many different soils and met many different gardeners on the way. Despite their differences I have found one universal truth that binds all productive gardeners – none of them like to spend any money! There is an old rhyme I have found which describes this feeling amongst the horticultural-minded folk:

What's the use of spending gold
On potatoes, seeds or kale
Money is always better spent
On a night of real ale!

Well, OK, so the rhyme is not so old, in fact it was written just a fraction of a moment before this! The point of it, however, is that there are always things you can spend your money on but gardening doesn't have to be one of them. Famously, prisoners in Guantanamo bay started a productive garden using nothing more than seeds taken out of their meals and the plastic cutlery they were given to eat them with. To my mind this goes to show that the desire to grow our own food is so innate and so woven into our genetic makeup that people will risk anything to do so.

In this modern society we're so conned into believing we need money to do anything, yet in other cultures around the world where there is no money people improvise and make do with what they have. I didn't set out

Nothing quite beats the taste of home-grown produce.

to write a book that would be a definitive guide to making everything possible in the fruit and vegetable garden. I did, however, aim to get people to think in a different way about how they garden and perhaps even how they view 'rubbish'.

I'd like to think this book will inspire a resourcefulness in some who may be lacking this quality and encourage those who are already resourceful to be more so. Thanks for buying this book; if you really enjoyed it why not lend a copy to a friend? (Although I'm sure my bank manager would prefer it if you bought your friend a copy!)

RESOURCES

BOOKS

Adams, C. R., Early, M. P. & Bamford, K. M. (5th edition, 2008) *The Principles of Horticulture*, Butterworth-Heinemann

Anthony, Diana (2000) *Creative Sustainable Gardening*, Centre for Alternative Technology
(The best gardening book I have ever come across.)

Boyle, Mark (2010) *The Moneyless Man*, Oneworld Publications

Crawford, Martin (2010) *Creating a Forest Garden*, Green Books

Hamilton, Dave & Andy (paperback edition, 2009) *The Self-sufficientish Bible*, Hodder & Stoughton

Jenkins, Joseph (3rd edition, 2006) *The Humanure Handbook: A guide to composting human manure*, Jenkins Publishing

Law, Ben (2001) *The Woodland Way: A sustainable approach to sustainable woodland management*, Permanent Publications

Mabey, Richard (2007) *Food for Free*, Collins

Phillips, Roger (2006) *Mushrooms*, Macmillan Reference
(A must for any mushroom hunters, but be sure to cross-reference with another guide to be absolutely confident of correct identification.)

Reader's Digest (1977) *Food from your Garden: All you need to know to grow, cook and preserve your own fruit and vegetables*, Reader's Digest
(Still relevant despite its age – just ignore the outdated information on pest and disease management. There is an updated version written in 2008 but I still prefer the original.)

Scott, Nicky (2009) *How to Make and Use Compost: The ultimate guide*, Green Books

Shepherd, Allan (2007) *The Organic Garden*, Centre for Alternative Technology / Collins
(The friendliest gardening book ever written – good sound advice.)

Thompson, Ken (2007) *No Nettles Required: The reassuring truth about wildlife gardening*, Eden Project Books

Tracey, David (2007) *Guerrilla Gardening: A manualfesto*, New Society Publishers

Whitefield, Patrick (2004) *The Earth Care Manual: A permaculture handbook for Britain and other temperate climates*, Permanent Publications
(An expensive book but worth saving up for.)

WEBSITES

The Freeconomy (Free Economy) Community
www.justfortheloveofit.org
A brilliant organisation set up by 'moneyless man' Mark Boyle.

Freecycle
www.freecycle.org
A fantastic worldwide forum where people offer unwanted items or ask for things they need.

Landshare directory
www.landshare.net
A forum connecting growers with people with land to share.

Making local food work
www.makinglocalfoodwork.co.uk
A very useful website for anyone interested in Community Supported Agriculture schemes, food co-ops or local food in general.

Preloved
www.preloved.co.uk
Similar to eBay but sells only second-hand goods.

Slug Off
www.slugoff.co.uk
A one-stop shop for the low-down on slug and snail elimination.

Transition Town Totnes 'how to set up a garden share scheme' http://transitiontown totnes.org/gardenshare/startupscheme

ORGANISATIONS
General
Centre for Alternative Technology
Machynlleth, Powys SY20 9AZ
01654 705950
www.cat.org.uk

Eden Project
Bodelva, Cornwall PL24 2SG
01726 811911
www.edenproject.com

Garden Organic
Coventry, Warwickshire CV8 3LG
024 7630 3517
www.gardenorganic.org.uk

Proper Job
Crannafords Industrial Park
Chagford, Newton Abbot, Devon TQ13 8DR
01647 432985
http://proper-job.typepad.com
(A well-managed recycling centre in Devon – it even has its own second-hand book shop!)

Wood
National Community Wood Recycling Project
39-42 East Street, Brighton BN1 1HL
01273 20 30 40
www.communitywoodrecycling.org.uk

Wood Recyclers' Association
Birdsong, Peach Grove, Palestine,
Hants SP11 7EP
07841 499856
www.woodrecyclers.org

Water butts
Smiths of the Forest of Dean Ltd.
The Orchard, Station Road,
Milkwall, Coleford, Gloucestershire GL16 8PZ
01594 833308
www.smithsofthedean.co.uk
(Sells every kind of recycled container you can imagine.)

Seeds
Beans and Herbs
The Herbary, 161 Chapel Street,
Horningsham, Warminster,
Wiltshire BA12 7LU
www.beansandherbs.co.uk
(Contributor Pippa Rosen's seed company.)

The Real Seed Catalogue
PO Box 18, Newport near Fishguard,
Pembrokeshire SA65 0AA

01239 821107
www.realseeds.co.uk
(Specialises in heritage seed and offers
advice on seed saving.)

Suttons Seeds
Woodview Road, Paignton,
Devon TQ4 7NG
0844 922 2899
www.suttons.co.uk
(Offers a good range of organic seeds.)

Tamar Organics
Cartha Martha Farm, Rezare,
Launceston, Cornwall PL15 9NX
01579 371182
www.tamarorganics.co.uk
(An excellent organic seed company.)

Allotments

**National Society of Allotments and Leisure
Gardens Ltd**
O'Dell House, Hunters Road, Corby
Northants NN17 5JE
01536 266576
www.nsalg.org.uk

Fruit trees

Adam's Apples (cheap fruit trees with
discounts for large orders)

Talaton Plants (incorporating Adam's Apples)
Egremont Barn, Payhembury,
Honiton, Devon EX14 3JA
01404 841196
www.talatonplants.co.uk

Hedges

Hopes Grove Nurseries
The Estate Office, Smallhythe Road,
Tenterden, Kent TN30 7LT
01580 765600
www.hopesgrovenurseries.co.uk
(Visits by appointment only; not open to
visitors in general.)

Metric/imperial conversions

Where possible, we have given imperial
conversions for metric values throughout
this book (note that these may be
approximate rather than exact). However,
readers in the US should note that pints,
gallons and fluid ounces given in these
pages are UK values, which differ slightly
from those in the US, as follows.

1 UK pint = 1.2 US liquid pints
1 UK gallon = 1.2 US liquid gallons
1 UK fluid ounce (fl oz) = 0.96 US fl oz

INDEX